Rogues in Black Robes

Destroying Lives and Committing Crimes with No True Accountability

BRIAN VUKADINOVICH

Red Penguin
BOOKS

Copyright © 2023 by Brian Vukadinovich

All rights reserved.

Published by Red Penguin Books

Bellerose Village, New York

ISBN: Print 978-1-63777-406-9 / 978-1-63777-447-2

Digital 978-1-63777-398-7

No part of this book may be reproduced in any form or by any electronic or mechanical means, including information storage and retrieval systems, without written permission from the author, except for the use of brief quotations in a book review.

For the People Who Have Been Denied Fairness and Justice by the American Courts

I dedicate this book to all of the people across the country who have been unfairly denied fairness and justice by the American judiciary. Everybody in our country deserves fairness and justice by the judiciary, but many never receive it because of a very infected judiciary. This book is a tribute to all of the victims who were judicially abused at the hands of miscreant judges.

WHAT READERS ARE SAYING

"People of this nation owe a debt of gratitude to Brian Vukadinovich. He has worked tirelessly to make this country a better place for the average American and for posterity. His books are not only informative, but show that ordinary people can stand up to the world's largest crime syndicate and prevail and show that the 'rogues in black robes' are truly a menace to society. Kudos to him. We give him a standing ovation!"
—Sara Naheedy and Tom Scott, authors of *Stack the Legal Odds in Your Favor*

"Brian Vukadinovich represents himself in court better than most lawyers could...Brian is not a lawyer, but I can't think of anyone in the business of litigation who deserves more applause....I've told Brian that if more of us could handle a courtroom the way he does, we'd have a justice system that worked for everyone."
—Sonja Ebron – CEO, Courtroom5, Durham, NC

"Vukadinovich is one of the few pro se's who managed to win in court."
—Reuters

"*Vukadinovich has plenty to say—a luxury many lawyers often don't have.*"

—The Indiana Lawyer

"*He's seen it all and is unafraid to call out evidence of corruption in our justice system.*"

—Sonja Ebron – CEO, Courtroom5, Durham, NC

"*Brian's is a wonderful American success story. He was never rich; he was never powerful. But he was determined, indomitable, fearless, and daring. And so he won. And he will go on winning.*"

—Richard A. Posner, Retired Judge of United States Court of Appeals for the Seventh Circuit, Chicago

"*Brian Vukadinovich is a very sophisticated and experienced pro se litigator.*"

—Judge Allen Sharp, United States District Court

"*Brian Vukadinovich should have been the one who coined the phrase 'it ain't over 'till it's over,' rather than baseball great Yogi Berra. The Valparaiso man never goes down without a fight...*"

—South Bend Tribune

"*Brian. Congratulations on your victory, you have gone against the age old saying an attorney who represents himself has a fool for a client.*"

—Robert Shapiro, Member of "Dream Team" in O.J. Simpson Trial

CONTENTS

Foreword	xi
Prologue	1
1. Tormenting by the Valparaiso Indiana Police	5
2. The Federal Judiciary's Manipulation of the Rules	15
3. The Disclosure by Judge Richard A. Posner of Case Fixing at the U.S. Court of Appeals in Chicago	34
4. Judicial Misconduct Complaint Swept Under the Rug	40
Chapter 4 - Continued	61
5. Petition to the Judicial Conference of the United States	68
Chapter 5 - Continued	81
6. The Attorney General Who Allows Case Fixing and Cover Up by Federal Judges	91
Chapter 6 - Continued	100
7. The Chief Justice of the United States is Perfectly Fine with Case Fixing and Cover Up by Federal Judges	103
Chapter 7 - Continued	116
8. The Stench on the 27th floor of the Dirksen Federal Building in Chicago	121
9. Government Officials Routinely Protect Corrupt Activities by Government Players	131
10. Routine Dismissals of Judicial Misconduct Complaints	139
11. Secrecy in the Judiciary	148
12. The Federal Judiciary is a Weapon of Mass Destruction!	157
13. Judges Should be Required to Take a Yearly Polygraph Test	170
14. How the Courts Fleece the Public	183
15. Who Died and Made Judges Kings?	189
16. Lifetime Appointments for Federal Judges	198

17. The Makeup of the Federal Court System is a Disgrace	203
18. The Chief Justice of the United States	207
19. The Judicial Confirmation Hearings Are A Joke	217
20. The Supreme Court is Essentially an Illegitimate Court	224
21. The Buying and Selling of the Supreme Court	238
22. Evidence of the Seventh Circuit's Systemic Discrimination	243
23. Evidence of the Supreme Court's Hypocrisy Regarding Systemic Discrimination	249
24. The Entire Judiciary Needs a Wholesale Cleansing	255
Epilogue	275
About the Author	279

FOREWORD
SAMANTHA GEIMER

Brian Vukadinovich writes of a journey that many may find shocking, even unbelievable. Sadly, his journey down the rabbit hole of judicial misconduct is far too common. In my case, much of it is very familiar. For example, a judge given a case for which they are not assigned but simply desire. This is something I know about. I witnessed such judicial corruption in the proceedings involving Roman Polanski in which Judge Rittenband, who was given the case upon request, not assignment, did not operate above board and refused to honor his own words. It was at that point that I began to lose my faith and trust in the judiciary when I saw that the judge could not be believed. This had a dramatic impact on how I viewed the judiciary after my experience in the Roman Polanski proceedings.

As Brian's book points out, a longtime and highly-respected federal court of appeals judge, Richard A. Posner, disclosed that an associate member of the court with a grudge against Brian, Judge Kanne, persuaded Judge Posner to decide in favor of the police in order that Brian would not prevail in the appeal. He points out the corrupt nature of the system when he writes about how he filed a misconduct complaint against the judge, and the complaint was dismissed without a determination on the merits. In my case, when the prosecutor, defense attorney, and my attorney, hired specifically to protect me from the judge, petitioned to have Rittenband removed, he simply stepped aside, avoiding any accountability. Brian details how officials of the federal judiciary and even the chief justice of the United States, John Roberts, turned a blind eye to the case fixing and cover up at the U.S. Court of Appeals in Chicago in order that the public not know how serious a problem we have in our country with judicial corruption.

Brian's book reminded me of how unfair and corrupt the judiciary can be—those in positions of power and trust acting for the benefit of their egos or agendas. Even worse, showing callous disregard for both the rule of law and citizens involved to advance their own ambition. Perhaps just a disregard for what should and can be done in favor of the safer path or no action. No matter who you are—defendant, plaintiff, or even a victim drawn into the justice system—you may suffer the same type of abuse. Once you are in the web, it is often too late to ever seek true justice. Acknowledging these circumstances, paying attention to our court systems, and demanding only the highest level of ethics from our police officers, prosecutors, and judges is critical. Our justice system is the foundation of our democracy, and it is in peril. When you or someone you care about is at its mercy, you may find you are powerless; the system runs itself and you are just a part of the machine.

These injustices come in many forms. It can be caused by ego or indifference. Whatever the initial cause and effect, once it is done the system serves itself. It will not acknowledge these bad and inappropriate actions. If someone of character does acknowledge it, you will be hard pressed to get any action. To do nothing is an easier path than stirring the pot for those who may be ethical and honest but pay a cost for not toeing the line. Why suffer the consequences of an unpopular decision? For some, it's just that there is no personal benefit in taking action to correct the misconduct of another in our justice system.

FOREWORD

Brian is shining a light on something everyone should be aware of. These corrupt judges act with impunity, and it's time we, the public, pay attention and demand better. When someone says they are being abused by the system, believe them. Demand what we ourselves fund and what we deserve as citizens.

Demand an honest and open judicial system. Demand the corrupt or unqualified judges, prosecutors, and police officers be forced out by those who have the power to remove them. Demand that only those with the highest degree of honor, honesty, and integrity are elected, placed, and hired for these positions. Citizens should trust that our justice system is fair and equitable and administered without any prejudice or ambition of those involved. The only way to change things is to speak out and demand better. I believe this is exactly what Brian is doing.

PROLOGUE

"The pen is mightier than the sword"
~ Edward Bulwer-Lytton

We, as an American society, are led to believe that we have the best justice system on planet Earth and that our judiciary is beyond reproach. As you will see when you read on in this book, both of these points are a fallacy. The purpose of this book is to sound the alarm and enlighten the public as to how unfair and corrupt the American judiciary is and how badly we are need of serious judicial reforms in our country. The judiciary has become the antithesis of what it is supposed to be. In this book, I will make the case for much needed judicial reforms, and I will challenge you, the reader, to decide if you believe we have an unfair and corrupt judiciary, and if we, as a country, need to implement serious judicial reforms. In a way, you will be a juror, so to speak.

To make my point, I will discuss a very serious matter of a civil rights case that I brought against an extremely rogue and out of control police department in Indiana—Valparaiso Police Department. A trial was held in March 1991 in the United States District

Court for the Northern District of Indiana, Hammond Division, before a very infected judge, James T. Moody, whereby protecting the unlawful activities of the Valparaiso police was basically the rule of the day. You will read about how this judge bent over backwards and departed from the governing rules of procedure to help the rogue police who had tormented me for years with numerous false arrests and brutalities for which not a single bogus arrest stood up in the state courts during the criminal proceedings that were filed against me. You will be amazed at the lengths that Moody went to in issuing blatantly corrupt rulings, basically ensuring that the police would escape liability for their obvious unconscionable and wrongful actions against me, and you will be equally or even more amazed at how the judiciary came running to that judge's rescue when I filed an appeal as to his nefarious rulings.

I will show how a retired, longtime federal court of appeals judge, Richard A. Posner, of the United States Court of Appeals for the Seventh Circuit, Chicago, who was on the panel, came clean after years of harboring the guilt of throwing a decision from the appeal of the police case. This was done as a favor to another federal court of appeals judge, Michael S. Kanne, who was on a mission to ensure that I did not prevail in the appeal so that the trial court's (Moody's) infected rulings would be affirmed in order that Kanne's personal animosity against me would be satisfied—which was done so in violation of the laws of the United States. And you will read about how the chief judge of the United States Court of Appeals for the Seventh Circuit, Diane S. Sykes, and her minions, came running to the rescue of their brethren judge, Michael S. Kanne, even though he (Kanne) didn't deny on the record that he had the appellate decision fixed after I submitted the information to the Seventh Circuit and even though Judge Posner, who was a member of the panel in the case, disclosed that Kanne persuaded him to fix the decision.

I will show how the attorney general of the United States, Merrick Garland, and the chief justice of the United States, John Roberts, both turned a blind eye to the fixing of the appellate decision in the face of the disclosure by the judge (Richard A. Posner) who acceded to the wishes of a corrupt brethren federal court of appeals judge (Michael S. Kanne) who put the fix in motion. I will also show how the Administrative Office of the United States Courts in Washington, D.C., is trying to sweep under the rug the information I have provided to that office regarding the case fixing and cover-up activities that took place in the U.S Court of Appeals in Chicago.

I will show the corrupt nature of the mechanisms that are in place to enable corruption that has permeated the judiciary, at every level, at every turn. I will show how each one of our branches of government—legislative, executive, and judicial—breach their responsibilities to the people and go out of their way to protect criminal activities of federal judges who basically have carte blanche to fix decisions and how the nefarious judges depend on the judicial hierarchy to sweep their judicial malfeasances under the rug. I will show that the judicial machinery is so corrupt in how it disregards judicial misconduct complaints, that in addition to judges protecting brethren judges, there is also an administrative mechanism set up to aid and abet the corruption that is going on in the federal judiciary through the Administrative Office of the United States Courts by its complicity. And you will read about how the federal judiciary keeps the information of the judicial corruptions concealed from the public with the help of elected officials who comprise the House and Senate Judiciary Committees who have the power to investigate corrupt judges—but choose to look the other way. I will prove all of these points without a shadow of a doubt.

You will read that we have a big problem in the federal judiciary in that it is overwhelmingly comprised of extremist judges who are put in place to protect the interest of corporations and government agencies rather than protecting the constitutional rights of the citizenry. You will read about the ridiculously high percentage of cases that are being routinely dismissed by the federal courts and how the people of our country are systematically being deprived of their fundamental right to a jury trial that is actually guaranteed by the Seventh Amendment of the United States Constitution, but the extremist judges in the federal judiciary simply ignore the Seventh Amendment and show their allegiance to the corporations and government agencies that are trampling over the rights of the citizens of our country. I will show that the judiciary has unwittingly given us a great deal of proof demonstrating without a shadow of a doubt that the American judiciary is a very unjust and corrupt enterprise—and that it is by design.

The history of the American judicial system, unfortunately, is replete with unfairness, skullduggery and corruption. I will make the case that for fairness and anti-corruption to enter the bloodstream of the judiciary, there will have to be significant judicial reforms. I will show that the hierarchy of the American judicial system, through its modus operandi of installing judges who routinely disregard their oaths of office and disregard the Constitution, has enabled the judiciary to metastasize into an organization of malfeasance bordering on a criminal enterprise.

CHAPTER 1
TORMENTING BY THE VALPARAISO INDIANA POLICE

"I'll tell you what Freedom is to me. No fear."
~ Nina Simone

While the essence of this book is not to draw attention to the problem of rogue police that we have been experiencing in the country for quite a long time, for decades actually, I feel that I must discuss the facts of what the police did to me back in the day and how the federal judiciary protected the unlawful acts of the rogue police in order to expose the degree of corruption in the federal judiciary—which is the primary purpose of this book.

September 25, 1981, started out like any other day. Little did I know that my life was about to change forever. My mother and I were out shopping and made a stop at the First National Bank in Valparaiso. As soon as we walked through the door, several police officers of the Valparaiso Police Department swarmed in, grabbed me, threw me against the wall, and started beating me. My mother was very scared and pleaded with the officers to stop. The bank employees attempted to intervene, but to no avail. We later learned that just before we arrived there had been a problem with somebody in the bank's parking lot and the bank had called the police. The officers, William "Buddy" Collins and Cosmo Hernandez, attacked me before finding out that the person who was causing the problem was still in the parking lot and that my mother and I didn't have anything to do with it. We were simply trying to do a bank transaction before our shopping trip. Unfortunately, the police officers were totally out of control and refused to listen to what the bank people were trying to tell them during the ordeal and ignoring our pleas that we didn't know what was going on. When officers Collins and Hernandez finally realized that the person they were supposed to be arresting was still outside in the parking lot, rather than letting the matter go with an apology, they instead charged me with "disorderly conduct," even though they knew that they had made a mistake. I had to appear in court on the bogus charge, and I hired a lawyer. On March 31, 1982, we appeared before Judge Bryce Billings who had a reputation as a tough but fair judge. My mother, I, and the officers, Collins and Hernandez, all testified, and Judge Billings ruled that I was not guilty of the disorderly conduct charge. He chastised the officers for bringing such a charge against me under those circumstances since they knew they made a mistake in falsely arresting me. Needless to say, the Valparaiso Police were not happy as they not only had egg on their face for the false arrest, but they were also publicly chastised by the presiding judge for what they did to me. Because of what I had to go through, I filed a false arrest and brutality case against the Valparaiso Police Department in the state court. The Valparaiso Police Department was represented by the high-powered insurance defense firm of Spangler, Jennings and Daugherty. I was ultimately awarded an out-of-court settlement of $3,500.00. At this point in time, I thought that the ordeal was over and that I could concentrate my efforts on my teaching and coaching career and move on with my life. Little did I know that the nightmare of my life was just in its beginning stages as the Valparaiso Police Department officers weren't willing to accept the fact that they were wrong.

On March 31, 1983, the same Valparaiso policeman, William "Buddy" Collins, encountered me once again, beat me, and falsely arrested me—this time in the WiseWay store parking lot in Valparaiso for an expired plate on my motorcycle. I tried to explain that I didn't know the license plate was expired, but it didn't matter. I was under arrest and was going to the police station. By this time, it looked like a major crime scene as several police cars arrived with lights flashing. Officer Collins pinned me against the hood of his squad car, beat me, handcuffed me, and then put me in the back seat of another officer's squad car with a police dog, a German Shepherd, with its teeth gritting. My hands were handcuffed behind my back, and I was left alone with the police dog in the back seat for what seemed like an eternity. It was terrifying as I couldn't have defended myself if the dog would have attacked me. I was taken to the Valparaiso Police Department where I was subjected to a great deal of verbal and physical abuse. I was then transported to the Porter County Jail and locked up, charged with resisting arrest. I was not allowed to make a telephone call. I had to stay in the jail cell for a long period of time without my family or friends knowing where I was. Fortunately, an acquaintance I knew who had officiated some of my basketball games, Richard Wendt, who was an administrator for a county agency, saw me in the jail cell and asked me what happened. He was kind enough to call my brother, Branko, to let him know what had happened. Branko then came to the Porter County Jail and bailed me out. I again hired James Tsoutsouris, the same lawyer as before, to defend me from the bogus charge. It was a very humiliating ordeal to have to go through.

Fortunately for me, a young lady employee of the WiseWay store, Amy Newlin, witnessed the incident. On September 1, 1983, Amy Newlin appeared at the Valparaiso Police Department, at their request, and gave a statement. The statement was taken by Captain John J. Widup. When Widup asked her what she saw, Amy Newlin stated that while she was taking out someone's groceries, she saw Collins push me up against the hood of the police car on my back and heard me say, "Call the police." She hurried up and went in and called police. Amy Newlin also testified to this fact during her deposition on March 2, 1987, testifying that she saw Buddy Collins "push him up against the hood of his car on his back..." something that Collins had denied doing during the false arrest, but this witness refuted his account of how things really happened. On February 10, 1984, Judge Bryce Billings dismissed the resisting arrest charge. Because I again had to hire a lawyer to defend me from the bogus charge and was again subjected to another malicious prosecution, I filed another state court lawsuit against Collins and the Valparaiso Police Department and was awarded a settlement of $2,500.00. I would later learn that Collins was no stranger to making false reports. On October 23, 1979, Collins was suspended for three days and lost the privilege of using his patrol car for thirty days for "making a false office report." It is mind boggling that police officers are allowed to remain on the force even after the department has evidence of officers making false reports—which is obviously a problem all around the country. I again found myself having to explain another false arrest, which was making things tougher for me in my life, both personally and professionally, let alone what it was doing to my mother.

Retaliation became the rule of the day, and the next vindictive move by the Valparaiso Police Department took place on February 19, 1986, when a speeding ticket made out to my brother, Branko, was placed on his parked car in the driveway of our home. This was very strange as everybody knows that when a person is caught speeding, the officer pulls the vehicle over right on the spot and issues the ticket. Branko then had to appear in Judge Billings' court. Because of this, Branko had to hire an attorney to represent him even though he did nothing wrong. The Valparaiso policeman who wrote the ticket and appeared at trial was Cosmo Hernandez, the same policeman who was involved in the initial beating and false arrest against me at the Valparaiso bank on September 25, 1981, with Buddy Collins, when this whole ordeal started. My brother was sitting at the defense table, and I was in the gallery watching the proceedings. When Hernandez was asked to identify the defendant, he pointed at me. Judge Billings immediately dismissed the charge and shook his head in disgust at what the Valparaiso police were doing. He was clearly upset at the shenanigans initiated once again by the Valparaiso Police Department. And again, rather than accepting legal defeat from their own calculated nonsense, the Valparaiso Police Department continued their harassment against me and refiled the charge, which I would then, of course, have to fight in court—yet another vindictive prosecution they would put me through. When Buddy Collins was deposed, my lawyer asked him if he was aware that Hernandez refiled against me after the bogus charge against my brother, Branko, was thrown out of court by Judge Billings. Collins responded, "That was common knowledge around the police department." That charge, just like all of the previous bogus charges, was eventually dismissed by Judge Billings. And, yes, there was more to come. Simply put, the Valparaiso Police were totally out of control.

On June 17, 1986, while driving away from a court hearing with my attorney, Calvin Hubbell, a Porter County deputy who had also attended the hearing radioed a Valparaiso policeman to intercept me. The officer put his lights on, stopped me, and verbally harassed me. When he realized that my attorney was with me, he let me drive away. It was the same officer who had put me in the back seat of his squad car with the police dog on March 31, 1983, during the second Buddy Collins incident at the WiseWay store. However, that was not the end of it, as the following day, another bogus charge of driving with a suspended license was filed against me. This was very strange because if my driver's license was actually suspended, he would not have let me drive away when he stopped me the day before. Clearly, this was another form of ongoing harassment that the Valparaiso police were subjecting me to. It seemed there was no end in sight. This bogus charge was also dismissed by Judge Billings. The plan was rather obvious; it was to file as many bogus charges against me as possible to make me look bad and to break me financially—obviously in retaliation for successfully standing up for my rights, which was an apparent problem with the Valparaiso police.

On October 15, 1986, I was again stopped and arrested by the Valparaiso police, this time by officer Rick Zentz, on Roosevelt Road while on my way home from my teaching job. I pulled over into the Family Tree Restaurant parking lot, and within seconds, the lot was swarming with Valparaiso police cars with lights flashing. I asked Zentz why he stopped me. He said I was driving with no headlights. During the course of the arrest, he said that my driver's license was suspended, but it wasn't. By now, Zentz had several more of his cohorts to assist him with the false arrest: Patrolman Ross, Patrolman Brickner, Lieutenant Utterback, and Sergeant Wilson. The people driving by and those in the restaurant had to think that this was a major crime scene because all of the squad cars had their flashing lights on. But it was just another one of the several Valparaiso police setups—this time orchestrated by Zentz and his cohorts. I had hidden a tape recorder in the car under the seat for just this type of situation so I could have proof of what was said. Zentz went ahead and arrested me for driving with a suspended license even though it was not, and he also filed a bogus charge of "failure to use headlights" at 4:37 p.m. My car was towed and impounded. The Valparaiso officers all gathered around, laughing and making incriminating comments, not realizing that they were being recorded during the false arrest that amused them so much. When they searched my car, I was sure that they would discover the tape recorder, which they did. Through their stupidity, they made several very ignorant comments which were caught on tape while they were discussing what they should do. I, of course, had to post bond in order to be released. My brother went to get the car out of impound the following day while I was teaching. When I got home from school, I was curious as to whether or not Zentz or any of his cohorts found the tape recorder. Branko told me the tape recorder was in the car and that it picked up the conversations between the Valparaiso police officers. These "Keystone Cops" were having so much fun enjoying the stop, my detention and arrest, and so forth, that they lost their senses, if they had any sense, that is, which was very questionable to say the least. I now had direct proof of the bogus stop. I had it in their own words and with their laughter. One of the Valparaiso officers said, "I'm goin' to get the son-of-a-bitch. F--- him." I again had to appear in court in front of Judge Billings. After I told the judge that my driver's license wasn't suspended and that the "failure to use headlights" was a bogus charge as it wasn't dark at the time Zentz stopped me—at 4:37 p.m.—the Valparaiso Police Department then altered the ticket to a later time so that the charge could nevertheless proceed against me. I had to yet again defend against another one of their ongoing false charges. Judge Billings ultimately dismissed both of the bogus charges. Clearly, he knew what was going on. They actually should have thanked Judge Billings because had he not thrown the bogus charges out of court, the Valparaiso Police Department would have been very embarrassed at the criminal trial when I played the tape recording to the jury. Finally, I had some tangible evidence of what was actually going on. It is extremely difficult—if not impossible—to overcome false charges when it is your word against several police officers who are up to no good. This time I had evidence: words spoken from out of their very own mouths. Judge Billings didn't even need to hear the tape. He knew that they set me up for another false arrest, and he didn't let the Valparaiso police play games with him. He was one of the very few judges who didn't allow police corruption to make its way into the courtroom. He was an honest judge of high honor.

A little over two weeks later on November 3, 1986, I was again stopped by Valparaiso Police officer Richard Zentz on Roosevelt Road in Valparaiso, just like two weeks earlier. It was déjà vu. It became very evident that he knew what time I would be driving home from school as he lived in an apartment building on Roosevelt Road and would see me driving to and from work when he was standing in the yard as I drove by. He just waited to put the plan into play. He again verbally accused me of driving with a suspended license, and I again tried to tell him that my license was not suspended. I then told him that I'd had enough of the nonsense and that was going home. I lived less than five blocks away from where he stopped me. When I got out of my car in my driveway, there were several Valparaiso police cars and officers waiting for me, including Officers Ronald Kurmis and John Ross. My mother and brother were home. To their horror, I was beaten in my yard by the Valparaiso police while my mother, brother, and neighbors watched. It was devastating for my mother and brother to have to watch this happen right in front of their eyes in our own yard. They tried to stop them but to no avail as they were threatened with arrest. I was put in the back seat of the squad car with my hands cuffed behind me, and Kurmis jumped on my back and pressed his knee into my back all the way to the Valparaiso Police Station. I couldn't breathe. I begged him to get off of me and to get his knee out of my back, but he wouldn't do so. When we arrived at the police station, I could hardly stand up for lack of oxygen as I couldn't breathe all the way there. I was helpless as they had my hands handcuffed behind my back. I thought for sure I was going to die because I couldn't breathe. I was taken into the Valparaiso Police Station for additional beating and finally was taken to Porter Memorial Hospital in Valparaiso where I was treated for injuries to my wrist, foot and nose. Then I was taken to the Porter County Jail. I was put in a cell but the jailors would not tell me what the charges were. They couldn't tell me what the charges were. This was because the Valparaiso police went to Judge Billings' court to attempt filing charges against me, but Judge Billings wouldn't accept the charges and threw the corrupt Valparaiso officers out of his courtroom. The Valparaiso Police then went to the Portage Court several miles away and filed charges of speeding, fleeing, resisting arrest, and battery on a police officer. I later learned that Buddy Collins signed the arrest report. Yes, the same Buddy Collins who had twice previously falsely arrested me and abused me with his cohorts, and yes, the same Buddy Collins who had previously been suspended for making a false report. My brother, Branko, bailed me out of the Porter County

Jail. It was a devastating day that took its toll not only on me, but also on my brother and mother. By this time, I began representing myself; and the judge, Mary R. Harper, dismissed all of the bogus charges ruling that there was no probable cause in fact and law for the stop, detention, and arrest, and that the stop, detention, and arrest were invalid.

BRIAN VUKADINOVICH

STATE OF INDIANA,)
          Plaintiff,)
     v.)
BRIAN VUKADINOVICH,)
          Defendant.)

CAUSE NO: 86-PSC-CD-M-820

FILED IN OPEN COURT

APR 20 1987

Mary R Harper
JUDGE PORTER SUPERIOR COURT
COUNTY DIVISION

<u>ORDER</u>

This cause coming on for hearing on the issue of probable cause for the stop, detention, and arrest of defendant; the deposition of the arresting officer having been published; the Court, having considered the evidence and having heard the arguments of counsel and being duly advised in the premises, now finds that there was no probable cause in fact and law for the stop, detention, and arrest of defendant, and that the stop, detention, and arrest of defendant were and are invalid, that all evidence against defendant concerning this prosecution should be and hereby is suppressed, and that, with consent of the STATE OF INDIANA, all criminal charges pending against defendant in this prosecution growing out of said stop, detention, and arrest of defendant should be, and hereby are, dismissed with prejudice.

Mary R Harper
MARY R. HARPER
Judge, Porter County Court No. 2

This is the order issued by Porter Superior Court Judge Mary R Harper on April 20, 1987, ruling that the Valparaiso police did not have probable cause in fact and law for the stop, detention, and arrest of Brian Vukadinovich in dismissing all of the bogus charges against him.

CHAPTER 2

THE FEDERAL JUDICIARY'S MANIPULATION OF THE RULES

THE JUDICIAL KISS OF DEATH TO FAIRNESS

"No man is above the law and no man is below it; nor do we ask any man's permission when we ask him to obey it.
Obedience to the law is demanded as a right, not asked as a favor."
~ Theodore Roosevelt

Because the situation had escalated to such a dangerously high level, I decided to take the Valparaiso Police Department to federal court to make them answer for what they were doing to me. I represented myself and was able to get the case to a jury trial which began on March 11, 1991, and ended on March 18, 1991. I had a very strong case but a very bad judge, James Moody, who had a reputation for being arrogant and belligerent and also for siding with the government. Unfortunately, I had no control over who presided, as judges are supposedly randomly selected, and it was a very unlucky thing that he was assigned to my case. In point of fact, the Lake County Bar Association conducts a survey every year following a presidential election, and in the March 18, 2013, survey, the disdain of Moody by the Lake County Bar Association showed when he received the lowest rating, 6.79. He had formerly been the city attorney for the City of Hobart, City of East Gary, and City of Lake Station. It is generally not a good thing to have a judge who has spent a good portion of his career representing governmental agencies when you are battling a government agency in court in a civil rights case against a governmental municipality. These judges have a great tendency to be inclined to side with the government. But it's what we are stuck with as a country as most appointments to the federal judiciary come from the governmental sector in one way or another.

In keeping true to his reputation as a pro-government type judge, the two-bit Moody set the table nicely for the corrupt Valparaiso police officers when he ruled that he was not going to allow the jury to see the order by state court Judge Mary Harper, who presided over the criminal case, when she determined that there was no probable cause to stop, detain, or arrest me when she threw out all of the bogus charges from the false arrest of November 3, 1986, by Officer Rick Zentz and his cohorts. It was mind boggling that a citizen would have so many obstacles put in the way of his ability to prove what was going on in a high stakes civil rights trial. No fair-minded rational person would have agreed that the order by Judge Harper should not be allowed into evidence in order that the jury, who was to make the ultimate decision in the case, would not have the benefit to see what the state court judge had, in fact, ruled. By disallowing the jury from seeing Judge Harper's order, Moody was, in essence, tacitly encouraging the Valparaiso police to argue that they had probable cause to stop and arrest me, when in fact a state court judge who had held a hearing on the matter determined that the Valparaiso police did not have probable cause to do so. When the Valparaiso police lawyer moved for a directed verdict, Moody granted their motion, stating that there was probable cause to arrest me on November 3, 1986, even though Judge Harper, the state court judge who adjudicated the criminal case, explicitly ruled that there was no probable cause to arrest me. It was very clear right then and there that Moody was a corrupt judge.

And then there are the nefarious judges on the United States Court of Appeals for the Seventh Circuit in Chicago who stated in the appeal that since Zentz followed me for several seconds in a car with a speedometer that no reasonable jury could conclude that he "guessed" at my speed, notwithstanding that Zentz, in fact, testified that he "guessed" at my speed. Needless to say, the Seventh Circuit reared its government-friendly face when it chose to cover the infected ruling by Moody which, in effect, was to approve a false arrest by a corrupt officer who testified that he "guessed" at my speed using his speedometer, a ridiculous assertion that the state court judge, Mary Harper, had the integrity to throw out in every respect. This was amazing. The misfits on the Seventh Circuit stated that although Zentz didn't have a radar device, that he was able to "estimate" my speed. And in helping Moody's infected ruling on giving a directed verdict on the probable cause issue, the misfits on the Seventh Circuit stated that Zentz followed me for "several seconds" with a "calibrated" speedometer and that no reasonable jury could conclude that Zentz "guessed" at my speed. This was a very interesting and telling statement by the misfits on the Seventh Circuit since what those judges said wasn't true, and quite frankly, was blatantly false. During the state court proceeding when the Valparaiso Police were pressing the false charges against me, at a hearing on March 23, 1987, I asked Judge Harper to order the Valparaiso Police Department to provide all records of calibration of the speedometer in Zentz's car since he was basing his arrest off of his speedometer reading. When Judge Harper asked Prosecutor Nancy Vaidik if she had those records, Vaidik responded, "I do not have those. I'm not even sure if they even exist or not." And yet the misfit judges on the Seventh Circuit based their decision on a "calibrated" speedometer which didn't even exist as was verified in the criminal proceeding of the matter. If this isn't judicial corruption, then we must be living on a flat planet! The federal judiciary is so corrupt in this way that common people don't have much of a chance for justice when they bring cases against government entities, particularly in Indiana.

Moody also ruled that there was no evidence establishing a custom or practice by the City of Valparaiso tolerating deprivations of my rights despite the significant evidence of the several previous false arrests and beatings inflicted on me. Moody also ruled that the evidence was "insufficient" to link Officer Buddy Collins to the conspiracy despite the evidence of his prior false arrests against me and even his participation of signing off on Zentz's false arrest of me on November 3, 1986. In other words, Moody refused to let the jury make the decision on Collins' involvements in the prior false arrests that he perpetrated against me and his continuing conduct in even signing Zentz's arrest report of the false arrest of November 3, 1986. It didn't matter to Moody that Collins had previously been suspended for making a false report, a point that the jury undoubtedly would have found very interesting. Had Moody not been so interested in protecting the corrupt Valparaiso police officers he would have allowed me to submit the evidence to the jury regarding the corrupt activities of the Valparaiso Police and let the jury make the decision, but he didn't want that to happen, and the reason is obvious—because the jury would have, in all likelihood, found in my favor—and Moody knew it. Moody well knew there was a very high likelihood that the jury would take Collins' previous false arrests against me and his personal involvement in signing Zentz's false arrest report of the November 3, 1986, arrest into consideration when the jury was weighing all of the evidence. Moody greatly assisted the corrupt Valparaiso Police Department in escaping liability for what they had done. During a couple of breaks, I saw Moody and the Valparaiso police's lawyer, William Kurnik, walking down the hall side by side and talking. I thought this was very inappropriate, but that's how it was. Never mind fairness if you're just a regular citizen, at least in Moody's court.

Moody did plenty to make sure that when the jury made its decision on March 18, 1991, that they would return a verdict in favor of the Valparaiso police on the remaining claims, as well. He did a great deal to help them along with this in a lot of different ways. One of the significant ways Moody helped the Valparaiso police escape liability was when he wouldn't allow me to play the tape recording of the October 15 arrest to the jury. It would have shown the jury that the Valparaiso police were conniving to get me. The evidence was right on the tape. The Valparaiso police were laughing, and one cop even said, "I'm goin' to get the son-of-a-bitch. F--- him." I was sure that once the jury heard the audiotape they would know right then and there what was going on. But Moody refused to allow the audio recording into evidence using the nonsense excuse that it was inaudible. I had a transcript of the audiotape prepared by the FBI that showed everything that was caught on the tape. If the tape was as inaudible as Moody was trying to make it look, then there couldn't have been a transcript made of the tape. It was more than obvious that Moody was not going to allow the jury to hear actual proof of what happened. Instead, the jurors were allowed to hear lies from the Valparaiso police that I would have been able to rebut with the audio recording—but Moody made sure that wouldn't happen. When I appealed to the Seventh Circuit Court of Appeals in Chicago, it stated, in keeping with its disdain of the rights of citizens, that a court has "broad discretion" in deciding whether to admit tape recordings, and will overturn its decision only in "extraordinary circumstances." The Seventh Circuit conceded that I "correctly" stated "that the parties included the tape recording in the pretrial order and that appellees failed to object to its inclusion as required by Local Rule 21(f)(6)", but then went on to say that Moody's decision to exclude the tapes at trial "nevertheless was proper" and that "we are reluctant to interfere with the trial court's determination not to hold the appellee[s] to the pretrial order" and "we perceive no injustice resulting from our reluctance to interfere with the court's decision to alter the pretrial order." This was a very interesting statement by the Seventh Circuit since Moody admonished in his Final Pretrial Conference Memorandum of September 7, 1990, that "The parties are reminded to adhere to this Court's Order controlling trial." The problem was that Moody himself wasn't willing to adhere to his own controlling order—and this was perfectly fine with the nefarious judges on the Seventh Circuit.

It was a corrupt process throughout the trial with Moody presiding and the Seventh Circuit brethren helping a judicial brother along with judicial malfeasance of the highest degree under the guise of so called "justice." And for icing on the proverbial governmental cake, the Seventh Circuit misfits went on to say that there was no evidence of bad faith on the part of defense counsel in not adhering to the pretrial order. No bad faith that lies being allowed by the defense counsel's clients to take place rather than the truth that would have come out if the tape was played if you consider such acceptance of lies to be "proper" as the Seventh Circuit allowed. So in essence, by Moody's and the Seventh Circuit's standards, governmental lies are acceptable in cases where citizens have evidence of government corruption. And to top it all off, the misfits on the Seventh Circuit went on to say that "even if the tape was improperly excluded" that it was "harmless error." And then the Seventh Circuit, in grasping at straws by trying to find ways to justify its obvious corruption, then stated that the case was "unique" and "we perceive no injustice resulting from our reluctance to interfere with the court's decision to alter the pretrial order." This pretty much told me all I needed to know about how corrupt our federal judiciary is—and make no mistake about it, it is very corrupt.

When a federal judicial system has rules governing trial proceedings that are explicitly spelled out beforehand, and when federal judges disregard those rules when citizens have properly listed their exhibits which were not objected to, and the federal judges disallow this proper evidence to be admitted into evidence and allow government defendants to lie while this evidence has been improperly disallowed, then we as a country are in big trouble. Make no mistake about it, when a federal appeals court condones such corruption to occur in a federal court proceeding, we as a country are definitely in trouble. It is sad, but true. In light of what Moody did in refusing to let me play my audio recording to the jury in my case and refusing to let me show the jury the transcript of the recording against the corrupt Valparaiso police, it is interesting that in a government case in United States v. John Buncich, Cause No. 216-CR-161, in August 2016, Moody allowed the government to play an audio recording of poor quality that the audience in the courtroom had problems hearing. Moody then allowed the government to show the jurors a transcript of the audio recording. I found this to be very interesting since Moody wouldn't let me play my audio recording or show the jurors the transcript showing that the Valparaiso police had a premeditated plan to, in their own words on the audio recording, to "get" me. The fact that Moody had no problem in letting the government play audio recordings of poor quality that can barely be heard and allowed the government to present transcripts of the audio recordings, but yet he would not permit me to play my audio recording or submit a transcript of the recording to the jury, speaks volumes as to how Moody operated to ensure that the unwritten rule in his corrupt court was that citizens who have tangible evidence of police corruption should not be allowed to present their evidence to a jury. It stands to reason that a federal judge who goes out of his way to be so favorable to the government and so biased against individuals who bring cases against the government to the point of disallowing the citizen's direct evidence of police misconduct is a corrupt judge who shouldn't be in the federal judiciary. But unfortunately, there are plenty of James T. Moody types infested in the federal judiciary—and that is a bad thing for our country.

And to further underscore Moody's corruption, it should be noted that after he refused to let me play my audio recording of the October 15, 1986, false arrest, he had no problem during a trial in July 1991 allowing the government to play an audio recording obtained through a government bug that had been placed in The Taste of Italy restaurant in Calumet City, Illinois, that the government wanted admitted as evidence against alleged reputed members of a crime syndicate in a federal investigation called Operation Lights Out. It is very interesting that when the government wants to play an audio recording in a trial in Moody's court, Moody is very gracious in accommodating the government, but when a citizen wants to play an audio recording to show evidence of governmental wrongdoing, then it is a no. In other words, Moody accommodates the government but goes against a private citizen who has direct evidence of governmental corruption spoken from their own mouths. One must wonder who the real crime syndicate really is?

Another example of how Moody went out of this way to put a roadblock in my case against the Valparaiso police was when he chose to ignore the governing rules as to depositions. When the Valparaiso Police Department lawyer, William Kurnik, took my mother's deposition and asked her a lot of very personal and inappropriate questions for her reasons of coming to the United States from Europe, which had absolutely nothing to do with the issues in the case and were simply brought up to upset her and to inappropriately make her justify her reasons for immigrating to the United States, Kurnik, after such abuse against my mother, never submitted the deposition for her review as he was required to do under Rule 30(e) of the Federal Rules of Civil Procedure. It was an explicit governing rule. And when Kurnik referred to the deposition at the trial and I objected on the grounds that the deposition was not provided to my mother for her review and signature as required by the rules, Moody again assisted the Valparaiso Police Department and its unsavory lawyer by allowing the deposition into the trial even though the governing rule was not followed by the Valparaiso Police Department and its lawyer. When I brought this issue up in the appeal to the Seventh Circuit, the misfit judges stated that "Although it may be said that the court improperly admitted unsigned depositions, doing so constituted at worst harmless error." The misfits of the Seventh Circuit said the same thing as it said with Moody's conduct of improperly excluding the tape recording of the October 15, 1986, arrest as "harmless error" by Moody. Thus, the

Seventh Circuit reinforced its very disturbing pattern of indifference to the governing rules when it stated that the improperly admitted unsigned deposition was "harmless error" by Moody. It is very interesting that when government agencies are caught red handed violating rules and laws, and when a citizen addresses those violations in a federal court, the federal court, rather than enforcing the governing rule or law, simply ignores them. Then the federal appeals court comes running to the rescue and covers the corruption by stating that the judge's conduct in doing so was "harmless error." If this wasn't a "screw the people and protect police corruption ruling," then there never has been one. There couldn't have been a more swampier swamp than the swamp infested by the two-bit Moody and the acquiescence by the misfits of the Seventh Circuit Court of Appeals in Chicago. And indeed a dirty swamp it was then—and still is.

I was very proud of how my mother handled herself with such courage and dignity when she testified at the trial. The two-bit lawyer, William Kurnik, tried his best to shake her, but he couldn't do it. My mother's will was too strong for him. Kurnik disrespected my mother when he took her deposition when he smiled and asked her very oppressive questions about her life in Europe and for her reasons of coming to the United States. He was very low class and obviously not raised well to have become this type of a low-life person. It bothered my mother when he disrespected her during her deposition with his oppressive questions about her European life. But I couldn't have been more proud of how she handled this low-life lawyer when he again resorted to his unsavory methods to try to intimidate her. She reduced him to the sewer rat that he was, and everybody in the courtroom saw it. I was very proud of my mother.

Another way that Moody greatly assisted the rogue Valparaiso police was when he denied my post-trial motion to vacate the judgment and impose sanctions against the City of Valparaiso for withholding evidence in violation of a court order. The City of Valparaiso was under a court order to submit to the court for what is called an "in camera" (in private) inspection of the officers' personnel files. The personnel files weren't submitted in compliance of the court order in camera inspection and consequently, because Moody allowed the damaging information in the officers' personnel files to be swept under the carpet, i.e., concealed from the proceedings, Moody allowed the rogue police to get away with a fast one by depriving me of what should have been my rightful opportunity to show the jury just how corrupt the Valparaiso officers were in other situations. Make no mistake about it, they were very corrupt. And Moody's allowance of the circumvention of the in camera inspection order of the personnel files also deprived me of the opportunity to present evidence that the City of Valparaiso failed to discipline and continued to employ rogue police officers, which undoubtedly would have resulted in a verdict against the City of Valparaiso for its custom of lack of disciplining its rogue officers, and its continual employment of rogue officers who should have been fired. And even though the City of Valparaiso was required to submit the officers' personnel files for the in camera inspection but didn't do so, and even though the disregard of the court's order to do so prevented me from using the evidence of the officers' corruption at the trial, the misfit judges on the Seventh Circuit amazingly stated that the burden was on me to show that the City of Valparaiso wrongfully withheld evidence and that the withheld evidence would have produced a different result. But Moody prevented me from doing so when he allowed the Valparaiso police to disregard the court order of the in camera inspection of the personnel files, which I addressed in my post-trial motions and arguments to the Seventh Circuit. And then after I conclusively showed that the City of Valparaiso failed to provide the evidence, and that the evidence would have helped me prove the officers' corruption, the misfits on the Seventh Circuit went on to state that I "failed to adduce any evidence that the City deliberately or wrongfully withheld evidence." This was amazing. I requested in discovery proceedings that the officers' personnel files be disclosed, and the City of Valparaiso objected knowing good and well that the officers' personnel files had significant information of the officers' corrupt activities. When Moody ordered the City to submit the information for an in camera inspection, the City ignored the order, and Moody simply looked the other way and allowed the graft to take place—and the misfits on the Seventh Circuit rubber stamped it. Because the City was able to conceal the evidence of the officers' corrupt activities from the jury—with Moody's help, of course—I consequently wasn't able to show the jury the evidence of the corrupt activities of the officers of the Valparaiso Police Department. It was a classic whitewash. Then after being screwed at the trial by Moody's graft, the misfits on the Seventh Circuit added to the corruption by stating that the burden was on me to show that evidence was withheld and would have produced a different trial result. Amazingly, they stated that I "failed" to do so when I most certainly did very conclusively show that the evidence was withheld and that this evidence would have produced a different trial result once the jury saw proof of the officers' history of corruption. But Moody wasn't at all interested in allowing me the opportunity to show the jury the evidence of the corrupt officers of the Valparaiso Police Department, and the misfits on the Seventh Circuit weren't interested in dispensing justice with a reversal of the graft. The case was highly publicized, and Moody and the Seventh Circuit were determined to stop me from proving that the Valparaiso Police Department was infested with corrupt officers. This is how things work in the American judiciary.

Sadly, the Seventh Circuit climbed right into Moody's bed in covering his judicial graft by stating in the appeal that I didn't show that the City of Valparaiso was deliberately indifferent to the constitutional rights of its citizens; and that I did not demonstrate that the City of Valparaiso "perfunctorily dismissed citizen complaints." The record was crystal clear that when I tried to submit such evidence as numerous citizen complaints, from which the City essentially just looked the other way, and did nothing time and time again, while the Valparaiso police were abusing people, and newspaper articles reporting on abuse by Valparaiso police against people, and copies of legal actions filed against the City of Valparaiso by people who were victimized by officers of the Valparaiso Police Department, and even a copy of a departmental investigative report of Officer Zentz, the Seventh Circuit misfits conveniently ignored the fact that Moody wouldn't allow me to submit any of this information into evidence at the trial. What a joke of an appellate circuit. Moody made sure that the jury didn't know about it, and yes, you guessed right, the misfits on the Seventh Circuit helped things along by stating in the appeal that the exclusions of this evidence by Moody was okay in its infected determination that a court's decision to exclude evidence is "generally accorded great deference because of the court's first hand exposure to the evidence and its familiarity with the course of the proceedings." In other words, if the truth were to be told, the "generally accorded great deference" because of the court's "first-hand exposure to the evidence" and its "familiarity" with the course of the trial proceedings in reality means that corrupt judges have the consent of the appellate courts to screw regular people over in civil rights trials when the citizenry has tangible evidence to show corruption by government employees if the evidence is capable of helping a person win a civil rights trial. Make no mistake about it, that is what the nonsense legal jargon from the Seventh Circuit really means—if the truth were told, that is. It was essentially totalitarianism by a city government that wasn't willing to listen to peoples' complaints against its corrupt police officers, and by its inaction, the City of Valparaiso essentially approved of the widespread abuses against people within the city limits. Unfortunately, people have very little recourse when a municipality is indifferent to the abuses against people when coupled with courts that have a very negative and indifferent attitude against people who seek justice in the courts by bringing civil rights cases against the governmental municipalities. This was certainly the case insofar as the City of Valparaiso was concerned with respect to its corrupt officers and the sadness with judges of the likes of James Moody and the misfits on the Seventh

Circuit who have little to no interest in being fair to peoples' cases against police agencies and who have very little to no interest in dispensing actual so called "justice." All one has to do is review the decisions by the Seventh Circuit Court of Appeals in Chicago to see how dramatically lopsided its decisions are in favor of government entities.

Here are some instances of citizens' complaints against the Valparaiso Police Department that Moody refused to admit into evidence which the Seventh Circuit stated that that I did not demonstrate that the City of Valparaiso "perfunctorily dismissed citizen complaints."

- Claim submitted by Mark Montgomery on March 25, 1986, against Valparaiso Police Officer Richard Zentz for Zentz using his authority as a police officer to harass and intimidate Mark Montgomery for several months. The notice to the City of Valparaiso stated, "Recently, Patrolman Zentz has contacted an individual by the name of Jeffrey Walker and ordered said individual to assist him in arresting Mr. Montgomery for possession of cocaine. Patrolman Zentz apparently was planning to make arrangements to plant the cocaine on Mr. Montgomery." Chief of Police at the time, Walter R. Lamberson, sent a memo to City Attorney Brad Koeppen on April 2, 1986, stating, "I really do not believe that there is any validity in Mr. Montgomery's contentions."

- Claim submitted on May 14, 1986, by Sandi Lee Leveritt who was a telecommunicator for the Valparaiso Police Department stating that while "at her duty station on the 4th day of May, 1986, at or about 10:00 p.m. that at said time and date, she was accosted by Corporal Ronald Kurmis, who without reason or provocation, grabbed a telephone from her hand and physically struck her, pushing her against an adjoining wall." The claim stated several witnesses to the incident.

- Taped statement by Mary Jo Hall taken at Valparaiso Police Department on February 26, 1987, regarding an incident involving Valparaiso Officer Richard Zentz and four individuals at Azar's Restaurant in Valparaiso, Indiana. When Mary Jo Hall was asked what condition Zentz and his friend were in, she answered, "Well, they might have been drinking, but I don't think they was drunk."

- Memorandum by Valparaiso Detective Sergeant Robert Taylor to Chief Walter Lamberson dated February 2, 1987, regarding an altercation involving Rick Zentz at Franklin House bar on January 29, 1987. Detective Taylor stated that he called the night bartender at the Franklin House to receive information about the Zentz altercation and "he stated that Rick had been drinking heavy but all that were involved were drunk." Detective Taylor went on to state "I advised Jerry that we had information from Attorney Charles Nightingale that Rick had pulled his revolver and was holding it in the air to scare people."

- Taped statement by C.I. (a confidential informant) on February 27, 1987, at Valparaiso Police Department regarding a tape containing information that Jon Cooros had about Rick Zentz's involvement in setting up a person, Mark Montgomery, on a drug deal. When the confidential informant was asked what type of information he had, the C.I. responded, "That Jon Cooros had a tape made and was going to give a copy to Mark Montgomery, stating that, ah...either Rick was supposed to set up Mark or they were gonna try to set up Rick on a drug deal." When the confidential informant was asked if the tape was made by Cooros to take to a lawyer, the informant responded, "Uh huh." When the informant was asked if it dealt with drugs, he responded, "Yeah." When the informant was asked, "Do you know of any lawyers that are involved in this?" the informant responded, "Uh...Chuck Nightingale." When the informant was asked, "Okay, does this attorney know that this is a set up and not a legitimate complaint, or do you think he's going along with the set up part?" the informant responded, "I have no idea." When the informant was asked, "Do you know whether our Special Officer, Clyde Riggins, was involved in this is any way?" the informant responded, "Uh huh...yeah...um-m-m, Clyde was supposed to give inside information about different things for Jon."

- Taped statement by C.I. II (another confidential informant) on February 27, 1987, regarding dispute between Richard Zentz and Jon Cooros. Statement stated, "This whole dispute between Jon Cooros and Rick Zentz started because Cooros was told by Patrolman Cos Hernandez that Rick Zentz had broken into Cooros' garage (located at 503 Glendale). Cooros got so mad about this reported incident that he fumed for several days about it. Jon started making a taped "statement" onto his tape recorder. He told me that he was documenting an incident involving Zentz and a Mark Montgomery. He said he was going to tell the truth and "hang" Rick's ass. Cooros also wrote about a three-page letter to Carol Batshauer (then of the *Post Tribune*). He said he had called her on the phone and discussed it with her, and he was going to send her a written copy so that he could have Gary Galloway do a report on it....It had accusations against Unit 90 of the Drug unit ref: to 5 different rape charges against him and it told of the incident involving Montgomery, where Zentz planted drugs on him. He said that Zentz wanted him (Cooros) to keep Montgomery busy so that Zentz could plant the drugs in his coat....I never heard Cooros make any threats on Zentz, other than hanging his ass on the Montgomery thing. This incident occurred in October, 1986. I have not seen Jon Cooros since."

- Claim submitted by Joy Ann Stoner on April 7, 1988, stating, "On or about the 15th day of November, 1987, the Complainant, Joy Ann Stoner, was taken to an apartment complex that she believes to be on Kentucky Street in Valparaiso, Indiana, by 2 individuals who identified themselves as Valparaiso Police Officers; namely, Robert Furst and Richard Zentz. Said individuals purportedly acting on behalf of the Valparaiso Police Department, and by implication on behalf of the City of Valparaiso, held Joy Ann Stoner captive, at gun point, and refused to allow her to leave the premises, and continued to criminally confine her at said address. Said individuals placed a loaded weapon to her head, and indicated to her that unless she cooperated with them, that she would never leave the apartment.

- Evidence of the $175,000 award to Michael Berkowski who was shot in the head during a scuffle in 1977 with off-duty patrolman Ivan Blackman.

- Evidence of an undisclosed settlement amount reached in a Hammond federal court with a watch repairman who claimed he was beaten by former Valparaiso city patrolman Joseph "Ton" Leon. The lawyers for both sides refused to say how much money was involved, but a confidential source told the *Vidette-Messenger* that Donald Whisler received $25,000 to drop his suit in U.S. District Court. The allegations in that case were that Whisler was driving on Campbell Street on March 12, 1979, when he was stopped and ticketed for speeding that resulted in some verbal sparring. According to the complaint, Leon then reached through the open driver's window and hit Whisler in the mouth which resulted in bleeding and a missing tooth. The suit stated that Leon then opened the pickup's door and started to beat Whisler. Leon then got a wooden night stick from his squad car and started hitting Whisler on the face, legs, and groin. Leon allegedly split the baton in two and continued to beat Whisler. After the beating, Whisler and his wife, Julie, were arrested on separate disorderly conduct charges. The charges against Julie Whisler were dropped that evening when police learned she was pregnant. The prosecutor later cited "prosecutorial discretion" and dismissed the charge against Whisler. The Whislers filed a claim with the City of Valparaiso which the city rejected. In 1981, after the claim was rejected by the city, the Whislers sued the city, the police department, and officers Leon and John J. Widup in federal court. The Whislers stated in their claim that it was a "matter of general knowledge" that Leon had used similar tactics to deprive other people of their rights.

And yet Moody and the misfits of the Seventh Circuit thought it was okay to keep this information from the jury in my trial on the issue of the Valparaiso Police Department's history of abusing citizens' rights. And the misfits of the Seventh Circuit had the audacity to state in their opinion in protecting Moody's unjust rulings that I didn't show that the City of Valparaiso was deliberately indifferent to the constitutional rights of its citizens and that I did not demonstrate that the City of Valparaiso "perfunctorily dismissed citizen complaints" after Moody refused to let me do so. Amazing!

And then there was Moody's cowardly act of refusing to let me put on the witness stand a former Valparaiso police officer, Jon Cooros, who had direct knowledge of the conspiracy of the Valparaiso Police Department officers to falsely arrest me until they could achieve their goal of obtaining a wrongful conviction against me in order to take my freedom away. Moody chose to protect the Valparaiso police by disallowing Cooros' testimony about his inside knowledge and information about what was taking place by the Valparaiso officers who were scheming to arrest me. This is something that the jury should have been allowed to hear from Cooros since he was a former Valparaiso police officer with direct knowledge about what was going on, but Moody wasn't going to let it happen. He was determined to keep Cooros' vital information away from the jury, and he certainly made sure that the jury wouldn't know about it. Moody knew that if he allowed Cooros to take the stand and spill the beans that the jury would rule against the Valparaiso police. Moody may as well have sat at the defendant's table with the lawyer and the nefarious officers—this is how bad it was.

Jon Cooros was a former Valparaiso police officer who also served in the undercover unit and had direct inside information about the Valparaiso Police Department's premeditations to falsely arrest me and was willing to testify about it. He let my brother, Branko, know that he had knowledge of what the Valparaiso police were trying to do to me and that he didn't like what was going on. He was one of the few honest officers on the Valparaiso Police Department who had integrity. He had had enough of the corrupt methods of the Valparaiso Police Department and left the department. I located him and asked about what he knew and if he would be willing to testify at the trial. He told me he heard the Valparaiso officers on several occasions talking among themselves about how they were looking for me and that they were going to get me one way or the other. He also told me that he heard them laughing and boasting after several of the false arrests. At first, he was reluctant to testify as he indicated to me that he would face retaliation from the Valparaiso police if he did; but eventually, he decided to do the right thing and take his chances with the retaliation that he expected to happen for doing so. In the federal courthouse on the morning that I planned to call him to the witness stand, he told me that his mother received a threatening call from somebody who refused to identify himself who told her it would be a bad idea for her son to testify at the trial. He was very worried about this but was still willing to testify. But the judicial coward Moody wouldn't let me put Cooros on the witness stand. Moody knew that once I put Cooros on the stand to testify about the conversations he overheard regarding the Valparaiso police officers discussing how they were planning to set me up, that it was game over. But Moody couldn't make himself do the right thing. The corrupt blood running through his veins dictated to him that it was more important to protect rogue police and help insulate them from liability from what they did to me. This is precisely how corrupt governments get away with things. They install corrupt judges to protect them, and Moody certainly did just that. He was just what the doctor ordered for the rogue police—a misfit judge who helped misfit police.

The United States Court of Appeals for the Seventh Circuit in Chicago issued a decision on June 9, 1993, reported as Vukadinovich v. City of Valparaiso, et al. 995 F.2d 750 (1993) by judges Richard A. Posner, Frank H. Easterbrook, and William H. Timbers, when it affirmed Moody's corrupt rulings. Moody gave my case the kiss of death, and the gargoyles on the Seventh Circuit sealed the deal with its kiss of death, as well. Never mind that the so called "Standards for Professional Conduct Within the Seventh Federal Judicial Circuit" explicitly states under standard number 6: "We will give the issues in controversy deliberate, impartial, and studied analysis and consideration." A more corrupt federal appellate court there is not.

CHAPTER 3

THE DISCLOSURE BY JUDGE RICHARD A. POSNER OF CASE FIXING AT THE U.S. COURT OF APPEALS IN CHICAGO

"Never be afraid to raise your voice for honesty and truth and compassion against injustice and lying and greed. If people all over the world...would do this, it would change the earth."
~ William Faulkner

As a country, we are unfortunately at a point in time where the federal judiciary has, in all reality, turned itself into a criminal enterprise system with the chief judges of the circuits serving in the role of head of the syndicate of the circuit. The definition of organized crime is a national centralized enterprise run by criminals to engage in illegal activity. The U.S. Court of Appeals for the Seventh Circuit in Chicago fits this definition. And the revelation that retired judge Richard A. Posner, himself formerly of the U.S. Court of Appeals for the Seventh Circuit in Chicago, essentially affirmed just how corrupt the Seventh Circuit is when he disclosed to me how a judge from the Seventh Circuit, Michael S. Kanne, persuaded him to throw a decision from a civil rights appeal that I had against the Valparaiso Police Department from Indiana. And I thereafter learned even more just how corrupt the Seventh Circuit is after I filed a judicial misconduct complaint against the miscreant case-fixing judge, Michael S. Kanne.

One may understandably wonder why it is that a retired federal judge would disclose a case-fixing activity that he himself was involved in at the request of a brethren judge. That is certainly a fair question. For starters, to answer that question, it started out when Judge Posner retired from the federal bench on September 2, 2017, after 35 years on the bench, after he became very disenchanted with the judges on the U.S. Court of Appeals for the Seventh Circuit over how unfairly the judges were treating—actually mistreating—the pro se litigants, i.e., litigants, who do not have lawyers. ("Pro se" is a Latin expression meaning "for yourself." In law, it means a litigant who has no lawyer and is therefore conducting his own litigation.) He decided he no longer wanted to be part of the judiciary and that he wanted to do something to advance the cause of the pro se litigants. Posner told the *New York Times* in an interview published on September 11, 2017, "…that about six months ago…I awoke from a slumber of 35 years." <u>An Exit Interview With Richard Posner, Judicial Provocateur - The New York Times (nytimes.com)</u>. In other words, he saw the light. In speaking as to how badly the judges on the Seventh Circuit were treating the pro se litigants and how systematically unjust the Seventh Circuit judges were, he said in the article "The basic thing is that most judges regard these people as kind of trash not worth the time of a federal judge." He said that the legal system was treating the unrepresented litigants impatiently, dismissing their cases over technical matters. He said, "I gradually began to realize that this wasn't right, what we were doing." And shortly thereafter, he founded the Posner Center of Justice for Pro Se's.

In March, 2016, I represented myself, pro se, in a five-day jury trial in the United States District Court for the Northern District of Indiana, Hammond Division, against my former public school corporation employer, Hanover Community School Corporation, which is in Cedar Lake, Indiana. At the end of the five-day trial, the federal jury decided in my favor and awarded me significant six-figure damages ($203,840.39) for the corporation's violation of my federal due process rights when it terminated my employment as a teacher. The case received significant national attention because it is essentially unheard of for a lay person to successfully represent himself in a federal jury trial and beat a corporation and its team of lawyers in a civil rights case. Judge Posner heard about how I won the federal jury trial by representing myself. He contacted me and asked me to join him in his newly founded organization, Posner Center of Justice for Pro Se's. Because he was on the panel that went in favor of the Valparaiso police in my appeal, I was naturally leery at the outset when he contacted me, but I read about how he came to "see the light" about how unfair his court—Seventh Circuit Court of Appeals—was to the pro se litigants through his public comments, so I thought it would be prudent to keep an open mind and see what he was really all about. We continued to communicate, and he invited me to come to Chicago for lunch several times and we ended up becoming good friends. He even wrote the foreword to my first book, *Motion for Justice: I Rest My Case*. In February, 2018, Judge Posner appointed me to serve as the executive director of the Posner Center of Justice for Pro Se's.

Our working relationship and our friendship grew very strong, and in March, 2018, I traveled to Chicago to meet Judge Posner for lunch. He wanted to come clean and disclosed that during the pendency of my appeal of my civil rights case against Valparaiso Indiana police years ago in which they had been tormenting me with numerous false arrests, none of which stood up in court, that Judge Michael S. Kanne had initiated an ex parte conversation with Judge Posner, calling me a "troublemaker" and that Kanne "had it in" for me. Judge Posner then disclosed that Judge Kanne had asked him in ex parte fashion—as a "favor" to Judge Kanne—to make sure that I did not prevail in my appeal against the Valparaiso police as Judge Posner was on the panel and Kanne was not. Judge Posner admitted that, regrettably, he had succumbed to Kanne's pressure and had accommodated Kanne's request to have the district court's rulings

(Moody's rulings) in favor of the Valparaiso police affirmed even though Judge Posner knew that the case "should have been reversed." Judge Posner confessed that he knew what he did "was wrong" but that this was "something that judges did for one another from time to time." Judge Posner then acknowledged to me that Kanne was a "corrupt judge" who fixed cases and that Kanne should have never been a member of the federal judiciary. He told me he carried a great deal of guilt for participating in the case-fixing scheme orchestrated by Kanne and needed to get it off his chest. And he did just that.

I could sense that the weight of carrying this had been wearing on him and that disclosing it to me tremendously relieved his mind as he was genuinely remorseful. It was clear to me that he wanted to walk off into the sunset with a clear mind once the point of inflection came to him about how unfair the Seventh Circuit judges were to the pro se's, to which he went public. He was then finally able to put his mind at ease when he disclosed to me how Kanne convinced him to throw the decision in the Valparaiso police case. It was clear to me that during this inflection point in his life that Judge Posner woke up to the fact that Kanne used him in convincing him to throw the decision in favor of the Valparaiso police even though, as Judge Posner told me, the case should have been reversed in my favor. And it is clear to me that Kanne preyed upon Judge Posner as a prime target who could be manipulated into disregarding the rules and case laws to throw decisions as Judge Posner, in a previous *New York Times* interview, publicly stated, "I pay very little attention to legal rules, statutes, constitutional provisions," and that "When you have a Supreme Court case or something similar, they're often extremely easy to get around." An Exit Interview With Richard Posner, Judicial Provocateur - The New York Times (nytimes.com). It stands to reason that Kanne knew this about Judge Posner and figured that he would be an easy mark. And it worked—unfortunately.

After Judge Posner disclosed this to me, I did some checking and discovered that Kanne and Moody were basically judicial bosom buddies as both were nominated to the federal judiciary by the same president, Ronald Regan, on the exact same date, December 4, 1981; and both were confirmed by the Senate on the exact same date, February 8, 1982, for a seat on the exact same court, the United States District Court for the Northern District of Indiana, where they both primarily served in the exact same building in Hammond. And on top of that, eerily enough, both were born just a few months apart in 1938. In terms of the "friendly factor" between these two judicial bosom buddies who both were playing on the same team in the game of "let's screw the person out of justice," I will leave it up to you, the reader, to form your opinion as to all of these "coincidences" —keeping in mind that Judge Posner let the cat out of the proverbial bag in disclosing the case fixing. Welcome to "justice" good ol' boy style created by two Indiana judges cut from the same cloth and even hatched in the same year.

After Judge Posner came clean, I filed a judicial misconduct complaint against Kanne with the U.S. Court of Appeals for the Seventh Circuit in Chicago, and I requested that the Seventh Circuit request that the Chief Justice of the United States transfer the proceeding to the judicial council of another circuit pursuant to Rule 26. And as you read on, you will see that the Seventh Circuit did not request that the Chief Justice of the United States transfer the proceeding to the judicial council of another circuit pursuant to Rule 26 and instead chose to keep the proceeding in-house where it could manipulate the proceeding. On September 30, 2021, Chief Judge Diane S. Sykes dismissed the judicial misconduct complaint on ridiculous technical grounds with no ruling on the merits. Sykes did this even though Kanne didn't deny—on the record—that he fixed the decision as disclosed by Judge Posner. As you read on, you will see that I followed procedure and filed a petition to the Seventh Circuit for a review of the decision and asked for a decision on the merits. This is how corrupt things are in the U.S. Court of Appeals in Chicago. And as you read on, you will see that I filed a petition with the Judicial Conference of the United States, and that judicial body chose to act as though the petition was never filed, and was so worried about the public scrutiny over the case-fixing activities and cover up that I brought to light upon Judge Posner's revelation of Kanne's case fixing, that not only would it not issue a decision—as it is required to do—but it wouldn't even acknowledge the fact that I filed the petition with the Judicial Conference of the United States addressing the corruption in the U.S. Court of Appeals in Chicago. A more nefarious judicial system there couldn't be.

CHAPTER 4

JUDICIAL MISCONDUCT COMPLAINT SWEPT UNDER THE RUG

"Judges are the weakest link in our system of justice, and they are also the most protected."
~ Alan Dershowitz

After Judge Posner revealed the case fixing by Judge Michael S. Kanne in having the appellate decision from my civil rights case against the rogue Valparaiso police fixed, I decided to file a judicial misconduct complaint against Kanne, which I filed with the Seventh Circuit in Chicago on July 26, 2021. Knowing that the U.S. Court of Appeals in Chicago is a corrupt court, I exercised my right to request to the Seventh Circuit that it request that the Chief Justice of the United States transfer the proceeding to the judicial council of another circuit pursuant to Rule 26. However Chief Judge Diane S. Sykes and her cohorts refused to request that the Chief Justice of the United States transfer the proceeding to another circuit, and chose instead to keep the complaint in house where they could sweep the matter under the rug.

On September 30, 2021, Chief Judge Diane S. Sykes issued a Memorandum and Order dismissing the judicial misconduct complaint in a very questionable and troubling fashion in many different ways. Sykes dismissed the complaint on ridiculous technical grounds with no ruling on the merits. The dismissal order contained no on the record statement of denial by Kanne of the allegations against him that he had the civil rights decision fixed as was disclosed by Judge Richard A. Posner. In explaining her dismissal of the misconduct charge, Chief Judge Sykes wrote, "When a complaint is filed so long after an alleged event that memory loss, death, or changes to unknown residences prevent a "proper investigation" and that a proper investigation was "impossible." That was utter hogwash because Sykes didn't point to any evidence of "memory loss," evidence of "death," or evidence of "changes to unknown residences" that would "prevent a proper investigation." Since Kanne was still a member of the Seventh Circuit at the time of the misconduct complaint against him, there shouldn't have been any problem with his "memory," as he would need to have a functioning memory to be able to perform as a judge. And since Kanne was still a member of the Seventh Circuit at the time of the misconduct complaint against him, he obviously wasn't dead, so that certainly wasn't a factor. And since Kanne was still a member of the Seventh Circuit at the time of the misconduct complaint against him, there shouldn't have been any problem in locating him for an interview as to the allegations against him. And although Judge Posner was no longer a member of the Court, he still lived in Chicago and could have been very easily interviewed with regard to the allegations. Another problem with Sykes' so called "Memorandum and Order" was her utilization of fiction as she wrote that I "...did not identify anything that would have precluded him [Brian Vukadinovich] from filing it immediately after he learned of the alleged misconduct." This was hogwash, and Sykes knew it was hogwash because my reasons were explicitly stated on pages 5-10 of the judicial misconduct complaint —which constituted six pages of the judicial misconduct complaint against Kanne. This is how judicial corruption works. Judges not only far too often get creative to advance their corruption, they actually will outright lie to achieve their corrosive goals—and Sykes certainly did do that. This is a consequence of judges having so much leeway to do whatever they want as they know they can simply make things up as they go along to achieve their goals of protectionism of judicial corruption by way of distorting court records—which is exactly what Sykes did. Sykes obviously knew she was on shaky ground as she well knew that there was no statute of limitations for filing a judicial misconduct complaint, so to counter that problem, she simply added in her pitiful balderdash.

It stands to reason that since the key players, Posner and Kanne, were available to be interviewed, but were not, the Seventh Circuit's interest was not in getting to the bottom of what happened with Kanne's fixing of the decision, but rather showed that the Seventh Circuit's central focus was in sweeping Kanne's corrupt activities under the rug—which is exactly what that court of corruption did.

As for Sykes' pitiful statement that a proper investigation was "impossible" for the bogus reasons she gave, the only thing that made a proper investigation "impossible" was the corrupt conduct by Sykes, as she was bound and determined to cover up the case-fixing activities of Kanne, as was disclosed by Judge Posner. It should be noted that Sykes' dismissal order of the complaint contained no on-the-record statement of denial by Kanne of the allegations against him. Sykes made it very convenient for Kanne by not taking a formal statement from him. By not requiring Kanne to make a formal statement, he didn't have to lie on the record by denying that he fixed the decision as Judge Posner disclosed—thanks to Sykes' protectionism.

Sykes' statements in her so called "Memorandum and Order" had no credibility and were utter hogwash, and when I say hogwash, I do mean hogwash. Sykes raised a nonexistent issue of "memory loss" but pointed to no evidence of anybody claiming "memory loss." Sykes raised a nonexistent issue of "death" but pointed to no evidence of "death"—nobody died. Sykes raised a nonexistent issue of "changes to unknown residences" but pointed to no evidence of "changes to unknown residences." In grasping for straws, she even lied and stated that I did not identify anything that would have precluded me from filing the complaint against Kanne immediately after I learned of Kanne's case fixing, when she knew that I, in fact, utilized six pages of my judicial misconduct complaint—pages 5-10—in explaining my reasons. If there were a grand prize awarded to a federal judge who showed the highest degree of corruption in covering for a miscreant judge, Sykes would have been the winner hands down.

Very strangely, the so called "Memorandum and Order" showed only Sykes' name on the top of the document as "Chief Judge" just under the letterhead, "The Judicial Council of the Seventh Circuit." The document did not show the names of any other judges of the so-called "Judicial Council of the Seventh Circuit" who may have participated in the decision. It was a very strange-looking order, as judicial orders generally contain the name of the judge and judges who were involved in the order, with the participating judge's names shown at the end of the order. This particular order didn't identify any judges at the end of the order. Only Sykes' name appeared at the top under the letterhead. The fact that the so-called "Memorandum and Order" didn't identify the judges who were involved in the order was a very clear indicator that the Seventh Circuit was operating in a very shady manner and wanted to conceal the identities of the judges who were involved in the corrosiveness of the proceeding. On October 4, 2021, I sent an email to Chris Conway, Clerk of the United States Court of Appeals for the Seventh Circuit, and requested that he provide the names of the participating judges to me, but he refused to comply. I received an unsigned letter from an unnamed "Deputy Clerk" dated November 10, 2021, stating, "The order speaks for itself..." But the problem was, the order didn't at all speak to who the judges were. This is what happens when secrecy is the rule of the day in corrupt courts in America—the courts hide the criminal judges. If they didn't have anything to hide, then they wouldn't have to hide. But that is what the coward judges at the Seventh Circuit do, they run and hide. In the days of the Old Wild West, the criminals would run and hole themselves up somewhere and wait until it was safe to come out. In the Seventh Circuit, the criminals wearing the black robes hole up in their offices and let their minions in the clerk's office provide their cover for them as Chris Conway did when I asked him to provide the names of the involved judges—which he refused to do.

No. 07-21-90056

Brian Vukadinovich <bvukadinovich@hotmail.com>

To: chris_conway@ca7.uscourts.gov <chris_conway@ca7.uscourts.gov>
Cc: cfitzpatrick@ca7.uscourts.gov <cfitzpatrick@ca7.uscourts.gov>
Dear Mr. Conway,
I am in receipt of the Memorandum and Order dated September 30, 2021 filed under No. 07-21-90056. The document shows Chief Judge Diane S. Sykes listed at the top of the document but does not list the names of the judges who were involved in the decision. Because this is an order from a United States Court I believe I have a right to know the names of the judges who made the decision in this matter. Accordingly, please provide the names of each of the judges who participated in the decision relative to this Memorandum and Order. Thank you.
Brian Vukadinovich

This is an email sent by Brian Vukadinovich to the Clerk of the United States Court of Appeals for the Seventh Circuit, Chris Conway, asking Chris Conway to provide the names of each of the judges who participated in the decision relative to the Memorandum and Order of September 30, 2021, of which order dismissed the judicial misconduct complaint that Brian Vukadinovich filed against Judge Michael S. Kanne.

ROGUES IN BLACK ROBES

United States Court of Appeals
for the Seventh Circuit
219 South Dearborn Street
Chicago, Illinois 60604

Christopher G. Conway
Clerk of Court
312-435-5850

November 10, 2021

<u>CONFIDENTIAL</u>

Brian Vukadinovich
1129 E. 1300 N.
Wheatfield, IN 46392

In Re: Email Correspondence of November 10, 2021

Dear Mr. Vukadinovich,

We have received your November 10, 2021, email. The order speaks for itself. *See* 28 U.S.C. 352(b)(1)(A)(iii).

Please send all future correspondence to the court in writing. The court will not respond to emails sent to individual email accounts.

Sincerely,

Deputy Clerk

This is an unsigned letter Brian Vukadinovich received from a Deputy Clerk of the United States Court of Appeals for the Seventh Circuit stating that the "order speaks for itself" but does not provide the names of the judges who participated in the decision to dismiss the judicial misconduct complaint against Judge Michael S. Kanne.

And since the Seventh Circuit refused to identify the judicial confederates who participated with Sykes in the infected Memorandum and Order protecting the criminal conduct of Michael S. Kanne, I must wonder if Judge Frank Easterbrook, who reportedly has a demonstrated history of utilizing falsehoods in rulings, was one of Sykes' judicial cohorts who participated in the unlawful cover up of Kanne's case-fixing activities with my case as was disclosed by Judge Posner. Quite frankly, I wasn't entirely surprised by what Sykes and her compadres did as utilizing falsehoods is the modus operandi as to how the Seventh Circuit operates. The "Easterbrook Syndrome" has obviously rubbed off on the Seventh Circuit as Diane S. Sykes and her unidentified judicial confederates on the joke of the so-called "Judicial Council of the Seventh Circuit" took a page right out of Frank Easterbrook's unsavory playbook as Sykes and her judicial cohorts quite obviously have no problem in doing exactly what has been reported about Frank Easterbrook's way of conducting judicial business in a miscreant way, as Easterbrook's judicial malfeasances are well documented. *Injustice Watch* reported many disturbing things about Judge Frank H. Easterbrook of the U.S. Court of Appeals for the Seventh Circuit in Chicago. Pattern of misstated facts found in opinions of renowned U.S. Judge Easterbrook | Injustice Watch. The article pointed out that University of Chicago Law School Professor Albert W. Alschuler wrote in a law-review article, "Judge Easterbrook persistently presents wildly inaccurate, made-up statements as unquestionable statements of fact," and that "The truth is not in him." That led *Injustice Watch* to conduct a review of Easterbrook's opinions, and the result was a documented pattern of misrepresented facts in Easterbrook's opinions. *Injustice Watch* uncovered 17 cases since 2010 in which opinions authored by Easterbrook misstated the facts, omitted facts, or made assumptions that were contrary to the trial record. The article pointed out that in many cases Easterbrook's errors seemed to play a significant role in the outcome. See Emily Hoerner and Rick Tulsky, Pattern of misstated facts found in opinions of renowned U.S. Judge Easterbrook, InjusticeWatch.org (April 4, 2017), available at https://www.injustice watch.org/projects/2017/pattern-of-misstatedfacts-found-in-probe-of-renowned-federal-judges-opinions/.

In one opinion authored by Easterbrook, he brushed aside one convicted murderer's challenge to his death sentence, which was based in part on the failure of his defense attorneys to present evidence that he had schizophrenia. Easterbrook wrote that the attorneys offered two specific reasons at a post-conviction hearing to explain their decision not to call an expert to the stand, but the transcript of that hearing shows that the lawyers gave no such explanation. In another opinion, Easterbrook refused to let a prisoner challenge his death sentence on the basis of government records showing that the defendant had an intellectual disability before the crime occurred. Easterbrook wrote that the records of his mental state were known to the defendant and his counsel long ago and could have been obtained sooner, but nothing in the record supported Easterbrook's conclusion. In yet another case, Easterbrook wrote in an opinion that there was not sufficient evidence to support holding two members of the Chicago police department responsible for events that led to the highly-publicized rape of a mentally disturbed woman. But the federal judge hearing the case recited a cascade of evidence in the record before the panel that sharply contradicted the Seventh Circuit's decision written by Easterbrook. *Injustice Watch* documented the pattern of errors by reviewing the trial record, listening to tape recordings of oral arguments, and interviewing attorneys. The review was then expanded to identify earlier complaints about the accuracy of what Easterbrook wrote. The coward Easterbrook declined an interview to discuss the *Injustice Watch* review. And then there is a law review article that even accused Easterbrook of telling repeated "whoppers." [How Frank Easterbrook Kept George Ryan in Prison (valpo.edu)](valpo.edu).

Easterbrook's legal reputation is so suspect that in 1994, in evaluating Chicago-area federal judges, the Chicago Council of Lawyers wrote that at times Easterbrook "acts like the worst of judges" when he disregards law and facts and went on to add that Easterbrook "appears less concerned about the actual facts and issues presented in the appeals before him than about advancing his own philosophy." A *Chicago Tribune* article pointed out that the Chicago Council of Lawyers report, which was an evaluation of the Seventh Circuit's federal appeals judges, devoted 12 pages to Easterbrook and noted Easterbrook's "obvious contempt of those he finds below his intellectual level." U.S. APPEAL JUDGES GET AN EARFUL - Chicago Tribune. And very interestingly that in characterizing Easterbrook as the "worst of judges," the council went on to state that Judge Michael S. Kanne, yes, the one and only Michael S. Kanne who Judge Posner disclosed as a case-fixing judge, "lacks objectivity or the necessary legal skills to serve with distinction."

Frank Easterbrook, in fact, was on the panel in which Kanne, through devious *ex parte* methods, actively had the civil rights decision fixed as was disclosed by Judge Posner. Brian Vukadinovich v. Richard Zentz, Ronald Kurmis, John Ross, William Collins, and City of..., 995 F.2d 750 – CourtListener.com. So when everything is taken into context, the Easterbrook factor also naturally comes into play regarding the Seventh Circuit's refusal to identify the judges who were involved in the two orders which protected Kanne from his case-fixing activities. Clearly, there is a legitimate need for an answer to the question as to whether Judge Frank Easterbrook participated in either or both of the two orders since Easterbrook was a member of the panel of the fixed decision, and it would therefore stand to reason that Easterbrook should not have participated in the decisions from either of the two orders. And if Easterbrook's dubious history as a judge is any indication, the cause for concern would actually be a cause for alarm—which would further shed light on the reason that the Seventh Circuit didn't want me to know who the judges were who participated in the two orders.

It is no wonder that the Seventh Circuit decided that it should keep its corrupt activities in house rather than asking the Chief Justice of the United States to have the matter transferred to another circuit. The fact that Chief Judge Diane S. Sykes chose not to request to the Chief Justice of the United States to have the matter transferred to another circuit speaks volumes, especially since she is on record in previously publicly stating that appellate courts have a responsibility to follow doctrine and frameworks by the Supreme

Court. But publicly saying something that sounds good is one thing, actually being true to the public statement is quite another—at least as far as Diane S. Sykes is concerned. In a *Newsweek* article titled "A look at Diane Sykes, Possible Trump SCOTUS Nominee" published on December 13, 2016, a YouTube video was included where Sykes commented that the lower appellate courts "have the responsibility to follow whatever doctrine and framework the Supreme Court gives to us," and yet Sykes chose not to do so when it came to requesting that the Chief Justice of the United States transfer the proceeding I filed against Kanne to the judicial council of another circuit pursuant to Rule 26. A Look at Diane Sykes, Possible Trump SCOTUS Nominee (newsweek.com).

It is obvious that Sykes and her cohorts wanted to be able to come running to Kanne's rescue, which she and her confederates indeed did. Sykes' public hyperbole about following "doctrine" and "framework the Supreme Court gives to us" leaves much to be desired, to put it mildly. Instead of honoring her public words, Sykes instead chose to honor the Seventh Circuit's history of proclivity toward flexing its judicial muscle to ensure that judicial malfeasance issues are swept under the rug, such as what she did as chief judge by protecting the criminal case-fixing conduct of Judge Michael S. Kanne, as addressed in the judicial misconduct complaint—as was disclosed by longtime and now retired federal court of appeals judge Richard A. Posner. The hypocrisy of Sykes' public statements from the 2014 State Bar of Wisconsin annual meeting, compared to her actions in the judicial misconduct proceeding I filed against Kanne, demonstrates Sykes' lack of judicial integrity and reveals her for the person and judge that she truly is, a judge who says one thing but does another. As John F. Kennedy once famously said, "As we express our gratitude, we must never forget that the highest appreciation is not to utter words, but to live by them." Clearly, Diane S. Sykes has not lived by her own words. It is not surprising that The Peace & Justice Center has characterized Sykes as "the country's worst judge." Meet the Worst Judge in America - Peninsula Peace and

Justice Center. The chicanery exhibited by Kanne, Sykes, and Sykes' confederates on the Seventh Circuit, and the stench of their corruption, was very strong. Make no mistake about it, what Sykes and her cohorts did was judicial corruption of the highest degree. The machinations from these cartoon character, so-called "judges" is sickening.

On November 9, 2021, I filed a petition to the judicial council of the Seventh Circuit for a review of Sykes' order dismissing the judicial misconduct complaint Against Kanne. I pointed out in great detail the significant flaws and improprieties of the September 30, 2021, order by Sykes and her unidentified cohorts. I provided the Seventh Circuit with specific details with my sworn affidavit of the facts submitted under the penalty of perjury. The petition was styled as "Petition to Judicial Council of the Seventh Circuit for Review of Order Dismissing judicial misconduct Complaint Against Judge Michael S. Kanne for His Case Fixing Activities." It was filed under No. 07-21-90056.

This is a verbatim of the petition that I filed with the Seventh Circuit:

No. 07-21-90056

PETITION TO JUDICIAL COUNCIL OF THE SEVENTH CIRCUIT FOR REVIEW OF ORDER DISMISSING JUDICIAL MISCONDUCT COMPLAINT <u>AGAINST JUDGE MICHAEL S. KANNE FOR HIS CASE FIXING ACTIVITIES</u>

I. The So Called "Memorandum and Order" Dismissing the judicial misconduct Complaint Against Judge Michael S. Kanne Has ZERO Integrity

On September 30, 2021, The Judicial Council of the Seventh Circuit via Chief Judge Diane S. Sykes issued a Memorandum and Order dismissing the judicial misconduct complaint in a very questionable and troubling fashion in many different ways. The so called "Memorandum and Order" stated "Although no statute of limitations bars the filing of a judicial misconduct complaint, "[i]f the passage of time has made an accurate and fair investigation of the complaint impractical, the complaint must be dismissed. RULES FOR JUD.-CONDUCT 7 JUD.-DISABILITY PROC. 9; *see also id*. R. 11 (stating in the commentary that dismissal is appropriate "when a complaint is filed so long after an alleged event that memory loss, death, or changes to unknown residences prevent a proper investigation"). Here, the delay in filing this complaint renders proper investigation impossible—the alleged events occurred almost 30 years ago. Furthermore, the complainant says he learned of the alleged events in 2018, but he waited three years to file this complaint and did not identify anything that would have precluded him from filing it immediately after he learned of the alleged misconduct. This too impedes a full, fair, and accurate investigation and prejudices the subject judge's ability to rebut the allegations in the complaint. In short, the extreme passage of time, accompanied by an unreasonable delay in filing the misconduct complaint, justifies dismissal." HOGWASH!

Where in the record is there evidence of "memory loss?" NOWHERE! Where in the record is there evidence of "death?" NOWHERE! Where in the record is there evidence of "changes to unknown residences" that would "prevent a proper investigation? NOWHERE!

Judge Kanne is still a member of the Seventh Circuit, so there should be no problem with his "memory" as he would have to have a functioning memory to be able to function as a judge. And since Kanne is still a member of the Seventh Circuit, he obviously isn't dead, so that certainly isn't a factor. And since Kanne is still a member of the Seventh Circuit, there shouldn't be any problem in locating him for an interview as to the allegations against him. And although Judge Posner is no longer a member of the Court, he still lives in Chicago and, thus, could very easily be interviewed with regard to the allegations. Interviewing Judges Posner and Kanne would seem to be a very easy and practical way for the Judicial Council to investigate the allegations in the Complaint. In asserting that any investigation would be "impractical" due to the passage of time, since the key players are available to be interviewed clearly shows that the Seventh Circuit's interest is not in getting to the bottom of what happened with Kanne's fixing of the decision, but rather shows the Seventh Circuit's interest in sweeping Kanne's corrupt activities under the rug which actually constitutes the aiding and abetting of a crime. The Petitioner's instant judicial misconduct complaint against Kanne demonstrates a very different set of facts that were set forth in Sykes' citing of *In re Complaint of Jud. Misconduct No. 09-01*, 591 F.3d 638, 643-45 (U.S. Jud. Conf. 2009). In the instant judicial misconduct complaint against Kanne, nobody is deceased and in fact Kanne still sits on the Seventh Circuit so he clearly was available for Sykes and her judicial council compadres to get a denial or confession from him, but didn't do so, which is drastically dissimilar from the facts and circumstances in *In re Complaint of Jud. Misconduct No. 09-01*, 591 F.3d 638, 643-45 (U.S. Jud. Conf. 2009), *supra*. which consequently renders the *In re Complaint of Jud. Misconduct No. 09-01*, 591 F.3d 638, 643-45 (U.S. Jud. Conf. 2009) decision as misplaced and inapplicable to the facts and circumstances to the instant judicial misconduct complaint. The fact of such misapplication of an inapplicable decision demonstrates this circuit's interest in conducting a sham proceeding rather than a proceeding of integrity in order to wrongfully and unlawfully protect the criminal conduct of case fixing of one of its own members, namely Michael S. Kanne.

As for the fictitious statement that Petitioner "…did not identify anything that would have precluded him from filing it immediately after he learned of the alleged misconduct.", **which was in fact a false statement by Diane S. Sykes and her undisclosed judicial minions**, further demonstrates this circuit's penchant for creating falsehoods in its rulings as Petitioner's reasons were explicitly stated at pages 5-10 of the judicial misconduct complaint, which constitutes six pages of the complaint. [emphasis added]. Utilizing false statements further demonstrates just how corruptly this circuit operates as the "Easterbrook Syndrome" is apparently rubbing off on this circuit as Diane S. Sykes and her unidentified judicial minions took a page right out of Frank Easterbrook's unsavory playbook as Sykes and her unidentified judicial minions quite obviously have no problem in doing exactly what has been reported about Frank Easterbrook in adopting Easterbrook's modus operandi of presenting "wildly inaccurate, made-up statements as unquestionable statements of fact" which was revealed by University of Chicago Law School Professor Albert W. Alschuler in a law-review article that "Judge Easterbrook persistently presents wildly inaccurate, made-up statements as unquestionable statements of fact," adding, "The truth is not in him." See Albert Alschuler, *How Frank Easterbrook Kept George Ryan in Prison*, University of Chicago Public Law & Legal Theory Paper Series, No. 589, at 15 and 49 (2016). Furthermore, the organization *Injustice Watch* conducted a review of Easterbrook's opinions and "documented a pattern of misrepresented facts" in them. See Emily Hoerner and Rick Tulsky, Pattern of misstated facts found in opinions of renowned U.S. Judge Easterbrook, InjusticeWatch.org (April 4, 2017), available at https://www.injusticewatch.org/projects/2017/pattern-of-misstatedfacts-found-in-probe-of-renowned-federal-judges-opinions/. And very interestingly Easterbrook was on the panel to which Judge Kanne actively through devious *ex parte* methods had the civil rights decision fixed of which case fixing by Kanne was disclosed to Petitioner by Judge Posner as is shown in the judicial misconduct complaint. And since the Seventh Circuit refuses to identify the judicial minions who participated with Sykes in the infected memorandum and order protecting the criminal conduct of Michael S. Kanne, one must wonder if Frank Easterbrook is one of Sykes' judicial minions who participated and continue to participate in the unlawful cover up of Michael S. Kanne's criminal conduct of which criminal conduct by Michael S. Kanne renders Kanne a criminal under 18 U.S. Code Sec. 2(a)(b). It is easy to see why this circuit didn't want to have this proceeding transferred to the judicial council of another circuit.

II. The Hypocrisy of Judge Diane S. Sykes

In a *Newsweek* article titled "A look at Diane Sykes, Possible Trump SCOTUS Nominee" published on December 13, 2016, a youtube video was included featuring Judge Diane Sykes and Judge David Hamilton. The video was titled "Methods of Appellate Judging" regarding a summary that the judges discussed as to their participation in a 2014 State Bar of Wisconsin annual meeting. Judge Sykes commented on the video that "Judge Hamilton made a very important point which is that in appellate judging we are not just deciding our cases, but we are writing precedent and it's really important when we're writing our opinions to be transparent about what our decision method in the case is and how we get from point A to B to C in the analysis so that.... the public understand the reasoning and rationale behind our decisions." Judge Sykes went on to comment "Most cases come to us with an established doctrine or decision framework for deciding the case and so, umm umm, it's very often in our cases that these, umm, global theories of interpretation won't be debated umm among the judges or among the lawyers because they're well established in our law and we as a lower appellate court have the responsibility to follow whatever doctrine and framework the Supreme Court gives to us." And yet Sykes' memorandum and order was far from "transparent" as it steered clear of explaining why it mysteriously chose not to require a written response from Michael S. Kanne, nor did it explain why it chose not to get a statement from Judge Richard A. Posner who disclosed Michael S. Kanne's criminal conduct. The chicanery was so bad that the so called "memorandum and order" cowardly omitted the names of the judges who participated in the decision to dismiss the complaint against Kanne in order to protect Kanne from his criminal conduct.

Diane S. Sykes commented in her interview that the lower appellate courts "have the responsibility to follow whatever doctrine and framework the Supreme Court gives to us" and yet Sykes chose to not follow the so called "doctrine and framework the Supreme Court gives to us" when it came to requesting that the Chief Justice of the United States transfer this proceeding to the judicial council of another circuit pursuant to Rule 26. Sykes' hyperbole leaves much to be desired. Instead of honoring her public words, Diane S. Sykes instead chose to honor this circuit's history of proclivity toward flexing its judicial muscle to ensure that judicial malfeasance issues are swept under the rug such as what it is currently doing by protecting the criminal conduct of Judge Michael S. Kanne under the leadership of Chief Judge Diane S. Sykes with the help of her undisclosed judicial minions who participated in the infected "memorandum and order" dismissing the complaint against Michael S. Kanne, but didn't attach their names to the infected memorandum and order for the cowards that they are. The hypocrisy of Diane S. Sykes' public statements from the 2014 State Bar of Wisconsin annual meeting compared to her actions in this proceeding demonstrates Sykes' lack of judicial integrity and reveals her for the person and judge that she truly is. As John F. Kennedy once famously said *"As we express our gratitude, we must never forget that the highest appreciation is not to utter words, but to live by them."* Clearly, Diane S. Sykes has not lived by her own words.

III. According to Federal Law the Conduct of Judge Diane S. Sykes and Her Judicial Compadres Who Have Taken Part in the Cover-Up of Judge Michael S. Kanne's Criminal Conduct of Fixing the Decision Constitutes an Engagement of Acts of Treason And the "Memorandum and Order" Dismissing the Complaint Against Michael S. Kanne is Void with No Legal Force Effect Effect

The conduct of Judge Diane S. Sykes and her undisclosed judicial minions who participated in the infected so called "Memorandum and Order" dismissing the complaint against Michael S. Kanne without seeking a written response from him (Kanne) and without interviewing him, and without interviewing Judge Richard A. Posner who disclosed Kanne's case fixing misconduct, constitutes clear evidence of a cover up by this circuit of Kanne's criminal activities of having the decision fixed just as was disclosed by Judge Posner as reflected in the judicial misconduct complaint against Kanne. It is very noteworthy that Michael S. Kanne has not denied the allegations of his case fixing activities that have been clearly stated in the judicial misconduct complaint against him. The fact that Sykes and her undisclosed minions didn't explain why they didn't take action on Petitioner's request for the Judicial Council of the Seventh Circuit to request that the Chief Justice of the United States transfer this proceeding to the judicial council of another circuit pursuant to Rule 26 given that the complaint implicates current and former Judges on the Seventh Circuit, to which the recent developments have demonstrated that Chief Judge Diane S. Sykes and her unidentified minions have engaged and continue to engage in criminal conduct by way of their protectionism of Michael S. Kanne's case fixing activities which are criminal violations of federal law as revealed by Judge Richard A. Posner, speaks volumes as to this circuit's corruption. When a judge acts as a trespasser of the law, when a judge does not follow the law, the judge *loses subject matter jurisdiction and the judge's orders are void, of no legal force or effect.* The U.S. Supreme Court, in *Scheurer v. Rhodes*, 416 U.S. 232, 94 S.Ct. 1683, 1687 (1974) stated that "when a state officer acts under a state law in a manner violative of the Federal Constitution, he "comes into conflict with the superior authority of that Constitution, and he is in that case stripped of his official or representative character and is subjected in his person to the consequences of his individual conduct. The State has no power to impart to him any immunity from responsibility to the supreme authority of the United States." By law, a judge is a state officer. The judge then acts not as a judge, but as a private individual (in his person). The U.S. Supreme Court has made clear that "No state legislator or executive or judicial officer can war against the Constitution without violating his undertaking to support it." *Cooper v. Aaron*, 358 U.S. 1, 78 S.Ct. 1401 (1958). Any judge who does not comply with his oath to the Constitution of the United States wars against that Constitution and engages in acts in violation of the Supreme Law of the Land. The judge is engaged in an act of acts of treason. *S. v. Will*, 449 U.S. 200, 216, 101 S.Ct. 471, 66 L.Ed.2d 392, 406 (1980); *Cohens v. Virginia*, 19 U.S. (6 Wheat) 264, 404, 5 L.Ed. 257 (1821).

This circuit, in *U.S. v. Murphy*, 768 F.2d 1518, 1531 (7th Cir. 1985) held that the Circuit Court of Cook County was a criminal enterprise by virtue of the judges' failure to report the criminal activities of other judges and thus the protective judges consequently became principals in the criminal activity. The conduct of Chief Judge Diane S. Sykes and her undisclosed compadres who were participating actors in the so called "Judicial Council" in protecting the criminal conduct of

Michael S. Kanne who violated federal law by his conduct of having a decision fixed of which criminal conduct is a violation of the United States laws renders Diane S. Sykes and her participating undisclosed judicial minions as trespassers of the law which constitutes acts of treason. *S. v. Will*, 449 U.S. 200, 216, 101 S.Ct. 471, 66 L.Ed.2d 392, 406 (1980); *Cohens v. Virginia*, 19 U.S. (6 Wheat) 264, 404, 5 L.Ed. 257 (1821).

This circuit's protectionism of Michael S. Kanne's criminal conduct of having a decision fixed in violation of the United States laws renders the United States Court of Appeals for the Seventh Circuit as a criminal enterprise pursuant to the standards that this circuit itself set in *U.S. v. Murphy*, 768 F.2d 1518, 1531 (7th Cir. 1985) when it held that the Circuit Court of Cook County was a criminal enterprise by virtue of the judges' failure to report the criminal activities of other judges, just as Chief Judge Diane S. Sykes and her undisclosed minions have likewise failed to report the criminal activities of Michael S. Kanne and are in fact involved in an attempted cover-up of Michael S. Kanne's criminal activities which is precisely why Sykes and her minions chose not to ask the Chief Judge of the United States to transfer this proceeding to the judicial council of another circuit pursuant to Rule 26 and instead chose to keep Kanne's criminal activities in house where it could protect Kanne from the appropriate punishment that should be handed to him for his criminal activities of having a decision fixed in violation of the United States laws.

18 U.S. Code Sec. 2

> (a) Whoever commits an offense against the United States or aids, abets, counsels, commands, induces or procures its commission, is punishable as a principal.
> (b) Whoever willfully causes an act to be done which if directly performed by him or another would be an offense against the United States, is punishable as a principal.

18 U.S. Code Sec. 3

> Whoever, knowing that an offense against the United States has been committed, receives, relieves, comforts or assists the offender in order to hinder or prevent his apprehension, trial or punishment, is an accessory after the fact.

18 U.S. Code Sec. 4

> Whoever, having knowledge of the actual commission of a felony cognizable by a court of the United States, conceals and does not as soon as possible make known the same to some judge or other person in civil or military authority under the United States, shall be fined under this title or imprisoned not more than three years, or both.

It is utterly ridiculous for Sykes and her judicial compadres to imply that interviewing Michael S. Kanne was somehow "impractical" regarding the allegations in the complaint since Kanne is still a member of the Court. That defies all logic. And in the face of Sykes' and her unidentified judicial minions' decision to not interview Kanne, or require Kanne to submit a written response to the complaint, it is utter hogwash for Sykes and her unidentified minions to say that a "proper investigation" is "impossible" since Kanne could have very easily been interviewed with regard to the allegations, and the fact that Sykes and her unidentified judicial minions chose not to do so demonstrates evidence of this diseased circuit's inherent inclination to cover up for judicial corruption as it is clearly doing in unlawfully protecting the criminal conduct of Michael S. Kanne.

It is noteworthy that Sykes' and her unidentified judicial minions citing of the matter *In re Complaint of Jud. Misconduct No. 09-01,* is a matter where the proceeding was transferred to the Third Circuit Judicial Council from the Ninth Circuit Judicial Council by the Chief Justice, which is something that this corrupt circuit refused to do in its quest to keep in house the criminal activities of Michael S. Kanne's case fixing as is alleged in the judicial misconduct complaint against him as revealed by a retired former member of this circuit, Judge Richard A. Posner. Since Sykes and her unidentified judicial minions have cited the matter of *In re Complaint of Jud. Misconduct No. 09-01,* 591 F.3d 638, 643-45 (U.S. Jud. Conf. 2009), then they should have done just as was done in that proceeding and requested that the Chief Justice of the United States transfer this proceeding to the judicial council of another circuit pursuant to Rule 26 as Petitioner requested. But Sykes and her unidentified minions preferred to keep Kanne's criminal conduct in house rather than having another circuit conduct an "actual" investigation such as what was done in *In re Complaint of Jud. Misconduct No. 09-01,* 591 F.3d 638, 643-45 (U.S. Jud. Conf. 2009) where after transfer of the proceeding in that matter the judicial council had the integrity to conduct a real investigation and issued a Memorandum Opinion and Order in J.C. 03-08-90050, finding misconduct accompanied by "appropriate corrective action" and summarized the events and created a public document containing the official minutes of Judicial Conference action. By its infected action in the instant matter in keeping Kanne's criminal conduct in house rather than having the Chief Justice of the United States transfer this proceeding to the judicial council of another circuit, Sykes and her unidentified judicial minions provided cover to Kanne's criminal conduct as shown in the judicial misconduct complaint against him, to which Kanne never denied on the record, and Sykes and her unidentified minions conveniently avoided another circuit's taking of "appropriate corrective action" and conveniently avoided a summarization of events and the creation of a public document of official minutes of Judicial Conference action as to Kanne's criminal conduct of unlawfully having a decision fixed in this circuit as shown in the judicial misconduct complaint filed against him and as disclosed by Judge Richard A. Posner.

IV. This Circuit Is Without Jurisdiction to Adjudicate this Proceeding By Virtue of Its Unlawful Protectionism of the Criminal Conduct of Case Fixing by Judge Michael S. Kanne and this Proceeding Should be Transferred to Another Judicial Council of Another Circuit

The facts are such that the allegations in Petitioner's judicial misconduct complaint against Michael S. Kanne's criminal conduct of having a decision fixed as was disclosed by Judge Richard A. Posner are well grounded and supported by affidavit. The facts are such that Diane S. Sykes and her undisclosed judicial minions dismissed the complaint without interviewing Judges Posner and

Kanne even though Kanne is a current active member of the circuit. The facts are such that Diane S. Sykes and her undisclosed judicial minions didn't direct Michael S. Kanne to submit a written response to the complaint. The facts are such that Diane S. Sykes and her undisclosed judicial minions falsely wrote in the infected memorandum and order that Petitioner "…did not identify anything that would have precluded him from filing it immediately after he learned of the alleged misconduct.", which was in fact a false statement by Diane S. Sykes and her undisclosed judicial minions as Petitioner's reasons were explicitly stated at pages 5-10 of the judicial misconduct complaint, which constitutes six pages of the complaint. The facts are such that Diane S. Sykes and her undisclosed judicial minions ignored Petitioner's request for the Judicial Council of the Seventh Circuit to request that the Chief Justice of the United States transfer this proceeding to the judicial council of another circuit pursuant to Rule 26. The facts are such that the memorandum and order by Diane S. Sykes and her undisclosed judicial minions does not indicate the names of any of the judges who participated in the memorandum and order to dismiss the complaint against Michael S. Kanne regarding his criminal activities of having a decision fixed. The facts are such that the Clerk of the United States Court of Appeals for the Seventh Circuit, Chris Conway, has refused to provide the names of the judges who participated in the memorandum and order by Diane S. Sykes and her undisclosed judicial minions notwithstanding that Petitioner requested in an email dated October 4, 2021, that the judges' names be provided to the Petitioner. (see email from Brian Vukadinovich to Clerk Chris Conway attached hereto and labeled as **Petitioner Exhibit 1**). The facts are such that Michael S. Kanne has not denied on the record the allegations contained within the judicial misconduct complaint against him of which allegations were supported by Petitioner's affidavit of which affidavit statements were not rebutted in any way. The facts are such that there is no dispute about the allegations contained within the judicial misconduct complaint and supporting affidavit against Michael S. Kanne for his criminal case fixing activities of having a decision fixed.

Under federal law which is applicable to all states, the U.S. Supreme Court stated that if a court is "without authority, its judgments and orders are regarded as nullities. They are not voidable, but simply void; and form no bar to a recovery sought, even prior to a reversal in opposition to them. They constitute no justification; and all persons concerned in executing such judgments or sentences, are considered, in law, as trespassers." *Elliot v. Piersol*, 1 Pet. 328, 340, 26 U.S. 328, 340 (1828).

When a judge acts as a trespasser of the law, when a judge does not follow the law, the judge loses subject matter jurisdiction and the judge's orders are void, of no legal force or effect. The U.S. Supreme Court, in *Scheurer v. Rhodes*, 416 U.S. 232, 94 S.Ct. 1683, 1687 (1974) stated that "when a state officer acts under a state law in a manner violative of the Federal Constitution, he "comes into conflict with the superior authority of that Constitution, and he is in that case stripped of his official or representative character and is subjected in his person to the consequences of his individual conduct. The State has no power to impart to him any immunity from responsibility to the supreme authority of the United States." By law, a judge is a state officer. The U.S. Supreme Court has made clear that "No state legislator or executive or judicial officer can war against the Constitution without violating his undertaking to support it." *Cooper v. Aaron*, 358 U.S. 1, 78 S.Ct. 1401 (1958).

If a judge does not fully comply with the Constitution, his orders are void. *In re Sawyer*, 124 U.S. 200 (1888), he/she is without jurisdiction, and he/she has engaged in an act or acts of treason. Whenever a judge acts where he/she does not have jurisdiction to act, the judge is engaged in an act or acts of treason. *S. v. Will*, 449 U.S. 200, 216, 101 S.Ct. 471, 66 L.Ed.2d 392, 406 (1980); *Cohens v. Virginia*, 19 U.S. (6 Wheat) 264, 404, 5 L.Ed. 257 (1821).

The Seventh Circuit Court of Appeals has held that the Circuit Court of Cook County is a criminal enterprise. *U.S. v. Murphy*, 768 F.2d 1518, 1531 (7th Cir. 1985). Since judges who do not report the criminal activities of other judges become principals in the criminal activity, 18 U.S.C. Section 1, and since no judges have reported the criminal activity of the judges who have been convicted, the other judges are as guilty as the convicted judges.

When judges act when they do not have jurisdiction to act, or they enforce a void order (an order issued by a judge without jurisdiction), they become trespassers of the law, and are engaged in treason. The Court in *Yates v. Village of Hoffman Estates, Illinois*, 209 F.Supp. 757 (N.D. Ill. 1962) held that "not every action by a judge is in exercise of his judicial function. ...it is not a judicial function for a judge to commit an intentional tort even though the tort occurs in the courthouse."

Given that the instant judicial misconduct complaint against Michael S. Kanne implicates current and former judges in this circuit, and given that Chief Judge Diane S. Sykes and her undisclosed judicial minions are involved in covering up and protecting Judge Michael S. Kanne's criminal conduct of having a decision fixed, Diane S. Sykes as Chief Judge and the Judicial Council of the Seventh Circuit should have requested that the Chief Justice of the United States transfer this proceeding to the judicial council of another circuit pursuant to Rule 26 of which rule expressly authorizes this transfer. The Commentary to Rule 26 states that "[s]uch transfers may be appropriate . . . where the issues are highly visible and a local disposition may weaken public confidence . . . ." The nature of the allegations in this Complaint are both highly visible and implicate several past and current members of the Seventh Circuit who are indeed involved in protecting and insulating Michael S. Kanne from any punishment(s) for his criminal conduct of having a decision fixed in violation of the laws of the United States. Therefore, transfer was then, and is now, appropriate. *See, e.g., In re Complaint of Judicial Misconduct* (Ninth Circuit Judge Alex Kozinski), 575 F.3d 279, 280 (3d Cir. Jud. Council 2009), and *In re Charges of Judicial Misconduct* (Fifth Circuit Judge Edith Jones), 769 F.3d 762 (D.C. Cir. Jud. Council 2014). Transfer to another judicial council of another circuit is certainly called for in the instant case since several undisclosed judges from this circuit are involved in the criminal activity of protecting Michael S. Kanne from his criminal conduct of having a decision fixed, criminal conduct to which Michael S. Kanne has not denied on the record in this proceeding. The continual efforts to keep Kanne's criminal activities in house in this diseased circuit to protect Kanne from appropriate punishment for his violation of the laws of the United States renders Diane S. Sykes and her unidentified judicial minions as "trespassers" under the law. *Elliot v. Piersol*, 1 Pet. 328, 340, 26 U.S. 328, 340 (1828).

V. The After the Fact Protectionism and Concealment of Michael S. Kanne's Criminal Activities by Diane S. Sykes Effectively Disqualifies Diane S. Sykes <u>From Any Future Consideration for Appointment to the Supreme Court</u>

The conduct of Diane S. Sykes in submitting false statements in the memorandum and order falsely purporting that Petitioner didn't provide an explanation for why he didn't "immediately" file his complaint against Michael S. Kanne, when Petitioner certainly did provide an explanation demonstrates Sykes' willingness to falsify information on an official order of judicial business to which falsification of information was done to conceal and protect the criminal activities of Michael S. Kanne along with the other matters of impropriety by Diane S. Sykes as heretofore written renders Diane S. Sykes, a criminal under the laws of the United States as an accessory after the fact under 18 U.S. Code Sec. 3. And by Diane S. Sykes' knowledge of Michael S. Kanne's criminal activities in having the decision fixed, which Kanne has not denied in this proceeding, and by Diane S. Sykes' concealment of Kanne's criminal activities by not making Kanne's felonious conduct known to some judge or other person in civil authority, renders Diane S. Sykes a criminal under 18 U.S. Code Sec. 4.

The stench of this sham proceeding as spearheaded by Judge Diane S. Sykes and her judicial council compadres in operating in such secrecy in the common scheme to protect the criminal conduct of Michael S. Kanne is such a strong stench that Sykes and her compadres will not identify the judges who participated in the infected memorandum and order dismissing the judicial misconduct complaint against the case fixing judge Michael S. Kanne. The stench of the corruption spearheaded by Chief Judge Diane S. Sykes in this sham proceeding is so bad that even the clerk of the court for the Seventh Circuit, Chris Conway, is participating in the common scheme to protect the corrupt actors as he refuses to identify the participating judges who took part in the memorandum order which was so obviously designed to protect the criminal judge Michael S. Kanne. See email from Petitioner to Clerk Chris Conway attached hereto and labeled as **Petitioner Exhibit 1** showing Petitioner's request for the names of the judges who participated in the memorandum and order protecting Kanne's criminal conduct.

The continual efforts to keep Kanne's criminal activities in house in this diseased circuit to protect Kanne from appropriate punishment for his violation of the laws of the United States renders Diane S. Sykes and her unidentified judicial minions as "trespassers" under the law. *Elliot v. Piersol*, 1 Pet. 328, 340, 26 U.S. 328, 340 (1828). Such conduct by Diane S. Sykes and her unidentified judicial minions in failing to fully comply with the Constitution are acts of treason according to the Supreme Court. *S. v. Will*, 449 U.S. 200, 216, 101 S.Ct. 471, 66 L.Ed.2d 392, 406 (1980); *Cohens v. Virginia*, 19 U.S. (6 Wheat) 264, 404, 5 L.Ed. 257 (1821).

Because of her abuse of power as Chief Judge of the United States Court of Appeals for the Seventh Circuit by violating the laws of the United States in protecting the criminal activities of a corrupt judge, Michael S. Kanne, who has not denied fixing the decision that is the subject of the complaint against him, Diane S. Sykes dangerously abused her power, and she has thereby disqualified herself from any future consideration for an appointment to the United States Supreme Court. *"The greater the power, the more dangerous the abuse"* ~ Edmund Burke.

VI. CONCLUSION

Due to the protectionism unlawfully afforded to the criminal conduct of Michael S. Kanne by Chief Judge Diane S. Sykes and her undisclosed judicial minions, of which protectionism is violative of the laws of the United States, the memorandum and order previously issued by Diane S. Sykes and her undisclosed judicial compadres, the memorandum and order dismissing the complaint against Michael S. Kanne is void with no legal force or effect, and due to the protectionism unlawfully afforded to the criminal conduct of Michael S. Kanne by Chief Judge Diane S. Sykes and her undisclosed judicial minions, of which protectionism is violative of the laws of the United States, this proceeding should be referred to the Chief Justice of the United States with a request that the Chief Justice transfer this proceeding to the judicial council of another circuit pursuant to Rule 26. *See, e.g., In re Complaint of Judicial Misconduct* (Ninth Circuit Judge Alex Kozinski), 575 F.3d 279, 280 (3d Cir. Jud. Council 2009), and *In re Charges of Judicial Misconduct* (Fifth Circuit Judge Edith Jones), 769 F.3d 762 (D.C. Cir. Jud. Council 2014).

/s/ Brian Vukadinovich
Brian Vukadinovich, Pro Se

Because the judicial misconduct complaint against Kanne implicated current and former judges in the Seventh Circuit, and because Sykes and her undisclosed judicial cohorts were involved in covering up and protecting Kanne's criminal conduct of having a decision fixed, Sykes as chief judge and the judicial council of the Seventh Circuit should have requested that the Chief Justice of the United States transfer the proceeding to the judicial council of another circuit pursuant to Rule 26 of which rule expressly authorizes such a transfer. The Commentary to Rule 26 states that "[s]uch transfers may be appropriate . . . where the issues are highly visible and a local disposition may weaken public confidence . . ." It goes without saying that the nature of the allegations in my judicial misconduct complaint against Kanne were both highly visible and implicated several past and current members of the Seventh Circuit who were involved in protecting and insulating Kanne from any punishment(s) for his criminal conduct of having a decision fixed in violation of the laws of the United States. Therefore, transfer was appropriate and should have happened—but it didn't. *See, e.g., In re Complaint of Judicial Misconduct* (Ninth Circuit Judge Alex Kozinski), 575 F.3d 279, 280 (3d Cir. Jud. Council 2009), and *In re Charges of Judicial Misconduct* (Fifth Circuit Judge Edith Jones), 769 F.3d 762 (D.C. Cir. Jud. Council 2014). Transfer to another circuit didn't happen because Sykes and her confederates chose instead to keep their corrupt activities in house where the criminals in the black robes could protect one of their own, a case-fixing judge, and could sweep their corruption under the rug.

On January 20, 2022, the so called "Judicial Council of the Seventh Circuit" issued an order denying the petition for review and affirmed Sykes' Memorandum and Order of September 30, 2021 (No. 07-21-90056). I can't say that I was surprised. This is how corrupt courts operate, and the U.S. Court of Appeals for the Seventh Circuit in Chicago indeed is a corrupt court without question. The order stated that it was a "final decision" and that "The complainant is not entitled to any further review" which was not at all true as federal law, in fact, provides that a complainant who files a judicial misconduct complaint against a federal judge which has been dismissed by a judicial council circuit has a right to file a petition for review. 28 U.S. Code Sec. 357(a) explicitly states that "A complainant or judge aggrieved by an action of the judicial council under section 354 may petition the Judicial Conference of the United States for review thereof. 28 U.S. Code Sec. 357(b) explicitly states that "The Judicial Conference, of the standing committee established under section 331, may grant a petition by a complainant or judge under subsection (a). 28 U.S. Code § 357 - Review of orders and actions | U.S. Code | US Law | LII / Legal Information Institute (cornell.edu). And in addition to falsely proclaiming in an order that people who have been aggrieved by corrupt actions of federal judges who report the judges' corrupt actions are not entitled to a further review of a judicial council's infected decision, which is belied by the law of 28 U.S. Code Sec. 357(a), the Seventh Circuit's misinformation is further belied by the Supreme Court's decision in *Marbury v. Madison*, 5 U.S. 137 (1803) where the Supreme Court stated, "The very essence of civil liberty certainly consists in the right of every individual to claim the protection of the laws whenever he receives an injury, and further stated "It is emphatically the province and duty of the Judicial Department to say what the law is." WILLIAM MARBURY v. JAMES MADISON, Secretary of State of the United States. | Supreme Court | US Law | LII / Legal Information Institute (cornell.edu). The Seventh Circuit contrarily says what the law "is not." So clearly, the Seventh Circuit operates nefariously in bad faith by cavalierly giving out false information in its orders insofar as the orders concern the peoples' right to redress—as it clearly did by falsely stating in its order to me that its order was a "final decision" and that "The complainant is not entitled to any further review." Providing this false information is not only further evidence of how the Seventh Circuit operates in trying to cover for its graft, it is conclusive evidence of its nefariousness.

The January 20, 2022, order stated that Sykes and Kanne did not participate in this particular decision. It is easy to see that Sykes and her cohorts were covering their tracks by making their graft look better if their names weren't on that particular order, so they obviously left it up to their confederates to do their dirty work for them. It is interesting that the previous order of September 30, 2021, didn't indicate that Kanne did not participate in the decision from that particular order, so that issue is certainly suspect as to whether or not Kanne participated in that order. I would be highly surprised if Kanne wasn't somehow involved with it. The fact that the Seventh Circuit made it a point to state in the January 20, 2022, order that Sykes and Kanne didn't participate in that decision but didn't at all make a point that Sykes and Kanne didn't participate in the original September 30, 2021, order when the misconduct complaint against Kanne was dismissed, strongly suggests that they participated in that decision. The omission was basically an admission. It was a substantial perversion of the law by perverse judges who have no regard for the rule of law.

Sykes' corruption in the handling of my judicial misconduct complaint against Kanne seems to be par for the course for her in terms of her lack thereof for judicial integrity. The Peace & Justice Center has characterized Sykes as "the country's worst judge." <u>Meet the Worst Judge in America - Peninsula Peace and Justice Center</u>. Marge Baker, executive vice president of People for the American Way, has been quoted as saying that Sykes is a "far-right" judicial activist and that "Her record shows she's willing to put women's lives at risk to further her personal ideology." Marge Baker also said, "She's also undermined principles fundamental to our Constitution throughout her career" and "For instance, she was the sole dissent in a case reversing a conviction because a juror did not understand English...She should not sit on the Supreme Court." With this information about her, I can't be very surprised that she had no problem in proceeding in a corrupt manner when it came to making a protective decision for one of her corrupt brethren judges who fixed the decision in my appeal. This is a consequence of having to endure an out of control and unmonitored federal judiciary. Make no mistake about it, we do indeed have a very corrupt federal judiciary. And one doesn't have to look beyond the U.S. Court of Appeals for the Seventh Circuit to see just how corrupt it is. It is judicial corruption by fiat.

And if it wasn't bad enough that Kanne was in the federal judiciary fixing cases in such an untouched manner as he did with having the appellate decision of my appeal against the Valparaiso police fixed, as was disclosed by Judge Posner, he had no problem getting into the political arena as well in flexing his corrupt muscle to the point of insisting who his successor would be upon his retirement—as if we as a country needed more Kanne types. But unfortunately for Kanne, and fortunately for our country, something Kanne tried to do drew attention to his ugly insider politics when he tried to exert his political muscle in an area where his political muscle wasn't welcome. Kanne's penchant for throwing decisions wasn't just something he did when he wanted a particular decision in a case fixed, but he also had a penchant for trying to fix the outcome of the political appointment of his successor by leveraging his retirement in order to make an inappropriate demand of the executive branch. While the custom has been that federal judges have long retired with no strings attached, that tradition began to crack near the end of the Trump administration in 2018 when Kanne startled the legal community by withdrawing his announced retirement out of pique that his former clerk wouldn't be selected as his replacement.

In January 2018, Kanne received a political call from the White House basically asking him to cooperate in the scheme of packing the court with conservative judges by asking him to take senior status because he was 78 at the time and the Trump White House could then be assured of naming another conservative judge to the federal judiciary. At the time, under the leadership of Don McGahn, the White House counsel's office under Trump was focused almost singularly on filling the federal bench with conservative judges, and in Kanne, Trump's lawyers saw an opportunity to enhance this goal if it could convince Kanne to take senior status and then it could lock in a conservative who could be on the federal bench for decades to come. Rob Luther, a McGahn deputy responsible for nominations, phoned Kanne to suggest that he retire and told Kanne that the White House had a successor in mind, Tom Fisher, Indiana's solicitor general and a former clerk for Kanne. Kanne was very open to the idea since he took it as an opportunity to flex his own muscle and call the shots as to who his successor would be. According to news reports, Kanne said, "I had not intended to take senior status because that wasn't my plan, but if I had a former clerk who had the chance to do it, then I would." He went on to say, "On the consideration that he would be named, I sent in my senior status indication to the president." This was vintage Kanne as it was all about his penchant to satisfy his thirst for power and had nothing to do with what was best for the federal judiciary and the people of our country who are to be served by the federal judiciary. This way Kanne knew he could have enough influence to add one of his own minions on the federal judiciary, who in essence was his trained lap dog, and would then be able to continue Kanne's infected legacy on the federal judiciary.

And it was working to plan, as taking senior status, which is a form of semi-retirement for judges, Kanne could continue working and infecting the federal judiciary as he did when he had the appellate decision fixed in my case against the Valparaiso Indiana police, while at the same time creating a vacancy on the bench for Trump to fill. It was a perfect plan—until Vice President Mike Pence's aides found out about it and put the kibosh to Fisher's nomination.

As it turns out, as solicitor general of Indiana, Fisher had defended Mike Pence's policies in court when Pence was governor, and aides to the then vice president were concerned that a Fisher nomination would dredge up events and information politically damaging to Pence. So in the end, after Pence's lawyers and his chief of staff, Nick Ayers, objected, Kanne's lap dog didn't get nominated.

It was fitting that the very kind of politics that Kanne liked to play as a judge, in abusing his powers as a federal judge by undermining peoples' rights in order to help influential corporations and government agencies, was the very kind of politics that doomed his thirst for power when he wanted to dictate who would be his successor on his personal terms. After Kanne's tactic didn't work, he took his ball and went home crying when he reportedly said, "A number of weeks later, I got a phone call from [Fisher] saying, 'It's off, I'm not going to be named,' " to which Kanne responded, 'If you're not going to be named, then I'm not going to take senior status.' " <u>Why Pence spiked a Trump judge - POLITICO, Judges are using retirements as leverage against Joe Biden. (slate.com)</u>.

So in other words, Kanne's position was that if he couldn't get his own way in getting one of his former clerk minions on there to replace him, and obviously carry on what he picked up from Kanne, then Kanne would take his ball and go home. This is the way Kanne operated, it was his way or no way. This political side of Kanne, actually devious side, was in clear display in how he attempted to manipulate the decision of who should be his successor, of which arm twisting showed what was in his mindset in terms of utilizing pressure tactics to get his own way, much the same as he did when he pressured Judge Posner to fix the decision of the case I had against the Valparaiso police. Rather than letting the judicial appointment process take its natural course, Kanne abused the process by stepping in and demanding that he should control the outcome as to who should be named as the judge to fill the vacancy when he retired; and just as he went out of his way to control that outcome, he did much the same thing by stepping in to control the outcome of my case against the Valparaiso police, this time by using Judge Posner as his pawn to do so in order to get what he wanted—and get what he wanted he did. He was able to get the decision in the case fixed, as was ultimately disclosed by Judge Posner. Had it not been for the inside politics that was going on, Kanne's plan would have worked and the country would have ended up with a Kanne disciple on the federal judiciary—and that would have been a bad thing for the country. The country already suffered enough with Kanne's presence in the federal judiciary and would have suffered even more had Kanne's plan to install his former clerk disciple as his replacement worked.

CHAPTER 5

PETITION TO THE JUDICIAL CONFERENCE OF THE UNITED STATES

CAUSING THE GOVERNMENT TO RUN AND HIDE

"Does the government fear us? Or do we fear the government? When the people fear the government, tyranny has found victory. The federal government is our servant, not our master!"
~ Thomas Jefferson

On February 5, 2022, I filed a petition to the Judicial Conference of the United States for a review of the Seventh Circuit's actions in dismissing my judicial misconduct complaint against Judge Michael S. Kanne for his case-fixing activities without a determination on the merits of the complaint, and for the Seventh Circuit's nefarious protectionism of Kanne, and also as to its failure to request to the Chief Judge of the United States to assign the matter to another judicial circuit. Here is a verbatim of the petition:

Seventh Circuit No. 07-21-90056

PETITION TO JUDICIAL CONFERENCE OF THE UNITED STATES FOR REVIEW OF ACTION OF JUDICIAL COUNCIL OF THE SEVENTH CIRCUIT AS TO ORDER OF INAPPROPRIATE DISMISSAL OF judicial misconduct COMPLAINT AGAINST <u>JUDGE MICHAEL S. KANNE FOR HIS CASE FIXING ACTIVITIES</u>

The Petitioner submits this petition pursuant to Sec. 357(a) for review of the Judicial Council of the Seventh Circuit's inappropriate dismissal of the judicial misconduct complaint against Judge Michael S. Kanne. Attached hereto for the Judicial Conference's ready reference is a copy of the "Complaint of Judicial Misconduct"-w/exhibits; "Memorandum and Order" of September 30, 2021 by Chief Judge Diane S. Sykes; "Petition to Judicial Council of the Seventh Circuit for Review..."; and "Order" by the Judicial Council of the Seventh Circuit entered on January 20, 2022.

I. The Judicial Council of the Seventh Circuit's Denial of Complainant's Petition For Review of Chief Judge Diane Sykes' Memorandum and <u>Order Was Clearly Erroneous and Clearly an Abuse of Discretion</u>

      A. The Seventh Circuit's Actions Were Contemptuous in Every Way and the Judicial Conference of the United States Should Not Acquiesce to Such <u>Judicial Corruption</u>

The Judicial Conference of the United States reviews circuit judicial council orders for errors of law, clear errors of fact, or abuse of discretion. See, e.g., In re Complaint of Judicial Misconduct, 747 F.3d 869, 871 (U.S. Jud. Conf. 2014) (finding that circuit judicial council did not abuse its discretion); In re Complaint of Judicial Misconduct, 664 F.3d 332, 334-35 (U.S. Jud. Conf. 2011) (deferring to findings of circuit judicial council and overturning them only if clearly erroneous). These cases admonished that the Judicial Conference's reviews necessarily depend on the record before it and gives deference to the Circuit Judicial Council's consideration of the Special Committee's review of the evidence. These decisions pointed out that Petitioners contended that the evidence clearly weighed in their favor, relying on the materials submitted in support of the Complaint—namely, six affidavits from individuals who attended Judge Jones's lecture (one attorney and five law students). These decisions further pointed out that the Petitioners argues that the Circuit Judicial Council and the Special Committee "ignored" the affidavits and relied "almost exclusively" on Judge Jones's statements and recollections. In these decisions the Judicial Conference stated that from the review of the record, it was clear that the Circuit Judicial Council and the Special Committee relied on the entire record rather than a narrow comparison of Petitioners' six affidavits and Judge Jones's own recollections. The Judicial Conference explicitly stated that the Special Committee's "exhaustive review" included: (1) contemporaneous documentation and documentation created soon after the lecture, including the handwritten notes of an Assistant Federal Defender who attended the lecture, as well as that Assistant Federal Defender's subsequent summary made upon returning to her office; the electronic notes of another Assistant Federal Defender; a student text message exchange quoting Judge Jones sent during the lecture;

a text message to a legal blog and 6 email to a student attendee sent by another student who attended the lecture after the Complaint was filed; and three photographs of the event; (2) materials provided by Judge Jones, including the handwritten notes Judge Jones brought to the lecture; Judge Jones's ex post recollections of the lecture; a letter from Judge Jones denying the alleged misconduct; another letter from Judge Jones containing an excerpt from a report from the Defender Services Committee of the Judicial Conference; and various news articles, blog posts, and legal documents; and (3) materials from third parties supporting Judge Jones, including a declaration from a recent law school graduate who attended the lecture; a character reference by a past president of the National Association of Criminal Defense Lawyers and the Texas Criminal Defense Lawyers Association; a letter from 62 of Judge Jones's former law clerks; and a separate letter from another former law clerk of Judge Jones. See Special Comm. Rep. 3-5, 20-22; see also id. 22 ("The Committee relies on all of this information, together with the Special Counsel's Report, in reaching the conclusions below.").

Contrarily, in the instant matter here, the record clearly reflects that neither Chief Judge Diane S. Sykes or the judicial council reviewed any evidence that was submitted by Petitioner. The record clearly also reflects that neither Chief Judge Diane S. Sykes or the judicial council requested that the judge in question, Michael S. Kanne, submit a response to the allegations, and the record clearly reflects that Judge Michael S. Kanne did not deny the allegations against him. There was absolutely no rebuttal to any of the information submitted by the Petitioner. The Seventh Circuit very obviously whitewashed the matter, which explains why it chose not to refer the matter to the Chief Justice of the United States with a request that the Chief Justice transfer this proceeding to the judicial council of another circuit pursuant to Rule 26. *See, e.g., In re Complaint of Judicial Misconduct* (Ninth Circuit Judge Alex Kozinski), 575 F.3d 279, 280 (3d Cir. Jud. Council 2009), and *In re Charges of Judicial Misconduct* (Fifth Circuit Judge Edith Jones), 769 F.3d 762 (D.C. Cir. Jud. Council 2014). The Commentary to Rule 26 states that "[s]uch transfers may be appropriate . . . where the issues are highly visible and a local disposition may weaken public confidence ...."

There could be no higher example of a weakening of public confidence than when a federal court protects the corrupt activities of a brethren judge such as what Diane S. Sykes and her judicial council associates have tried to do by protecting Judge Kanne's case fixing activities—case fixing activities to which he himself has not even denied on the record. By keeping the matter in house, rather than allowing another circuit to conduct an unbiased and honest investigation and decision, the Seventh Circuit felt comfortable enough that it could get away with its malfeasance of protecting the unlawful case fixing activities of its brethren judge, Michael S. Kanne—to which Kanne did not deny anywhere on the record of this matter. The continual efforts to keep Kanne's criminal activities in house in the diseased Seventh Circuit in order to protect Kanne from appropriate punishment for his violation of the laws of the United States renders Diane S. Sykes and her judicial council partners to the cover up as "trespassers" under the law. *Elliot v. Piersol*, 1 Pet. 328, 340, 26 U.S. 328, 340 (1828).

B. **Falsity by Chief Judge Diane S. Sykes**

In the September 30, 2021, Memorandum and Order by Chief Judge Diane S. Sykes, she stated "Although no statute of limitations bars the filing of a judicial misconduct complaint, "[i]f the passage of time has made an accurate and fair investigation of the complaint impractical, the complaint must be dismissed. RULES FOR JUD.-CONDUCT 7 JUD.-DISABILITY PROC. 9; *see also id*. R. 11 (stating in the commentary that dismissal is appropriate "when a complaint is filed so long after an alleged event that memory loss, death, or changes to unknown residences prevent a proper investigation"). Here, the delay in filing this complaint renders proper investigation impossible—the alleged events occurred almost 30 years ago. Furthermore, the complainant says he learned of the alleged events in 2018, but he waited three years to file this complaint and did not identify anything that would have precluded him from filing it immediately after he learned of the alleged misconduct. This too impedes a full, fair, and accurate investigation and prejudices the subject judge's ability to rebut the allegations in the complaint. In short, the extreme passage of time, accompanied by an unreasonable delay in filing the misconduct complaint, justifies dismissal." Stating that Petitioner "…did not identify anything that would have precluded him from filing it immediately after he learned of the alleged misconduct." was a patently false statement as **Petitioner's reasons were explicitly stated at pages 5-10 of the judicial misconduct complaint, which constitutes six pages of the complaint.** [emphasis added]. Making such a false statement on an official court order in and of itself should be cause for alarm and the Judicial Conference of the United States should take appropriate judicial notice of such blatant falsehood by the chief judge in this matter. § 358 of the Act explicitly states that '[n]o rule promulgated under this section may limit the period of time within which a person may file a complaint under this chapter." This blatantly false statement by the chief judge is a bright red flag demonstrating the corrupt nature of how the Seventh Circuit proceeded in this matter in its quest of protecting the corrosive conduct of Judge Michael S. Kanne as demonstrated in the complaint—to which Kanne did not deny.

The conduct of Chief Judge Diane S. Sykes in submitting false statements in the memorandum and order falsely purporting that Petitioner didn't provide an explanation for why he didn't "immediately" file his complaint against Michael S. Kanne, when Petitioner certainly did provide an explanation demonstrates tangible evidence of criminal conduct on the part of Diane S. Sykes under the laws of the United States as an accessory after the fact under 18 U.S. Code Sec. 3 by virtue of Sykes' knowledge of Michael S. Kanne's criminal activities in having the decision fixed—which Kanne has not denied in this proceeding—and by Diane S. Sykes' concealment of Kanne's criminal activities by not making Kanne's felonious conduct known to some judge or other person in civil authority, renders Diane S. Sykes a criminal under 18 U.S. Code Sec. 4. The judicial corruption here is quite evident and the Judicial Conference of the United States has an obligation to act on it.

C. **The Chief Judge and Judicial Council's Determination that a Proper Investigation Was "Impossible" Borders on the Preposterous**

In the September 30, 2021, Memorandum and Order Chief Judge Diane S. Sykes stated "Although no statute of limitations bars the filing of a judicial misconduct complaint, "[i]f the passage of time has made an accurate and fair investigation of the complaint impractical, the complaint must be dismissed. RULES FOR JUD.-CONDUCT 7 JUD.-DISABILITY PROC. 9; *see also id*. R. 11 (stating in the commentary that **dismissal is appropriate "when a complaint is filed so long after an alleged event that memory loss, death, or changes to unknown residences prevent a proper investigation").** [emphasis added]. But Chief Judge Sykes pointed to no information or evidence of "memory loss" as to any relevant parties, pointed to no information or evidence of "death" as to any relevant parties, and pointed to no information or evidence of "changes to unknown residences preventing a proper investigation" as to any relevant parties. In point of fact, Judge Kanne is still a member of the Seventh Circuit, so there should be no problem with his "memory" as he would have to have a functioning memory to be able to function as a judge—which vitiates that part of Sykes' faulty reasoning, and since Kanne is still a member of the Seventh Circuit, he obviously isn't dead, so that certainly isn't a factor—which vitiates that part of Sykes' faulty reasoning, and since Kanne is still a member of the Seventh Circuit, there shouldn't have been any problem in locating him for an interview as to the allegations against him—which vitiates that part of Sykes' faulty reasoning, and although Judge Posner is no longer a member of the Court, he still lives in Chicago and, thus, very easily could have been interviewed, so the false reliance as to "unknown residence" certainly isn't a factor there—which vitiates that part of Sykes' faulty reasoning. Interviewing Judges Posner and Kanne would have been a very easy and practical way for the Judicial Council to investigate the allegations in the Complaint, but Sykes and her so called judicial council compadres chose not to do so. In asserting that any investigation would be "impossible" due to the passage of time, in the face of the key players' availability to be interviewed, clearly shows that Chief Judge Sykes and the Seventh Circuit Judicial Council's interest clearly was to not get to the bottom of what happened with Kanne's fixing of the decision, but rather shows the Seventh Circuit's interest in sweeping Kanne's corrupt activities under the rug—which actually constitutes the aiding and abetting of a crime. It is beyond belief, utterly inconceivable, that Chief Judge Diane S. Sykes chose not to interview Judge Richard A. Posner, a longtime member of the Seventh Circuit, who disclosed the case fixing conduct of Judge Michael S. Kanne—conduct that Kanne has not denied on the record of this matter.

D. Chief Judge Diane S. Sykes's Reliance of *In re Complaint of Jud. Misconduct No. 09-01*, 591 F.3d 638, 643-45 (U.S. Jud. Conf. 2009) Was Woefully Misapplied and Inapplicable

The Petitioner's judicial misconduct complaint against Kanne demonstrates a very different set of facts and circumstances than were set forth in Sykes' citing of *In re Complaint of Jud. Misconduct No. 09-01*, 591 F.3d 638, 643-45 (U.S. Jud. Conf. 2009) which clearly do not support an application of that decision to the instant case before the Judicial Conference of the United States as to Judge Michael S. Kanne. In *In re Complaint of Jud. Misconduct No. 09-01*, 591 F.3d 638, 643-45 (U.S. Jud. Conf. 2009) the Judicial Conference pointed out that the Complainant from that case argued that none of the many complaints and charges that were raised against the subject judge were considered or disposed of with finality by the Judicial Conference. The Judicial Conference noted that "none" of the alleged "many charges" were "raised" at the time, nor were the subject of a misconduct complaint in 2001 (or for that matter until 2008) which is why the Executive Committee Chair stated accurately in early 2008 that the matter was properly concluded seven years earlier with no finding of judicial misconduct. The Judicial Conference wrote that it was true that no specific allegations of misconduct against the subject judge by the Judicial Conference in 2001, but that was because "**none was filed.**" [emphasis added]. This is drastically dissimilar from the instant complaint where Petitioner indeed did raise specific charges against the subject judge—Michael S. Kanne—where there was **no finding whatsoever**—either way—of judicial misconduct, and instead, chicanery was utilized to sweep the complaint against Kanne under the rug via a poorly thought out mechanism tantamount to a non-existent statute of limitations for reasons that had no validity whatsoever, i.e., memory loss, death, or changes to unknown residences—none of which applied in any way, but yet were used in an infected way to wrongfully dismiss Petitioner's complaint in order to protect the corrupt activities of their brethren judge, Michael S. Kanne—who did not deny the allegations. § 358 of the Act explicitly states that '[n]o rule promulgated under this section may limit the period of time within which a person may file a complaint under this chapter." The interjection of false reasons that in no way apply, i.e., "memory loss, death, or changes to unknown residences" to somehow justify a dismissal of a complaint for time period reasons is a form of judicial chicanery clearly displayed by Chief Judge Diane S. Sykes and the Judicial Council of the Seventh Circuit. *In re Complaint of Jud. Misconduct No. 09-01*, 591 F.3d 638, 643-45 (U.S. Jud. Conf. 2009) the Judicial Conference noted that with the chief justice unavailable as a witness—due to death—that a full and fair investigation was not possible. As the Judicial Conference can clearly see in Chief Judge Sykes's memorandum and order, there was no issue with any witnesses either dying or otherwise being unavailable. The Judicial Conference should make short work of the chicanery by Chief Judge Diane S. Sykes and her compadres of the Judicial Council of the Seventh Circuit by their conduct of wrongfully protecting the unsavory case fixing activities of their brethren judge, Michael S. Kanne, who has not denied the allegations in the obvious sham proceeding undertaken in the Seventh Circuit.

In the judicial misconduct complaint against Kanne, nobody is deceased and in fact Kanne still sits on the Seventh Circuit so he clearly was available for Sykes and her judicial council compadres to get a denial or confession from him, but didn't do so, which is drastically dissimilar from the facts and circumstances in *In re Complaint of Jud. Misconduct No. 09-01*, 591 F.3d 638, 643-45 (U.S. Jud. Conf. 2009), *supra*. which consequently renders the *In re Complaint of Jud. Misconduct No. 09-01*, 591 F.3d 638, 643-45 (U.S. Jud. Conf. 2009) decision as misplaced and inapplicable to the facts and circumstances to the instant judicial misconduct complaint. The fact of such misapplication of an inapplicable decision demonstrates the Seventh Circuit's interest in conducting a sham proceeding rather than a proceeding of integrity in order to wrongfully and unlawfully protect the criminal conduct of case fixing of one of its own members, Judge Michael S. Kanne, who has not denied the allegations as the record clearly demonstrates, a record to which the Judicial Conference of the United States must base its determination in this matter. *"What just is, isn't always Jus-tice."* ~ Amanda Gorman.

II. According to Federal Law the Conduct of Judge Diane S. Sykes and Her Judicial Compadres Who Took Part in the Cover-Up of Judge Michael S. Kanne's Criminal Conduct of Fixing the Decision Constitutes an Engagement of Acts of Treason and the "Memorandum and Order" By Chief Judge Diane S. Sykes Dismissing the Complaint Against Michael S. Kanne and the Order of the Judicial Council of the Seventh Circuit Affirming Chief Judge Sykes's Memorandum and <u>Order Are Void with No Legal Force or Effect</u>

The undisputed facts are such that the allegations in Petitioner's judicial misconduct complaint against Michael S. Kanne's criminal conduct of having a decision fixed as was disclosed by Judge Richard A. Posner are well grounded and supported by affidavit. The undisputed facts are such that Chief Judge Diane S. Sykes dismissed the complaint without interviewing Judges Posner and Kanne even though Judge Posner continues to reside in Chicago and even though Kanne is a current active member of the circuit. The undisputed facts are such that Chief Judge Sykes didn't direct Michael S. Kanne to submit a written response to the complaint. The undisputed facts are such that Michael S. Kanne has not denied on the record the allegations contained within the judicial misconduct complaint against him of which allegations were supported by Petitioner's affidavit of which affidavit statements were not rebutted in any way. The undisputed facts are such that there is no dispute about the allegations contained within the judicial misconduct complaint and supporting affidavit against Michael S. Kanne for his criminal case fixing activities of having a decision fixed. The undisputed facts are such that Diane S. Sykes falsely wrote in the infected memorandum and order that Petitioner "…did not identify anything that would have precluded him from filing it immediately after he learned of the alleged misconduct," which was in fact a false statement by Chief Judge Diane S. Sykes as Petitioner's reasons were explicitly stated at pages 5-10 of the judicial misconduct complaint—which constitutes six pages of the complaint. The undisputed facts are such that Chief Judge Diane S. Sykes ignored Petitioner's request for the Judicial Council of the Seventh Circuit to request that the Chief Justice of the United States transfer this proceeding to the judicial council of another circuit pursuant to Rule 26.

It is well settled that when a judge acts as a trespasser of the law, when a judge does not follow the law, the judge loses subject matter jurisdiction and the judge's orders are void, of no legal force or effect. The U.S. Supreme Court, in *Scheurer v. Rhodes*, 416 U.S. 232, 94 S.Ct. 1683, 1687 (1974) stated that "when a state officer acts under a state law in a manner violative of the Federal Constitution, he "comes into conflict with the superior authority of that Constitution, and he is in that case stripped of his official or representative character and is subjected in his person to the consequences of his individual conduct. The State has no power to impart to him any immunity from responsibility to the supreme authority of the United States." By law, a judge is a state officer. The U.S. Supreme Court has made clear that "No state legislator or executive or judicial officer can war against the Constitution without violating his undertaking to support it." *Cooper v. Aaron*, 358 U.S. 1, 78 S.Ct. 1401 (1958).

If a judge does not fully comply with the Constitution, his orders are void. *In re Sawyer*, 124 U.S. 200 (1888), he/she is without jurisdiction, and he/she has engaged in an act or acts of treason. Whenever a judge acts where he/she does not have jurisdiction to act, the judge is engaged in an act or acts of treason. *S. v. Will*, 449 U.S. 200, 216, 101 S.Ct. 471, 66 L.Ed.2d 392, 406 (1980); *Cohens v. Virginia*, 19 U.S. (6 Wheat) 264, 404, 5 L.Ed. 257 (1821).

Under federal law which is applicable to all states, the U.S. Supreme Court stated that if a court is "without authority, its judgments and orders are regarded as nullities. They are not voidable, but simply void; and form no bar to a recovery sought, even prior to a reversal in opposition to them. They constitute no justification; and all persons concerned in executing such judgments or sentences, are considered, in law, as trespassers." *Elliot v. Piersol*, 1 Pet. 328, 340, 26 U.S. 328, 340 (1828).

The Seventh Circuit Court of Appeals has held that the Circuit Court of Cook County is a criminal enterprise since the judges who did not report the criminal activities of other judges become principals in the criminal activity, 18 U.S.C. Section 1, and since no judges have reported the criminal activity of the judges who have been convicted, the other judges are as guilty as the convicted judges. *U.S. v. Murphy*, 768 F.2d 1518, 1531 (7th Cir. 1985).

When judges act when they do not have jurisdiction to act, or they enforce a void order (an order issued by a judge without jurisdiction), they become trespassers of the law, and are engaged in treason. The Court in *Yates v. Village of Hoffman Estates, Illinois*, 209 F.Supp. 757 (N.D. Ill. 1962) held that "not every action by a judge is in exercise of his judicial function. ...it is not a judicial function for a judge to commit an intentional tort even though the tort occurs in the courthouse."

The continued efforts to keep Kanne's criminal activities in house in the diseased Seventh Circuit to protect Kanne from appropriate punishment for his violation of the laws of the United States renders Diane S. Sykes and her judicial compadres on the Judicial Council of the Seventh Circuit as "trespassers" under the law. *Elliot v. Piersol*, 1 Pet. 328, 340, 26 U.S. 328, 340 (1828). Such conduct by Diane S. Sykes and her judicial compadres in failing to fully comply with the Constitution are acts of treason according to the Supreme Court. *S. v. Will*, 449 U.S. 200, 216, 101 S.Ct. 471, 66 L.Ed.2d 392, 406 (1980); *Cohens v. Virginia*, 19 U.S. (6 Wheat) 264, 404, 5 L.Ed. 257 (1821).

The conduct of Judge Diane S. Sykes in issuing an infected so called "Memorandum and Order" dismissing the complaint against Michael S. Kanne without seeking a written response from him (Kanne) and without interviewing him, and without interviewing Judge Richard A. Posner—who disclosed Kanne's case fixing misconduct, and the conduct of Sykes's judicial council compadres who simply rubber stamped Sykes's infected decision to let Kanne off the hook for his corrupt case fixing activities—which he did not deny—without any investigation into the facts, and without a single denial of anything contained in the complaint, constitutes clear evidence of a cover up by the Seventh Circuit of Kanne's criminal activities of having the decision fixed, just as was disclosed by Judge Posner as reflected in the judicial misconduct complaint against Kanne—which Kanne did not deny on the record.

The Seventh Circuit's protectionism of Michael S. Kanne's criminal conduct of having a decision fixed in violation of the United States laws renders the United States Court of Appeals for the Seventh Circuit as a criminal enterprise pursuant to the standards that the Seventh Circuit itself set in *U.S. v. Murphy*, 768 F.2d 1518, 1531 (7th Cir. 1985) when it held that the Circuit Court of Cook County was a criminal enterprise by virtue of the judges' failure to report the criminal activities of other judges, just as Chief Judge Diane S. Sykes and her judicial compadres of the Judicial Council of the Seventh Circuit have likewise failed to report the criminal case fixing activities of Michael S. Kanne. It stands to reason that the cover-up of Michael S. Kanne's undisputed criminal activities and protectionism of his criminal activities in this proceeding is precisely why Sykes and her judicial compadres chose not to ask the Chief Judge of the United States to transfer this proceeding to the judicial council of another circuit pursuant to Rule 26 and instead chose to keep Kanne's criminal activities in house where it could protect Kanne from the appropriate punishment that should be handed to him for his undisputed criminal activities of having a decision fixed in violation of the United States laws.

18 U.S. Code Sec. 2

> (a) Whoever commits an offense against the United States or aids, abets, counsels, commands, induces or procures its commission, is punishable as a principal.
> (b) Whoever willfully causes an act to be done which if directly performed by him or another would be an offense against the United States, is punishable as a principal.

18 U.S. Code Sec. 3

> Whoever, knowing that an offense against the United States has been committed, receives, relieves, comforts or assists the offender in order to hinder or prevent his apprehension, trial or punishment, is an accessory after the fact.

18 U.S. Code Sec. 4

> Whoever, having knowledge of the actual commission of a felony cognizable by a court of the United States, conceals and does not as soon as possible make known the same to some judge or other person in civil or military authority under the United States, shall be fined under this title or imprisoned not more than three years, or both.

> *"No man is above the law and no man is below it; nor do we ask any man's permission when we ask him to obey it. Obedience to the law is demanded as a right, not asked as a favor."*
> ~ Theodore Roosevelt.

It is noteworthy that in dismissing the complaint Chief Judge Sykes cited *In re Complaint of Jud. Misconduct No. 09-01*, a matter where the proceeding was transferred to the Third Circuit Judicial Council from the Ninth Circuit Judicial Council by the Chief Justice, which is something that the Seventh Circuit refused to do in its quest to keep in house the criminal activities of Michael S. Kanne's case fixing as is alleged in the judicial misconduct complaint against him as revealed by a retired former member of this circuit—Judge Richard A. Posner. Since Sykes cited the matter of *In re Complaint of Jud. Misconduct No. 09-01,* 591 F.3d 638, 643-45 (U.S. Jud. Conf. 2009), then she as chief judge should have done just as what was done in that proceeding and requested that the Chief Justice of the United States transfer this proceeding to the judicial council of another circuit pursuant to Rule 26 as Petitioner requested. But Sykes instead inappropriately chose to keep Kanne's criminal conduct in house rather than having another circuit conduct an "actual" investigation such as what was done in the very case she cited in her infected memorandum and order, where after transfer of the proceeding in that matter, the judicial council had the integrity to conduct a real investigation and issued a Memorandum Opinion and Order in J.C. 03-08-90050, finding misconduct accompanied by "appropriate corrective action." Chief Judge Sykes cannot have it both ways, either she relies on the decision she cited, and if so, she was duty bound to proceed under its principles, but she didn't, as she chose instead to keep the malfeasance activities in house and protected Kanne's case fixing activities—case fixing activities revealed by Judge Posner—rather than asking the Chief Judge of the United States to transfer the matter to another circuit, as should have been done under Rule 26, as was done in the decision cited by Sykes.

Chief Judge Sykes's conduct in protecting the undisputed case fixing activities by Judge Michael S. Kanne reeks of judicial malfeasance and is a classic example of what a committee led by Supreme Court Justice Stephen Breyer warned us in 2006 when it admonished the potential dangers of a system in which judges are judging judges when it concluded that "A system that relies for investigation solely upon judges themselves risks a kind of undue 'guild favoritism' through inappropriate sympathy with the judge's point of view or de-emphasis of the misconduct problem." **The Breyer committee found that complaints were not handled properly and the main problem detected, in high visibility and other complaints, was chief judges' failure to conduct "adequate" inquiries before dismissing a complaint or to submit "clear factual discrepancies" to investigators to pursue**. [emphasis added].
https://www.cnn.com/2018/01/25/politics/courts-judges-sexual-harassment/index.html.

To say that Chief Judge Diane S. Sykes did not handle the complaint in this matter properly and that her failure to conduct "adequate inquiries"—of which there were no inquiries at all conducted—before dismissing the complaint would be an understatement for the ages!

History demonstrates the very troubling record of the federal judiciary where almost all complaints against federal judges are dismissed outright. In 2015, there were 1,214 complaints filed against federal judges, and not a single one resulted in remedial action against the judge. https://www.motherjones.com/politics/2016/03/time-merrick-garland-was-accused-protecting-fellow-judge-charged-ethics-violations/. A record of 0 for 1,214 hardly does much to preserve the public's trust in the federal judiciary. This type of record is ridiculous and borders on the ludicrous. Not even one single case resulted in remedial action against a judge! Amazing! What Chief Judge Diane S. Sykes and the Judicial Council of the Seventh Circuit did here underscores the significance of this apparent culture problem of wide proportion. This Petitioner cannot, and will not, allow such unacceptable culture rule the day in this matter where the chief judge and judicial council provided such protectionism to a case fixing judge who didn't even have to deny his corrupt case fixing activities to obtain cover for his illicit acts. Protectionism of Case Fixing is Alive and Well in U.S. Court of Appeals in Chicago (brianvukadinovich.com), The "Stench" of the Seventh Circuit Under Chief Judge Diane S. Sykes (brianvukadinovich.com), The Federal Judiciary is an Affront to the Peoples' Right to Justice (brianvukadinovich.com).

    Petitioner does not know if Judge Frank Easterbrook was a member of the Judicial Council of the Seventh Circuit as to the January 20, 2022, order affirming Chief Judge Sykes's memorandum and order as the order does not identify the participating members who took part in the issuance of the order. To the extent that if Judge Frank Easterbrook was a member of the judicial council that issued that order, that would have been entirely inappropriate as Judge Easterbrook would have had a substantial conflict of interest as he was on the panel with Judge Posner of the case that is the subject of Kanne's *ex parte* case fixing activities of which case fixing was disclosed by Judge Posner as reflected in the complaint. A close analysis of the decision indicates how the decision was corrupted as revealed by Judge Posner. Brian Vukadinovich v. Richard Zentz, Ronald Kurmis, John Ross, William Collins, and City of..., 995 F.2d 750 – CourtListener.com. And in light of Judge Posner's revelation of the fixing of the decision, of which Frank Easterbrook was on the panel, it would have been entirely inappropriate for Easterbrook to have been a member of the Judicial Council of the Seventh Circuit which issued the order affirming Chief Judge Sykes's dismissal of the complaint against Michael S. Kanne, if indeed Easterbrook was a member of that Judicial Council.

    If Frank Easterbrook was a member or the Judicial Council which issued the order affirming Chief Judge Sykes's dismissal of the complaint against Kanne, there is a very serious consequential problem in terms of the integrity of the process, not only as to the conflict of interest issue, but also in terms of the judicial credibility of Frank Easterbrook which is in substantial doubt as there has been reporting of many disturbing things about Easterbrook's judicial integrity—or lack thereof. For example an article by *Injustice Watch* reported pointed out that Albert W. Alschuler, a highly respected law professor, wrote in a law review, "Judge Easterbrook persistently presents wildly inaccurate, made-up statements as unquestionable statements of fact," and added "The truth is not in him," and accused Easterbrook of telling repeated "whoppers." That led *Injustice Watch* to conduct a review of Easterbrook and the result was a documented pattern of misrepresented facts in Easterbrook's opinions. *Injustice Watch* uncovered 17 cases since 2010 in which opinions authored by Easterbrook misstated the facts, omitted facts, or made assumptions that were contrary to the trial record. The article pointed out that in many cases Easterbrook's errors seemed to play a significant role in the outcome. Pattern of misstated facts found in opinions of renowned U.S. Judge Easterbrook | Injustice Watch.

    In one opinion authored by Easterbrook, he brushed aside one convicted murderer's challenge to his death sentence, which was based in part on the failure of his defense attorneys to present evidence that he had schizophrenia. Easterbrook wrote that the attorneys offered two specific reasons at a post-conviction hearing to explain their decision not to call an expert to the stand, but the transcript of that hearing shows that the lawyers gave no such explanation. In another opinion

Easterbrook refused to let another prisoner challenge his death sentence on the basis of government records showing that the defendant had an intellectual disability before the crime occurred. Easterbrook wrote that the records of his mental state were known to the defendant and his counsel long ago and could have been obtained sooner, but nothing in the record supported Easterbrook's conclusion. In another case, Easterbrook wrote in an opinion that there was not sufficient evidence to support holding two members of the Chicago police department responsible for events that led to the highly publicized rape of a mentally disturbed woman. But the federal judge hearing the case recited a cascade of evidence in the record before the panel that sharply contradicted the Seventh Circuit's decision written by Easterbrook. *Injustice Watch* documented the pattern of errors by reviewing the trial record, listening to tape recordings of oral arguments and interviewing attorneys. The review was then expanded to identify earlier complaints about the accuracy of what Easterbrook wrote. How Frank Easterbrook Kept George Ryan in Prison (valpo.edu).

In 1994, in evaluating Chicago-area federal judges, the Chicago Council of Lawyers wrote that at times Easterbrook "acts like the worst of judges" when he disregards law and facts, and went on to add that Easterbrook "appears less concerned about the actual facts and issues presented in the appeals before him than about advancing his own philosophy." A Chicago Tribune article pointed out that the Chicago Council of Lawyers report, which was an evaluation of the Seventh Circuit's federal appeals judges, devoted 12 pages to Easterbrook and noted Easterbrook's "obvious contempt of those he finds below his intellectual level." U.S. APPEAL JUDGES GET AN EARFUL - Chicago Tribune. The council went on to state that Judge Michael S. Kanne "lacks objectivity or the necessary legal skills to serve with distinction."

It is no wonder that the people in our country are expressing a drastic decline in their trust in the federal judiciary at an historical low level. This was shown in a very enlightening article recently out by Gallup showing a steep decline over the past year in the percentage of Americans who express "a great deal" or "fair amount" of trust in the overall judicial branch of the federal government, from 67 percent in 2020 to 54 percent today. https://news.gallup.com/poll/354908/approval-supreme-court-down-new-low.aspx. What Chief Judge Diane S. Sykes and the Judicial Council of the Seventh Circuit did in this matter is a prime example of why the public is expressing such a distrust in the federal judiciary. The Judicial Conference of the United States has an opportunity to right a wrong here and instill a measure of public confidence back into the federal judiciary—and it clearly should do so.

What the Seventh Circuit did here is a real time example of why the public is becoming more and more disenchanted with the federal judiciary as shown in the recent Gallup Poll. Creatively fashioning a decision to somehow exonerate what the Seventh Circuit did would only further erode the public's confidence in the federal judiciary to an even lower level than it already is. This is a given. Oaths are given for a reason, and judges are expected to honor their oaths, not dishonor them. Rules and laws are implemented for a reason, and judges are obligated to respect and follow the governing rules and laws, not disrespect and ignore them. Putting on a black robe carries with it a high responsibility for judges to respect the oath of office and to respect and follow the governing rules and laws. Putting on a black robe does not give license for judges to act in a corrupt manner in judicial undertakings, which clearly took place here with Michael S. Kanne's case fixing activities as revealed by Judge Posner—which Kanne has not denied on the record. None of the information submitted in the judicial misconduct complaint and supporting affidavit has been disputed or contradicted in any way, and that is what the record is before the Judicial Conference of the United States. The Judicial Conference of the United States should now correct this grave miscarriage of justice and take appropriate steps in effecting appropriate discipline against Judge Michael S. Kanne for the undisputed case fixing activities as revealed by Judge Posner, and the Judicial Conference should take notice of what Chief Judge Diane S. Sykes and the Judicial Council of the Seventh Circuit did in attempting to cover up Kanne's corruption by implementing a sham proceeding in order to protect the malfeasance of Kanne and the infected customary way in how the Seventh Circuit conducts its business in acquiescing to such protectionism, all of which conduct is contrary to law and contrary to public policy. "The time is always right to do what is right." ~ Martin Luther King, Jr.

III. **CONCLUSION**

The Judicial Conference of the United States should review the record of this matter and issue appropriate disciplinary action(s) against Judge Michael S. Kanne for his corrupt activities of case fixing as has been revealed by Judge Richard A. Posner—and were not denied by Judge Kanne—of which undisputed corruption was swept under the rug by Chief Judge Diane S. Sykes who ignored the undisputed detailed information submitted in the judicial misconduct complaint against Judge Michael S. Kanne and inappropriately dismissed the complaint of which the Judicial Council of the Seventh Circuit inappropriately affirmed, notwithstanding that Judge Kanne did not deny the allegations against him, and notwithstanding that there were no disputes about any of the facts as set forth in the complaint and within Petitioner's affidavit.

Respectfully submitted,
/s/ Brian Vukadinovich
Brian Vukadinovich, Petitioner

I haven't heard back in any way. I have messaged the Administrative Office of the United States Courts and asked for a status of my petition to the Judicial Conference of the United States, but it won't answer. After it became evident to me that the Administrative Office of the United States Courts wasn't going to provide me with a status regarding the petition I filed with the Judicial Conference of the United States, and obviously was more interested in sweeping the corruption issues under the rug, I went to the website of the chair of the Senate Judiciary Committee, Dick Durbin, and informed him as to what was going on. I asked him to investigate the case fixing and cover up taking place in the U.S. Court of Appeals in Chicago and requested that he hold public hearings on the matter and allow me to testify. Durbin didn't respond back. The Senate Judiciary Committee, chaired by Dick Durbin of Illinois, is a committee that has the power to hold hearings, subpoena witnesses, and even initiate judicial impeachment processes; but when it comes to investigating case-fixing judges, Durbin and the other members of the Senate Judiciary Committee have deserted their posts and are basically missing in action, i.e., AWOL.

Durbin has yet to meet a television camera that he doesn't like, but when it comes to addressing case fixing by federal judges, Durbin makes an exception and prefers to stay away from the television cameras. As for the other minions on the Senate Judiciary Committee, they love the spotlight and the idea of being on such a powerful and influential committee, but they don't love the idea of taking to task federal judges who fix cases. Pretty much the only time we see or hear from any of them is when there is a political controversy about a nominee to the Supreme Court, and then we see them running in front of the television cameras spouting their political party's fodder. What you will never see Dick Durbin or any of the minions on the Senate Judiciary Committee do is publicly discuss the rampant problem our country has with case-fixing judges that have permeated the federal judiciary. That is a taboo topic for all of them —the political cowards that they are. The slogan for Durbin and the other minions on the Senate Judiciary Committee should be "Don't ask, don't tell" when it comes to issues of case-fixing federal judges and judges who participate in cover up of case-fixing activities.

It would be a great thing if Dick Durbin and the other members of the Senate Judiciary Committee would come out of hiding, report for duty, and start investigating the case fixing that is going on with federal judges. They should start holding public hearings in order to do a public service for the people of America by eradicating the judiciary of the case-fixing judges who permeate our federal justice system. But unfortunately, when political cowards are faced with doing the right thing, they generally choose instead to do the wrong thing; they run and hide—and that is exactly what the political coward Dick Durbin did.

On April 4, 2022, I asked Indiana Senator Todd Young to contact the Administrative Office of the U.S. Courts to obtain the status from this federal agency as to my petition to the Judicial Conference of the United States regarding the Seventh Circuit's case fixing and cover-up activities, inasmuch as this federal agency had ignored my requests.

The question begging an answer is where does one go when a federal judge discloses that the decision of person's civil rights case was fixed by a federal judge and the chief judge sweeps it under the rug, and then the administrative agency of the United States federal court system—the Administrative Office of the U.S. Courts—refuses to provide a status or explanation as to why the Judicial Conference of the United States is looking the other way? I went to a United States Senator in my state, Todd Young of Indiana, who boasts on his website that "Navigating the federal bureaucracy can be a difficult task. My staff and I can offer help for Hoosiers who can't get an answer from a federal agency in a timely manner..." I made the request for assistance to Senator Young on April 4, 2022, after it became evident that the Administrative Office of the U.S. Courts and the Judicial Conference of the United States was interested in keeping the case fixing and cover-up activities of the U.S. Court of

Appeals in Chicago close to the vest and away from the public's knowledge.

On April 7, 2022, I received an email from Senator Young stating, "...I have contacted the appropriate officials to express my interest on your behalf. I will be in touch with you as soon as I receive a response...." On May 2, 2022, I sent an email to Young's aide, a Melisa Shoots, Constituent Services Representative for Senator Todd Young, asking her to provide me with a copy of the so called "contact" that Senator Young said he made on my behalf to the "appropriate officials." I informed her that I was very concerned about the manner in which this federal agency does its business, of which concern is certainly underscored, and in how it ignored my request for a status report as to my petition. I made it clear that this was something that needed to be addressed. I received an email reply from Melisa Shoots stating, "We do not provide copies of those letters to our constituents. These letters have Congressional liaisons' contact info that we do not share. Other Federal agencies are not obligated to provide us the information we request. They do this as a courtesy." That was a poppycock response, to say the least.

BRIAN VUKADINOVICH

Senator Young Correspondence

Melisa_Shoots@young.senate.gov <Melisa_Shoots@young.senate.gov>
Thu 4/7/2022 1:42 PM
To: bvukadinovich@hotmail.com <bvukadinovich@hotmail.com>

Dear Mr. Vukadinovich,

Thank you for contacting my office regarding your petition. I understand that this matter is of great importance to you.

In an effort to be of service, I have contacted the appropriate officials to express my interest on your behalf. I will be in touch with you as soon as I receive a response.

In the meantime, if you have any additional information that would assist me as I pursue this issue for you, please contact my office.

Sincerely

Todd Young
United States Senator

This is an email that Indiana Senator Todd Young sent to Brian Vukadinovich stating that he (Todd Young) has contacted the appropriate judicial officials on behalf of Brian Vukadinovich, but he (Senator Todd Young) refused to provide to Brian Vukadinovich copies of any correspondence as to the purported contact that he said he made.

I responded to her that it was very disappointing to hear that Senator Young refuses to provide his constituents with copies of letters that he has purported to have sent out on their behalf. I told Ms. Shoots that if Congressional liaison contact information was truly a concern, then that particular information could be redacted from the letters. I told her that it would seem that a constituent should be entitled to a copy of a document that has been purportedly sent by an elected representative on the constituent's behalf as basic transparency 101. I told her that I do not accept proceedings undertaken in secret insofar as issues that are matters of public concern and direct concern to the constituent to be viable proceedings when there is a refusal against providing verifiable copies of the information to the constituent. The refusal of Senator Young to provide a copy of the purported correspondence he allegedly made on my behalf is cause for alarm, and such refusal calls into serious question whether he did indeed send the letter.

I sent several follow up emails to Melisa Shoots but all for naught, as every response was pretty much the same, so it became very evident to me that Senator Todd Young wasn't going to be of any help.

On May 15, 2022, I emailed Melisa Shoots and expressed my concern that the refusal of the federal agency to respond as well as the refusal of Senator Young to provide me with copies of letters that he purports were sent on my behalf mirrored how things were done in Russia and China. I told her that we cannot have government agencies and government officials in our country operating in such secret fashion without any accountability, and that two things needed to happen: a) Senator Young needed to introduce a senate bill requiring federal agencies to respond to senators' inquiries on behalf of their constituents, and b) Senator Young needed to request that the Chair of the Senate Judiciary Committee, Dick Durbin, and the other members of the Committee, hold public hearings as to the case fixing and cover up that is taking place in the U.S. Court of Appeals in Chicago, and to include in the public hearings the issue of the Judicial Conference of the United States' conduct of sweeping my petition as to the corruption in the U.S. Court of Appeals under the rug. I made it clear that this was a formal request and that she should let me know whether or not Senator Young would be honoring my requests as to these two issues.

On May 18, 2022, I emailed Melisa Shoots and asked if Senator Young was going to honor my requests, but she did not respond. On September 16, 2022, I sent another email and stated that I forthwith needed an answer specific to the reason(s) that Senator Young had not honored my request for him to call for public hearings before the Senate Judiciary Committee regarding the cover up of the case fixing that took place in the U.S. Court of Appeals in Chicago as well as the conduct of the Administrative Office of the United States Courts in refusing to provide a status of my petition to the Judicial Conference of the United States regarding the case-fixing activities and cover up at the U.S. Court of Appeals in Chicago. I advised her that Senator Young's silence on the matter was not helpful and indeed quite telling. But Young continued to play his games and wouldn't provide an answer as to whether or not he was going to honor my request. It became clear that Todd Young was choosing to continue with his little game of hide and seek. So I had to take steps to bring him out of hiding—and I did so. As they say: Where there's a will, there's a way. I certainly had the will, all I needed was the way; and that wasn't difficult as politicians do not like to be publicly exposed for the rats that they are.

After giving Todd Young plenty of chances to come clean and provide me with a copy of the communication that he said he sent on my behalf and to also offer an explanation as to why he wouldn't honor my request to contact the Senate Judiciary Committee, I decided to expose him on Twitter. I included in my posts an article I had written about him which I published on my website on May 20, 2022. The article was titled, "Senator Todd Young of Indiana Should Demand Public Senate Judiciary Hearings on Judicial Corruption." The tweets certainly had an impact because Young's office, lo and behold, quickly contacted me which was clearly an attempt by Young to do some damage control.

On September 19, 2022, I received an email from a Jessica Helmers explaining that she worked in Senator Young's D.C. office and would be willing to speak to me about my messages and asked for my telephone number. I emailed her back and explained to her that transparency was very important and preferred all communications to be in writing to preserve an accurate record of Senator Young's actions in the matter.

On October 20, 2022, I received an email from Jessica Helmers of Todd Young's office stating: "I understand your interest in having a written record of the actions taken with respect to your concern. It is not our practice to share correspondence between Senators with the public. However, I am happy to provide you with email confirmation once I pass along your cover letter and petition copy to let you know that I sent it. Alternatively, if you prefer to have copies of all direct communications, you could mail the documents directly to the Chairman and Ranking Member of the Committee, respectively, at 224 Dirksen Senate Office Building, Washington, DC 20510. I can then follow up with the Committee to confirm receipt. I will note that things sent by mail can be delayed in the Senate's mail opening security processes, so it may take several weeks until the Committee receives a paper mailing (even for something sent via FedEx overnight, for example)."

I replied on the same day that she was completely missing the point. I didn't contact Senator Young for him to "confirm" to me that the Senate Judiciary Committee received my documents, I contacted him for the express purpose of having the senator request to the Senate Judiciary Committee that it hold public hearings on the case fixing and cover up that is going on at the U.S. Court of Appeals in Chicago, and for the express purpose that the senator get to the bottom of why the Administrative Office of the United States Courts is trying to sweep under the rug my petition to the Judicial Conference of the United States where I addressed the case fixing and cover-up issues at the U.S. Court of Appeals in Chicago. I responded that her email centered on a simple "confirmation" that she was willing to provide that the Senate Judiciary Committee had received my documents, and that, quite frankly, her email was insulting given the magnitude of the issue. I informed her that I didn't need the senator to "confirm" that the Senate Judiciary Committee received my documents as I could get a confirmation of the Committee's receipt of my communication simply by sending it via certified mail. I also stated that her email was an insult to my intelligence, which I did not appreciate, and that she should save that for somebody else, as it wouldn't work with me.

As for the ridiculously stated position that "It is not our practice to share correspondence between Senators with the public," I reminded Jessica Helmers that United States senators are public servants, and it is the people who pay for the senators' very existence. Accordingly, I would not accept such a misguided position that senators should not share correspondence between senators on issues of public concerns that affect the very public they are supposed to be representing. I said that I could understand such a position of secrecy as utilized by authoritarian leaders such as China's Xi Jinping and Russia's Vladmir Putin where governmental control of peoples' lives is the rule of the day; but the last I checked, this is the United States, and in the United States, the people are to be informed of governmental affairs, not kept in the dark about governmental malfeasance issues, including judicial corruption issues, that are going on and helped along by elected officials by complicity. I underscored that it certainly appeared that that is exactly what was going on with the secrecy tactics preferred by Senator Young. I made it clear to her that the secrecy of such basic information is a red flag and cause for alarm.

I reminded Jessica Helmers that on October 16, 2022, in the senatorial debate in Indianapolis, Indiana, that in responding to a political issue, Senator Young said, "We need to increase transparency into the system." I asked her why the so-called "transparency" didn't apply here as to the issues of case fixing and cover up at the U.S. Court of Appeals in Chicago and complicity by the Administrative Office of the United States Courts? I told her that Senator Young should hardly be claiming to be a champion of "transparency" at a public political debate while at the same time refusing the principles of "transparency" when it comes to a constituent's concerns. I also told her that publicly declaring the championing of "transparency" to score political points during a political debate while at the same time opposing "transparency" when it comes to issues important to a constituent was not only distasteful, but immoral, and that Senator Young should be ashamed for such double talk and hypocrisy. Needless to say, I was appalled to see such brainwashing of the public at a public debate with such fake championing of the importance of "transparency" for scoring political points, but yet not espousing "transparency," but rather rejecting it, when it came to how he actually did his business. These types of politicians who talk out of both sides of their mouths are a dime a dozen, and Todd Young is certainly one of them.

I went on to say that I strongly suspected that Senator Young probably didn't even read the petition that I submitted to the Judicial Conference of the United States, and made it clear that I didn't need Senator Young to provide "confirmation" that my documents were received by the Senate Judiciary Committee. I needed Senator Young to make a specific request to the Senate Judiciary Committee to hold public hearings as to the case fixing and cover up going on at the U.S. Court of Appeals in Chicago that I addressed in my petition to the Judicial Conference of the United States. I told her that it was actually Senator Young, and not me, who should write the so-called "cover letter" to the Senate Judiciary Committee, and that he should be stating his concern as a United States senator as to the case fixing and cover up going on at the U.S. Court of Appeals in Chicago, and the need for public hearings on the matter. I told her if Young was not willing to do that, then he should just say so and not try to insult my intelligence any further. I also told her that if Young chose to not make a specific request to the Senate Judiciary Committee to hold public hearings on the case fixing and cover up going on at the U.S. Court of Appeals in Chicago AND provide me with a copy of the request, then I would have to assume that Young was perfectly fine with case fixing and cover up in the federal judiciary. On October 21, 2022, I received an email from Jessica Helmer stating that Young's office would be willing to "pass along" my request to the Judiciary Committee but nothing about Young making a statement to the Judiciary Committee emphasizing the importance for the Committee to hold public hearings on the matter. So, in the end, Indiana Senator Todd Young showed his true colors in refusing to make a statement to the Judiciary Committee as to the importance of the Committee to get to the bottom of the case fixing and cover up going on at the U.S. Court of Appeals in Chicago, which also reaffirmed my belief that he never sent a letter on my behalf as he had earlier purported.

Senator Todd Young's refusal to provide a copy of the alleged letter and his failure to say whether or not he would honor my requests for him to introduce a bill that would require federal agencies to respond to senators' inquiries on behalf of their constituents, as well as the failure to honor my request that he ask the Chair of the Senate Judiciary Committee, Dick Durbin, and the other Committee members to hold public hearings as to the case fixing and cover up that is going on in the U.S. Court of Appeals in Chicago, constitutes a blatant failure of Todd Young in his role as a United States senator. Young clearly breached his duty to me, as a constituent, by his refusal to provide me with a copy of a letter that was purportedly sent, calling into substantial question whether Young actually sent it, and a further breach against the people of our country by his refusal to request that the Senate Judiciary Committee hold public hearings as to the case fixing and cover up going on in the U.S. Court of Appeals in Chicago. Our country is infested with political cowards, and Indiana Senator Todd Young is a classic example.

CHAPTER 6

THE ATTORNEY GENERAL WHO ALLOWS CASE FIXING AND COVER UP BY FEDERAL JUDGES

LOOKING THE OTHER WAY

"If you are neutral in situations of injustice, you have chosen the side of the oppressor."
~ Desmond Tutu

After Joe Biden won the presidency and appointed Merrick Garland as Attorney General of the United States, I thought perhaps Garland had a measure of integrity where he might actually be interested in doing the right thing and get to the bottom of what was going on. So I decided to write to him and ask that he hold grand jury proceedings and indict the criminal judges on the U.S. Court of Appeals in Chicago who were involved in case fixing and cover up of the appeal I had against the Valparaiso, Indiana, police which had been disclosed by Judge Richard A. Posner. I provided Garland a great deal of information for him to chew on. Here is the verbatim letter that I wrote to Garland:

BRIAN VUKADINOVICH
XXXXXXXXXXXXXXXX
XXXXXXXXXXXXXXXX
XXXXXXXXXXXXXXXX

April 22, 2021

Honorable Merrick B. Garland, Attorney General
U.S. Department of Justice
950 Pennsylvania Avenue, N.W.
Washington, DC 20530-0001

Re: Public Corruption by Law Enforcement and State and Federal Judges Need for Grand Jury Proceedings and Criminal Indictments

Dear Mr. Attorney General Garland:

First, please allow me to congratulate you on your recent appointment as our country's new attorney general. It is an appointment very well deserved on your part. We as a country will be better for it. The U.S. Department of Justice website states that you, as the chief law enforcement officer for the United States, are "dedicated to the fair and impartial administration of justice on behalf of the American people." I am therefore writing to you to ask you to reopen a what was a very infected investigation undertaken by the Department of Justice some years ago into several instances of harassments and brutalities that were perpetrated against me by various law enforcement agencies in northwest Indiana, several of which I was physically brutalized and falsely arrested and vindictively prosecuted, from which each and every false arrest resulted in a jury acquittal, dismissal of charges, or a pardon by the Indiana governor of the lone conviction which was obtained by infected means. The law enforcement agencies involved were the Valparaiso Police Department, Porter County Sheriff's Department, Porter County Prosecutor's Office in concert with the Westville Police Department and LaPorte County Prosecutor's Office, Wheatfield Police Department and Jasper County Prosecutors Office, all of which were located as adjoining counties to Porter County, from which there is a substantial documented paper trail clearly demonstrating a conspiracy between these law enforcement agencies to deprive me of my civil rights by actively cooperating with each other to falsely arrest me and vindictively prosecute me in retaliation for my actions of successfully defending myself of several false and fictitious charges from several false arrests involving these police departments and acquiescence by the prosecutor's offices in Porter, LaPorte and Jasper Counties.

During court proceedings on March 23, 1987, in the matter of State of Indiana v. Brian Vukadinovich, Cause No. 86-PSC-CD-M-820 in the Porter County Court II, Judge Mary R. Harper presiding, Porter County Deputy Prosecuting Attorney Nancy Vaidik made false representations regarding my request for production of communications between the various law enforcement agencies about me. Vaidik argued [lied] that there was no correspondence between Porter County officials and other law enforcement officials. When I responded to Judge Harper that it was my belief that Vaidik's office was intentionally withholding evidence, Judge Harper stated *"First of all, I'm not sure whether or not there was correspondence. The State says there was not."* I responded back *"There absolutely was."* Judge Harper stated *"Apparently, it is not in the Prosecutor's file."* Vaidik then responded *"And then he responded and indicated that he couldn't find it."* Judge Harper then stated *"And then he responded and he indicated that it didn't exist. That's what we are stuck with. The State has responded."* I can of course provide a transcript to you. After Nancy Vaidik's lies and shenanigans, I subpoenaed the various law enforcement officials that Vaidik was inappropriately trying to protect with her lies, and Judge Harper dismissed all of the fabricated criminal charges with prejudice on April 20, 1987. (copy of dismissal order enclosed herein).

Vaidik's lies denying that there was correspondence between various law enforcement agencies about me are belied by several letters. In point of fact a letter was written by then Porter County Sheriff Tim McCarthy to LaPorte County deputy prosecutor Robert Szilagyi in February 1986 where McCarthy stated in his letter to Szilagyi that he had *"an extensive file"* on me and adding in a comment that somebody was fleeing police and *"It may very well have been Brian Vukadinovich"* implying that it was me, when in fact it was not me. (copy of letter is enclosed herein). The event probably never even happened as it stands to reason that if there would have been an incident of "fleeing police" there would have been some kind of police report about it with some details of which McCarthy would have undoubtedly cited in his letter when he made such an outlandish and irresponsible statement, which was essentially a lie. When I took McCarthy's deposition my lawyer asked him if he (McCarthy) had any occasion to write any letters to any prosecuting attorneys about me and McCarthy answered *"Not that I can recall."* After testifying that he couldn't recall writing any letters to any prosecutors about me, when he was further pressed on it, McCarthy then said *"There was some correspondence I can't recall."*

On the very next day after McCarthy's deposition, LaPorte County deputy prosecutor Robert Szilagyi (who McCarthy had written to) then wrote to Porter County deputy prosecutor A. James Sarkisian, stating *"It would also appear that Vukadinovich creeps into the gray area of the law quite often."* (copy of letter is enclosed herein). These co-conspirators worked it out so they could apply a double whammy against me by making me have to defend myself in two trials in back to back months with the LaPorte County trial in May 1986 and the Porter County trial in June 1986. On May 23, 1986, Westville Marshal Michael J. Lindsay wrote a letter to Porter County Sheriff Tim McCarthy stating "Officer Spears would be willing to speak with your prosecutor about being a witness for the prosecution on this subject." (copy of letter enclosed herein). After a two day jury trial in Porter County, the jury found in my favor and issued a not guilty verdict. (copy of verdict enclosed herein). The conspirators knew they were going to lose the trial as Porter County Sheriff Tim McCarthy testified on his deposition *"I felt that they would lose that case because there simply wasn't the evidence there to prove that he was under the influence."* But yet McCarthy allowed his department to press a prosecution against me from the bogus charge by his officer knowing that they were going to lose at trial.

Honorable Merrick B. Garland, Attorney General
U.S. Department of Justice
April 22, 2021 – Page 3

    On October 25, 1988, Dan Berning, Prosecuting Attorney of Porter County Indiana at the time, who was Nancy Vaidik's boss by the way, wrote a letter to Indiana Deputy Attorney General James Clark in response to information that Clark was requesting about me. Berning told Deputy Attorney General Clark that "in the past" his office would respond to such informational requests by "sending a copy of a letter authored by James Sarkisian to the LaPorte County Prosecutor's Office." (Sarkisian was one of Berning's deputy prosecutors in the Porter County Prosecutor's Office). Berning went on to state in his letter to Deputy Attorney General Clark that he asked his secretaries "to locate and pull all of the files on Vukadinovich." and that "As it turns out" the files on me have been "misplaced" and that his secretaries "have not been able to locate those files." And then Berning said "Even if we were able to locate the files on Vukadinovich," "our answer" to the motion to produce "would be that no such information exists." This was a lie from one state official to another state official in a scheme of concealing and covering up information by stating that it didn't matter if the information existed, that they would lie and say that "no such information exists." And in the face of all of these frauds and setups, John Bolton would determine that there was no wrongdoing by these so called law enforcement officials who did everything they could outside the bounds of the law to persecute me with numerous false arrests and vindictive prosecutions.

    Out of the ten false arrests, the minions were able to obtain one (tainted) conviction in LaPorte County based on a switched affidavit that I later discovered. The switched affidavit showed that the arresting officer, Michael Spears of the Westville Police Department lied at the trial when he testified that he observed empty beer cans in my car as the switched affidavit showed that he found "Empty 7-up" cans and not empty beer cans leaving the jury to surmise that Spears found empty beer cans when in fact there were no empty beer cans in my car. When I asked LaPorte County deputy prosecutor in a post-conviction proceeding if Robert Szilagyi had any conversations with Spears about the *"mistake"* in not turning evidence over to me during the criminal proceedings, Szilagyi answered *"He may have said something in passing when I found about the document in question."* And yet Szilagyi never disclosed this exculpatory evidence in order to get an infected conviction against me which would cost me my teaching job and thirty days in jail. The governor of Indiana, Mitch Daniels would later issue a pardon after I presented the information about how Spears switched affidavits and lied at the trial with Szilagyi's knowledge. (copy of Executive Order of Pardon enclosed herein).

    In his political campaign for prosecutor, Szilagyi would subsequently publicly boast to the Michigan City News Dispatch and LaPorte Herald Argus newspapers in April 2010 that he obtained a conviction against me for resisting law enforcement (which was not true) calling it his "most memorable case." Several people called me and told me about it so I took immediate steps to have both newspapers publish a retraction. The correction by the News Dispatch of Michigan City on April 27, 2010 headlined the correction as "Szilagyi provides false information." The LaPorte

Honorable Merrick B. Garland, Attorney General
U.S. Department of Justice
April 22, 2021 – Page 4

County Herald Argus on April 27, 2010 published a "Correction" as to Szilagyi's false statement as well. Both newspapers pointed out that former prosecutor Szilagyi provided "false information" in his discussion of my case. In addressing Szilagyi's false statement about me, the newspapers wrote "According to Clerk of the Circuit Court Lynne Spevak, Vukadinovich was not charged with or convicted of resisting law enforcement." So not only did Szilagyi lie to the jury to get a conviction against me, he also lied to the public in a political campaign so he could get elected as the county prosecutor falsely stating that he obtained a conviction against me for resisting law enforcement in what he said was his "most memorable case."

There are a great deal more things to talk about that I will not be able to address in this letter in the interest of brevity, but if you will grant a meeting with me in order that I can show you the very substantial and significant information that the U.S. Department of Justice chose to disregard and ignore under John Bolton's direction in Bolton's infected so called investigation, which was a blatant sham from which only police were interviewed and no independent witnesses were interviewed, although there were several independent witnesses who had information and knowledge about what happened including a member of the Valparaiso Police Department who had listened to conversations between Valparaiso police officers who were scheming to falsely arrest and brutalize me. The type of investigation that the FBI and U.S. Department conducted that included only interviewing police personnel and didn't involve interviewing known independent witness was sham investigation to say the least. On October 1, 1994, I wrote a critical piece in the "Voice of the People" in the Post-Tribune where I wrote about several questionable deaths that occurred in the Porter County Jail (the same jail where I was taken after the multiple false arrests and brutalities). I later learned that the FBI was monitoring my free speech rights and faxed my piece to the Department of Justice. The "Originator's Name" according to the FBI Facsimile Coversheet was Dennis P. Hyten, the FBI agent that I met with and reported what the police were doing to me. (copy of "Voice of the People" piece and FBI Facsimile Coversheet is enclosed herein). It is clear by this facsimile that the FBI was more interested in monitoring my free speech rights than it was in investigating what the rogue police were doing to me, a fact made clear when Bolton cleared the rogue police without interviewing independent witnesses and only interviewing police.

The situation became worse and worse by the day to the point that I couldn't go to the grocery store without getting stopped and arrested and prosecuted to no end. The situation became very high profile with major news media reporting. (copies of several articles enclosed herein). The numerous false arrests cost me a great deal in terms of loss of employment of teaching jobs as the police actually went to my places of employment and talked to school officials for which I later was terminated from my teaching jobs. (copies of several articles enclosed herein). There were several state and federal lawsuits that resulted from the goings on from the false arrests and brutalities and loss of employment where state and federal judges chose to run to the rescue of the law enforcement players. A few years ago after I successfully represented myself, pro se, in a federal civil rights jury trial against my former public school corporation employer, Hanover Community

Honorable Merrick B. Garland, Attorney General
U.S. Department of Justice
April 22, 2021 – Page 5

School Corporation, where the jury ruled in my favor and awarded me significant damages for the corporation's violation of my due process rights when it terminated my employment, Judge Richard A. Posner, retired judge of the United States Court of Appeals for the Seventh Circuit in Chicago, heard about how I successfully represented myself at the federal jury trial and asked me to join him in his newly created company, Posner Center of Justice for Pro Se's, and he shortly thereafter appointed me as the executive director. Judge Posner confided to me that when he was on the bench that his fellow judge, Michael S. Kanne, told him that he (Kanne) didn't like me and asked him (Judge Posner) to do him and district judge James T. Moody a favor and rule against me in an appeal that I had filed against Moody's rulings from a trial involving the Valparaiso Police Department. Judge Posner told me that Kanne "had it in for you." Judge Posner admitted to me that he accommodated Kanne's request and made sure that I would not prevail in the appeal. The appeal involved Moody's actions of disallowing me from putting a Valparaiso police officer, John Cooros, on the witness stand to testifying about how he heard certain Valparaiso police officers scheming to falsely arrest me and brutalize me. Moody also refused to let me play a tape recording of one of the false arrests of which tape recording caught the Valparaiso police laughing and bragging about arresting me and even stating *"I'm goin' to get the son-of-a-bitch. F--- him."* The recording was listed on the controlling pre-trial order as an admissible exhibit, but at trial, Moody refused to let me play it to the jury. Moody also refused to let me show the jury the evidence of prior acts of corruption and the many citizens' complaints against the Valparaiso Police Department. (copies of newspaper articles enclosed herein). Judge Posner told me that the case clearly should have been reversed but that he succumbed to Kanne's pressure on him to fix the decision to make sure that I didn't prevail. Judge Posner apologized to me and asked for my forgiveness. He said he knew it was wrong but it was something that judges did for one another from time to time. When Judge Posner told me about it, I had a flashback to an oral argument that took place on September 10, 2002, under Case No. 01-1625 in Chicago where I was appealing a decision about the loss of my teaching job from the North Newton School Corporation and Kanne called me a "troublemaker" and then wrote the adverse decision against me on January 22, 2002. Later I learned that Kanne was doing a favor for his wife who was a co-worker of a principal defendant/appellant in the case in writing the decision in his favor. After I learned about this, I filed papers in the Seventh Circuit and then Kanne recused himself on September 26, 2002, which was of course well after he wrote the adverse decision. (copy of complaint form and relevant documents enclosed herein). After Judge Posner told me about how Kanne pressured him to do what he had to do in order that I not prevail in my case against the Valparaiso Police, it all became very clear as to what was going on and how Kanne orchestrated the decisions against me. Judge Posner made that clear to me.

After the numerous false arrests and brutalities, including when an officer of the Porter County Sheriff's Department falsely arrested me (I was acquitted by a jury) and broke my jaw during the false arrest, and put me in jail overnight while refusing my request for medical attention, and

Honorable Merrick B. Garland, Attorney General
U.S. Department of Justice
April 22, 2021 – Page 6

refusing my request for a telephone call, from which the FBI saw no problem, I went to my congressman, Jim Jontz, and asked him to contact the Department of Justice, which he did. On August 3, 1097, Congressman Jontz wrote a letter to John R. Bolton, an assistant attorney general at the time, and asked for a review of what happening to me. (copy of letter enclosed herein). On October 13, 1987, John Bolton wrote a letter to Congressman Jontz and stated that "An investigation was conducted by the Federal Bureau of Investigation into Mr. Vukadinovich's complaints" and that "We have carefully reviewed the reports of the FBI as well as documents submitted by Mr. Vukadinovich and have concluded that the facts presented do not support a prosecutable violation of federal civil rights laws." (copy of letter enclosed herein). I thereafter made a request for records from the Department of Justice and received some information, mostly which was redacted, but the information made it clear to me that the FBI only interviewed police personnel and did not interview any independent witness who had knowledge and information about what the police did to me. On February 18, 1988, I wrote a letter to Bolton outlining the problems with his infected letter making it very clear to Bolton that review of the information was a far cry from a "carefully reviewed" process as Bolton put it and I asked for a meeting with him to discuss the matter. (copy of letter enclosed herein). Bolton did not grant my request for a meeting with him, so his distortions and lies stand to this day.

    Such a sham investigation reeks of corruption tantamount to the false report disseminated by the Minneapolis Police just after Chauvin murdered George Floyd when the Minneapolis police publicly submitted that Mr. Floyd had a medical condition and died at the hospital with no mention of Chauvin pressing his knee into Mr. Floyd's neck for over nine minutes killing him. This is precisely what Bolton did in putting out a letter with false information covering for the corrupt and unlawful actions of the police.

    It is more than clear that there was a cover up of the police's concerted actions in falsely arresting me and brutalizing me on numerous occasions and such cover up involved high levels of government including John R. Bolton who ultimately covered up the information and evidence in order to protect unlawful police misconducts against me for which state prosecutors and state judges acquiesced in the scheme of things. It is clear that a grand jury proceeding is in order against all players involved in the overall scheme. I realize that there is a substantial time period that has elapsed since these events, but it was only recently that I was told by Judge Richard A. Posner about the fraud by judge Michael S. Kanne to protect the corrupt actions of Judge James T. Moody. Accordingly, I request that a grand jury be empaneled and witnesses be subpoenaed for grand jury testimony and indictments to be sought against all of the government employees and officials including the judges who were involved in the grand scheme of things.

    Just after the Chauvin verdict you publicly stated that the U.S. Department of Justice is "unwavering in its pursuit of equal justice under law" in addressing the issues surrounding the

Honorable Merrick B. Garland, Attorney General
U.S. Department of Justice
April 22, 2021 – Page 7

Minneapolis Police Department as to its infected practices and customs in violating peoples' civil rights. If what you publicly said is true, that the Department of Justice is "unwavering in its pursuit of equal justice under law," then you will do the right thing and order a meaningful investigation into what the police did to me and an investigation into the conduct of Michael S. Kanne and James T. Moody in their obstructions of justice. Judge Richard A. Posner is a man of integrity and I believe he would step up to the plate and disclose to the Department of Justice how Michael Kanne asked him for a favor to ensure that Moody's infected actions from the federal trial against the Valparaiso police not be reversed. Federal judges who conduct themselves in such an unlawful manner so as to obstruct justice in order to protect wrongful and unlawful police conduct and to deprive a person's fundamental right to redress of grievances for civil rights violations against him should be put in front of a federal grand jury and indicted. I therefore request that you investigate these matters and take steps to indict judges Michael S. Kanne and James T. Moody. If you subpoena Judge Richard A. Posner to testify before a federal grand jury the grand jury would without question issue indictments against Michael S. Kanne and James T. Moody for their wrongful and unlawful acts of interfering with my civil rights and obstruction of justice to the point of persuading a federal court of appeals judge, Richard A. Posner, to throw a decision as a favor for two corrupt federal judges, Michael S. Kanne and James T. Moody.

I will look forward to hearing from you as to your decision to impanel a grand jury for indictments as to these matters. I believe you would agree that as a country we cannot, and should not, stand for corrupt activities by rogue police and law enforcement officials and that we cannot and should not stand for corrupt activities on the part of state and federal judges. To look the other way here and allow this type of public corruption to go without consequence would render the axiom that "nobody is above the law" as a meaningless phrase. Derek Chauvin killed George Floyd by pressing on his neck, we cannot allow these corrupt police and law enforcement officials and judges to kill justice by pressing on its neck. John Bolton suffocated justice when he covered for the unlawful actions of the police when he chose to disregard evidence and not interview known witnesses, the police suffocated justice when they acted in concert in their schemes to falsely arrest and brutalize me, the state prosecutors and state judges suffocated justice by their acquiescence to the police schemes, Michael S. Kanne suffocated justice when he persuaded Richard A. Posner to throw the case as a favor to him in order that James T. Moody would not be reversed, James T. Moody suffocated justice when he decided to throw the civil rights trial for the Valparaiso police by refusing to let me put a Valparaiso officer on the witness stand to testify about his knowledge of the schemes to falsely arrest and brutalize me and by not allowing me to play to the jury the tape recording of the false arrest, and by not allowing me to show the jury the evidence of prior acts of corruption and the many citizens' complaints against the Valparaiso Police Department.

The fact that a federal judge, Richard A. Posner, has disclosed that a brethren federal judge, Michael S. Kanne, asked him to throw a decision from a federal court of appeals case as a favor to another judge is public corruption of the highest degree. It would be inconceivable to look the other way and not hold a grand jury proceeding in order to protect those corrupt federal judges from criminal indictments. Michael S. Kanne and James T. Moody should be brought before a grand jury and indicted.

Sincerely,
Brian Vukadinovich
Enclosures

Needless to say, Garland did nothing. In all honesty I wouldn't have bet the ranch that he would actually do something, but I thought that it might be worth a try to see if he was any different from the other political cronies who pledge to work on behalf of justice but who simply are interested in nothing more than having an important title and collecting a hefty government salary along with the associated perks. As it turned out, Garland came from the same mold. Merrick Garland likes to publicly talk about the so-called "rule of law." In his press conference addressing the warrant served at Trump's property at Mar-a-Lago and the confiscating of boxes of documents, Garland said, "Faithful adherence to the rule of law is the bedrock principle of the Justice Department and of our democracy. Upholding the rule of law means applying the law evenly without fear or favor. Under my watch, that is precisely what the Justice Department is doing." Garland must have conveniently forgotten that he didn't take such a posture about the rule of law, which he likes to talk about so much, when he was a judge and was put in charge of ruling on an ethics complaint against Texas judge Edith Jones of the 5th Circuit Court of Appeals. She was accused of an ethics violation for making public derogatory comments against Blacks and Hispanics, including suggesting that Blacks and Hispanics were "predisposed to crime" and "prone" to violence" during a 2013 speech at a Federalist Society-sponsored event held at the University of Pennsylvania Law School. Several groups filed an ethical complaint against Jones for her derogatory public comments. The matter ended up before Garland, who then appointed a special committee that included himself to handle the complaint.

Only two people were allowed to testify before Garland's committee during the investigation: Jones herself and Marc Bookman, a Philadelphia death penalty lawyer who attended her speech and helped file the complaint. Maurie Levin, one of the lawyers for the complainants, said the investigation was "blanketed in secrecy and bias." Levin has pointed out that although Bookman was cross-examined by Jones' attorney, Jones testified in secret, without any of the complainants in the room. Garland's panel refused to disclose a transcript of Jones' testimony or the documents she filed in her defense. He and his appointed cohorts ultimately found that Jones hadn't violated the judicial code of ethics and recommended that the D.C. Circuit's judicial council, which had final say in the matter, dismiss the complaint, which it did. https://www.motherjones.com/politics/2016/03/time-merrick-garland-was-accused-protecting-fellow-judge-charged-ethics-violations/.

According to Maurie Levin, "The judicial panel that investigated the complaint—presided over by Judge Garland—twisted itself into a pretzel to find that Judge Jones would face no consequences and dismissed the complaint." Levin said the process raises the question of whether Garland and his fellow judges were "more interested in protecting [their] brethren than rooting out bias in the administration of justice." In the end, Garland's involvement in protecting his "brethren" judge hardly constituted a "Faithful adherence to the rule of law," as he likes to say.

Civil rights groups wrote, "At its core, the decision of the [judges] serves to undermine any faith the public may have in the fairness and impartiality of the judiciary, the federal judicial discipline system or a system free of race bias." Luis Roberto Vera Jr., LULAC's national general counsel, said in a press release, "Just as concerning as these instances of bias, the one-sidedness and secrecy surrounding the ethics complaint process and the untoward deference to the judge's denials makes it unlikely that any claims of judicial misbehavior can be handled in a way that gives the public confidence that justice is being served."

Andrew Cohen, a CBS commentator and lawyer, tweeted at the time: "Farce of the Day: How federal judges herded together to protect 5th Circuit Judge Edith Jones, a national disgrace."

And now, as Attorney General of the United States, Garland is once again showing his preference of looking the other way as to the judicial corruption that I reported to him—just as Attorney Maurie Levin previously stated in the aftermath of the Edith Jones matter when Ms. Levin said that Garland and his fellow judges were "more interested in protecting [their] brethren than rooting out bias in the administration of justice." This time around, Garland has chosen to protect a case-fixing judge in the U.S. Court of Appeals for the Seventh Circuit in Chicago, and is also protecting the chief judge and the other complicit judges on the Seventh Circuit who took part in the cover up. Strikingly similar as to how Garland conducted the proceeding against the Texas judge, Chief Judge Sykes also proceeded with a blatant bias and one-sidedness and secrecy. Based on the comments by these civil rights advocates, Garland's actions here likewise don't at all sound anything akin to "Upholding the rule of law...evenly without fear or favor" as Garland likes to publicly profess.

Actually, Sykes' conduct in protecting Kanne was even worse than the situation with the Texas judge that Garland protected—the Texas judge asserted denials of wrongdoing, contrarily to Kanne who didn't deny on the record that he fixed the decision in the civil rights case as disclosed by Judge Posner. Sykes' conduct of dismissing a well-grounded judicial misconduct complaint, supported by affidavit, to which she chose to not even interview the judge who disclosed the case fixing conduct, and chose to not even interview the subject of the complaint in her secret proceeding, certainly does not demonstrate "public confidence that justice is being served." And just as in the case of the Texas judge that was investigated by Garland, which was characterized by CBS commentator and lawyer Andrew Cohen as the "Farce of the Day: How federal judges herded together to protect 5th Circuit Judge Edith Jones, a national disgrace," so too is the case against Judge Michael S. Kanne with Chief Judge Diane S. Sykes starring as the head of the herd to protect its brethren case-fixing judge, another "Farce of the Day" and "national disgrace"—something that Attorney General Merrick Garland obviously has no problem with. So much for Garland's professing of "Upholding the rule of law...evenly without fear or favor."

CHAPTER 7

THE CHIEF JUSTICE OF THE UNITED STATES IS PERFECTLY FINE WITH CASE FIXING AND COVER UP BY FEDERAL JUDGES

*"Power concedes nothing without a demand.
It never did and it never will."*
~ Frederick Douglass

After Chief Judge Diane S. Sykes and her confederates on the U.S. Court of Appeals in Chicago swept under the rug the case fixing and cover up of the appeal, on October 4, 2021, I wrote a letter to the Chief Justice of the United States, John Roberts, and let him know what was going on. As chief justice, Roberts is the nation's highest ranking judicial official and speaks for the judicial branch of the federal government, and also serves as the chief administrative officer for the federal courts. I thought it would be appropriate to contact Roberts to advise him of the corruption in the Seventh Circuit with the case fixing by Kanne and cover up by Sykes and her cohorts in the hope that he might actually give a care about the corruption in that court, but I knew that was wishful thinking at best, as he has a terrible track record for monitoring and actually taking action against judges in the federal judiciary, including

Supreme Court justices. Case in point, an article by NBC News reported that because of many judicial improprieties, there have been increased calls that the Supreme Court be subject to a code of ethics, like all other U.S. courts, but that Chief Justice John Roberts has consistently defended the court s refusal to adopt one, rejecting all suggestions of congressional or other oversight. The article points out that the Supreme Court has refused for over 50 years to adopt the Judicial Conference code, or any other code, making it the only court in the United States without a formal set of ethics rules. Roberts stated position is that the Supreme Court has "no reason to adopt the Code of Conduct as its definitive source of ethical guidance." Roberts spews that "every justice seeks to follow high ethical standards" and that they may turn to "judicial opinions, treatises, scholarly articles and disciplinary decisions," and also seek advice from one another. https://www.nbcnews.com/think/opinion/supreme-court-chief-justice-john-roberts-gives-incomplete-history-lesson-ncna1286943.

This borders on the hilarious. But his idiotic statement does show one thing for sure, Roberts has no interest in having any formal guidelines for conduct when it comes to his sidekicks on the Supreme Court. This tells us a lot about him. Roberts has also been quoted as saying that the nation s federal courts are doing a better job of policing themselves, which he called essential for the ability of the judicial branch to maintain its independence. He also said that the judiciary s power to manage its own internal affairs "insulates courts from inappropriate political influence and is crucial to preserving public trust in its work as a separate and co-equal branch of government." https://nypost.com/2022/01/01/chief-justice-john-roberts-warns-against-inappropriate-political-influence-in-federal-courts/. He should be a stand up comedian as that line would undoubtedly get him a lot of laughs at a comedy club. So since we have a chief justice who doesn't believe in having a code of conduct for Supreme Court justices and also believes that the federal judiciary should manage its own internal affairs in order to "preserve public trust in its work"—which would also be a great one liner at a comedy club—it came as no surprise to me that Roberts chose to look the other way as to the case fixing and cover up going on in the U.S. Court of Appeals in Chicago. This is a verbatim of a letter I wrote to Roberts:

BRIAN VUKADINOVICH
XXXXXXXXXXXXXXXX
XXXXXXXXXXXXXXXX
XXXXXXXXXXXXXXXX

October 4, 2021

Honorable John Roberts, Chief Justice of the United States
Supreme Court of the United States
1 First Street, NE
Washington, DC 20543

        Re: Whitewash of Judicial Corruption by Judge Michael S. Kanne, United States Court of Appeals for the Seventh Circuit

Dear Chief Justice Roberts:

    I am writing to you to advise you about a very serious issue of case fixing of a decision of a civil rights case by Judge Michael S. Kanne that took place in the United States Court of Appeals for the Seventh Circuit in Chicago and for the Seventh Circuit's sweeping under the rug the information properly submitted in a judicial misconduct complaint against Judge Kanne, a copy of which judicial misconduct complaint is attached hereto. On September 30, 2021, The Judicial Council of the Seventh Circuit via Chief Judge Diane S. Sykes issued a Memorandum and Order dismissing the judicial misconduct complaint in a very questionable and troubling fashion, a copy of which order is attached hereto. You may recall publicly stating in your *2019 Year-End Report on the Federal Judiciary* "I ask my judicial colleagues to continue their efforts to promote public confidence in the judiciary, both through their rulings and through civic outreach." and "We should reflect on our duty to judge without fear or favor, deciding each matter with humility, integrity, and dispatch." 2019year-endreport.pdf (supremecourt.gov).

    This is certainly an inflection point in your legacy as Chief Justice of the United States, for your response and action, or lack of response and action, will determine in the public's eye whether or not your reign as Chief Justice of the United States was worthy or unworthy, and this determination will be based not on your rhetoric, but by your actions, or inactions as Chief Justice, for as you admonished your judicial colleagues when you publicly stated "We should reflect on our duty to judge without fear or favor, deciding each matter with humility, integrity, and dispatch" the public at large expects you as Chief Justice of the United States to follow your own publicly stated words where you stated the importance to "promote public confidence in the judiciary." You now have a golden opportunity to demonstrate, not through words, but by action, if you truly believe the importance of promoting "public confidence" in the judiciary. As President John F. Kennedy once said *"As we express our gratitude, we must never forget that the highest appreciation is not to utter words, but to live by them."*

On July 26, 2021 I submitted a judicial misconduct complaint against Judge Michael S. Kanne for his conduct of *ex parte* case fixing of a decision from a civil rights case in which I represented myself, pro se, in the case titled as *Brian Vukadinovich, Appellant, v. Richard Zentz, Ronald Kurmis, John Ross, William Collins, and City of Valparaiso*, Appellees, Case No. 92-2957, 995 F.2d 750 (7th Cir. 1993). The information submitted in the judicial misconduct-complaint against Judge Kanne is based on information that I obtained from my personal communication in 2018 with Judge Richard A. Posner who was on the panel and who has since retired from the Court on September 2, 2017. Judge Posner was a member of the three-judge appellate panel assigned to adjudicate the decision, Judge Kanne was not. Instead, the other two members of the appellate panel were Judge Frank Hoover Easterbrook of the Seventh Circuit and Judge William H. Timbers of the U.S. Court of Appeals for the Second Circuit, sitting by designation. As the Complaint demonstrated, although Judge Kanne was not a member of the appellate panel he previously knew me from when he (Judge Kanne) was a U.S. District Court Judge. In 1986 Judge Kanne granted summary judgment against me (when I represented myself *pro se*) in a First Amendment case against my former public-school employer. In that same case, Judge Kanne also denied my motion for a preliminary injunction to stop the school from replacing me as a teacher.

In March 2016, I successfully represented myself *pro se* in a five day jury trial against my former public-school employer before the United States District Court for the Northern District of Indiana, where I won a six-figure verdict. The presiding judge was the Honorable Philip P. Simon. This case was titled *Brian Vukadinovich v. Hanover Community School Corporation, et al.*, Cause No. 2:13-CV-00144-PPS (N.D. Ind.). Because I made history as a successful *pro se* litigant, the case received national attention. As a result, in October 2017 when Judge Posner was creating a company that eventually came to be called The Posner Center of Justice for Pro Se's Nonprofit Company, see http://www.justice-for-proses.org/, Judge Posner telephoned me for advice. In another telephone call in November 2017, I told Judge Posner that I was writing a book about my previous pro se litigation, which included the aforementioned case of *Brian Vukadinovich v. Richard Zentz*, et al., of which book, titled MOTION FOR JUSTICE: I REST MY CASE, was in fact published on June 6, 2018. After reading a manuscript of my book, in November 2017 Judge Posner wrote the Foreword to MOTION FOR JUSTICE: I REST MY CASE. In February 2018, Judge Posner appointed me to serve as Executive Director of the Posner Center of Justice for Pro Se's. As Judge Posner explained in the Foreword to MOTION FOR JUSTICE: I REST MY CASE: "I retired . . . as a federal judge after more than 35 years on the bench because I had come to realize albeit belatedly that my court was systematically unjust to pro se's, i.e., litigants who do not have lawyers. . . . I felt that the pro se's who number literally in the millions, deserved more consideration than we were giving them, and I was determined to help them…" After writing the Foreword to my book, Judge Posner invited me to meet with him to discuss the Posner Center. On March 19, 2018, I traveled from my home in Indiana to Chicago to meet Judge Posner. There, Judge Posner treated me to lunch at a restaurant called Petterino's, located at 150 North Dearborn Street, Chicago, IL 60601. During my lunch with Judge Posner at Petterino's, Judge Posner continued in the same vein that he had begun in the Foreword to my book by discussing his disgust concerning the mistreatment that pro se litigants, such as I, had suffered at the hands of his former Court, the Seventh Circuit. Judge Posner then went on to disclose to me that, although Judge Michael Kanne had not been a member of the appellate panel in my civil rights case against the Valparaiso police, that Judge Kanne was behind the panel's decision to rule against me in that case. Specifically, Judge Posner told me that, during the pendency of my appeal of the civil rights case against the Valparaiso Indiana police, that Judge Kanne had initiated an *ex parte* conversation with Judge Posner about me and the case. During the conversation Judge Posner told me that Judge Kanne told him (Judge Posner) that I was a "troublemaker" and, in a reference to my earlier case before Judge Kanne when he (Kanne) was a District Court Judge, that Judge Kanne stated that he (Judge Kanne) apparently "didn't get the job done" by having ruled against me in that earlier case. Explaining that Judge Kanne had it in for me , Judge Posner then revealed that Judge Kanne had asked Judge Posner—as a "favor" to Judge Kanne—to make sure that the I did not prevail in my appeal against the Valparaiso police. Next, Judge Posner admitted that, regrettably, he (Judge Posner) had succumbed to Judge Kanne's "pressure" and therefore had accommodated Judge Kanne's "request" to have the district court's decision in favor of the Valparaiso police affirmed even though Judge Posner knew that it "should have been reversed." Judge Posner apologized to me for having "fixed" the decision and asked me for forgiveness, which I of course granted, as I could see that Judge Posner's remorse was genuine and heartfelt. Judge Posner added that he knew what he did "was wrong," but that this was "something that judges did for one another from time to time." Judge Posner then acknowledged that, because Judge Kanne was a "corrupt judge" who fixed cases, Judge Kanne should have never been a member of the federal judiciary. Judge Posner also stated that it was "unjust situations" like the one that had happened to me that motivated Judge Posner to retire from the bench.

Accordingly, Judge Kanne's actions violated the Judicial Conduct and Disability Act, the Rules for Judicial-Conduct and Judicial-Disability Proceedings, and the Code of Conduct for United States Judges because Judge Kanne initiated an improper *ex parte* communication with a fellow judge (Judge Posner) in which Judge Kanne asked that other judge to corruptly fix a case against a party (me) for whom Judge Kanne had a strong personal dislike. Because Judge Kanne was not a member of the appellate panel assigned to adjudicate that case and had no other responsibilities regarding this case, Judge Kanne was acting outside the performance of his official duties. As such, Judge Kanne engaged in conduct outside the performance of his official duties that was prejudicial to the effective and expeditious administration of the business of the courts, undermined public confidence in the integrity and impartiality of the judiciary, and created a strong appearance of impropriety. The Judicial Conduct and Disability Act allows "[a]ny person alleging that a judge has engaged in conduct prejudicial to the effective and expeditious administration of the business of the courts" to file a complaint against the judge. See 28 U.S.C. § 351(a). To implement that Act, as amended, the Judicial Conference of the United States promulgated the Rules for Judicial-Conduct and Judicial-Disability Proceedings. Rule 4(a)(1)(C) defines "cognizable misconduct" as including "engaging in improper ex parte communications with parties or counsel for one side in a case." Rule 4(a)(7) defines "cognizable misconduct" as including "conduct occurring outside the performance of official duties if the conduct is reasonably likely to have a prejudicial effect on the administration of the business of the courts, including a substantial and widespread lowering of public confidence in the courts among reasonable people." Canon 2 of the Code of Conduct for United States Judges provides:

"A Judge Should Avoid Impropriety and the Appearance of Impropriety in all Activities." The Commentary to Canon 2A states that "An appearance of impropriety occurs when reasonable minds, with knowledge of all the relevant circumstances . . . would conclude that the judge's honesty, integrity, impartiality, temperament, or fitness to serve as a judge is impaired. Public confidence in the judiciary is eroded by irresponsible or improper conduct by judges. . . . A judge must avoid all impropriety and appearance of impropriety. This prohibition applies to both professional and personal conduct."

It should be noted that Judge Frank Easterbrook was on the panel to which Judge Kanne actively through devious *ex parte* methods had the civil rights decision fixed. It is noteworthy that University of Chicago Law School Professor Albert W. Alschuler wrote in a law-review article that, in his judicial opinions, Seventh Circuit "Judge Easterbrook persistently presents wildly inaccurate, made-up statements as unquestionable statements of fact," adding, "The truth is not in him." See Albert Alschuler, *How Frank Easterbrook Kept George Ryan in Prison*, University of Chicago Public Law & Legal Theory Paper Series, No. 589, at 15 and 49 (2016). After Professor Alschuler's article came out, the organization *Injustice Watch* conducted a review of Judge Easterbrook's opinions and "documented a pattern of misrepresented facts" in them. See Emily Hoerner and Rick Tulsky, Pattern of misstated facts found in opinions of renowned U.S. Judge Easterbrook, InjusticeWatch.org (April 4, 2017), available at https://www.injusticewatch.org/projects/2017/pattern-of-misstatedfacts-found-in-probe-of-renowned-federal-judges-opinions/.

Indeed the case fixing orchestrated by Judge Kanne and the manner in which the decision as to the judicial misconduct complaint was reached precisely fits the modus operandi of Judge Easterbrook in the widely reported articles about how Easterbrook "persistently presents wildly inaccurate, made-up statements as unquestionable statements of fact," and that "The truth is not in him." and also the review of Easterbrook's opinions reporting a "documented a pattern of misrepresented facts" demonstrates Easterbrook's unfitness to be a federal judge.

A close review of the fixed decision strongly reveals Easterbrook's infected thumbprint and how the decision was fixed exactly how Judge Kanne wanted it done, and in fact, had it done, according to Judge Posner. With regard to the issue of the district court's, (James Moody) refusal to follow the pretrial order in disallowing me from admitting into evidence a tape recording of a tape record of a false arrest I was subjected to, where the tape caught the Valparaiso police laughing and one cop even said *"I'm goin' to get the son-of-a-bitch. F--- him."* which of course would have shown the jury evidence of the game that the rogue police were playing with the false arrest. The infected panel wrote that I *"correctly"* stated "that the parties included the tape recording in the pretrial order and that appellees (police) failed to object to its inclusion as required by Local Rule 21(f)(6)," but then the infected panel then went on to say that Moody's decision to exclude the tapes at trial *"nevertheless was proper"* and that *"we are reluctant to interfere with the trial court's determination not to hold the appellee[s] to the pretrial order"* and *"we perceive no injustice resulting from our reluctance to interfere with the court's decision to alter the pretrial order."* This was a very interesting statement by the panel since Moody admonished in his Final Pretrial Conference Memorandum of September 7, 1990 that *"The parties are reminded to adhere to this Court's Order controlling trial."* And for icing on the proverbial government cake, the infected panel of the 7th Circuit went on to say that there was no evidence of bad faith on the part of defense counsel in not adhering to the pretrial order. And to top it all off, the infected panel went on to say that *"even if the tape was improperly excluded"* that it was *"harmless error."* And then the infected panel in grasping at straws in trying to find ways to justify its obvious corruption then stated that the case was "unique" and *"we perceive no injustice resulting from our reluctance to interfere with the court's decision to alter the pretrial order."*

Another example in how the decision was fixed was how the poisoned panel of the 7th Circuit went out of their way to cover for the infected ruling by the district court judge, James T. Moody went out of this way to put a roadblock in my case against the Valparaiso Police was when he chose to ignore the governing rules as to depositions. When the Valparaiso police's lawyer took my mother's deposition and asked her a lot of very personal and inappropriate questions for her reasons of coming to the United States from Europe, which had absolutely nothing to do with the issues in the case and were simply brought up to my mother to upset her and to inappropriately make her justify her reasons for immigrating to the United States, their lawyer, after such abuse against my mother, never submitted the deposition for her review as he was required to do under Rule 30(e) of the Federal Rules of Civil Procedure, an explicit governing rule. When the lawyer referred to the depositions at the trial and I objected on the grounds that the deposition was not provided to my mother for her review and signature as required by the rules, Moody again assisted the Valparaiso Police Department and its unsavory lawyer by allowing the deposition into the trial even though the governing rule was not followed by the Valparaiso Police Department and its lawyer. When I brought this issue up in the appeal to the 7th Circuit, the infected panel stated that *"Although it may be said that the court improperly admitted unsigned depositions, doing so constituted at worst harmless error."* Thus, the infected panel reinforced its very disturbing pattern of indifference to the governing rules and acquiescence to Kanne's case fixing of the decision when the infected panel wrote that the improperly admitted unsigned deposition was *"harmless error"* in order not to do the right thing in reversing the fixed ruling.

Another way that the infected panel operated in fixing the decision was in how it greatly assisted the Valparaiso Police in not reversing the denial of my post-trial motion to vacate the judgment and impose sanctions against the City of Valparaiso for withholding evidence in violation of a court order. The City of Valparaiso was under a court order to submit to the court for an *in camera* (in private) inspection of the officers' personnel files. The personnel files weren't submitted for the court ordered in camera inspection and consequently, and because Moody allowed the damaging information in the officers' personnel files to be swept under the rug, I never got the opportunity to show the jury just how corrupt the Valparaiso officers were. And even though the City of Valparaiso was required to submit the officers' personnel files for the *in camera* inspection, but didn't, and even though the disregard of the court's order to do so prevented me from using the evidence of the officers' corruption at the trial, the infected panel stated that the burden was on me to show that the City of Valparaiso wrongfully withheld evidence and that the withheld evidence would have produced a different result, which I indeed did do by my post-trial motions and arguments to the 7th Circuit. And then after I showed that the City of Valparaiso failed to provide the evidence and that the evidence would have helped me prove the officers' corruption, the infected panel went on to state that I "failed to adduce any evidence that the City deliberately or wrongfully withheld evidence." This was utter hogwash.

And in its case fixing scheme as disclosed by Judge Posner, the infected panel of the Seventh Circuit wrote that I didn't show that the City of Valparaiso was deliberately indifferent to the constitutional rights of its citizens and that I did not demonstrate that the City of Valparaiso "perfunctorily dismissed citizen complaints." This was entirely false and had Easterbrook's fingerprints all over it, no doubt with case fixer Kanne's blessing. I had substantial evidence of numerous citizens' complaints that the City of Valparaiso essentially just looked the other way and did nothing time and time again while the Valparaiso Police were abusing people. The record very clearly showed that I tried to submit into evidence newspaper articles, and copies of legal actions filed against the City of Valparaiso by people who were victimized by officers of the Valparaiso Police Department and even a copy of a departmental investigative report of Officer Zentz, but Moody wouldn't allow me to submit any of this information into evidence at the trial, and then the infected panel in its creative case fixing helped things along by stating in its order that the exclusions of this evidence by Moody was okay writing that a court's decision to exclude evidence is *"generally accorded great deference because of the court's first hand exposure to the evidence and its familiarity with the course of the proceedings."* The infected panel also chose to disregard the evidence that Moody wouldn't let me put a former Valparaiso police officer, John Cooros, on the witness stand to testify about how he listened to conversations between corrupt Valparaiso police officers discussing plans on how they were going to falsely arrest me and brutalize me. It was all in the record. This is precisely how Kanne convinced the panel to fix the decision, just as Judge Posner said they did, and Judge Posner would know since he was on the panel corrupted by Kanne. But the infected panel through its creative case fixing methods and Easterbrook's penchant for persistently presenting "wildly inaccurate, made-up statements as unquestionable statements of fact," and his reported conduct of resorting to a "documented a pattern of misrepresented facts," Kanne's case fixing worked and he got just the result he sought when he made clear to Judge Posner that the decision was to be fixed against me.

Given that the Complaint implicates current and former Judges on the Seventh Circuit, the Judicial Council of the Seventh Circuit should not have adjudicated the Complaint. I requested that, pursuant to Rule 26 of the Rules for Judicial-Conduct and Judicial-Disability Proceedings, that the Judicial Council of the Seventh Circuit request that the Chief Justice of the United States transfer this proceeding to the judicial council of another circuit. Rule 26 expressly authorizes such a transfer. The Commentary to Rule 26 states that "[s]uch transfers may be appropriate . . . where the issues are highly visible and a local disposition may weaken public confidence . . . ." and the continued infected actions of the Seventh Circuit has most certainly weakened public confidence in how it has tried to sweep Judge Kanne's criminal conduct of case fixing under the rug. The nature of the allegations in the Complaint are both highly visible and implicate several past and current members of the Seventh Circuit, and therefore, transfer should have taken place instead of the ongoing cover up of the Seventh Circuit's criminal activities spearheaded by Judge Kanne. Such transfer procedure has been used before for Complaints involving only one Judge. See, e.g., In re Complaint of Judicial Misconduct (Ninth Circuit Judge Alex Kozinski), 575 F.3d 279, 280 (3d Cir. Jud. Council 2009), and In re Charges of Judicial Misconduct (Fifth Circuit Judge Edith Jones), 769 F.3d 762 (D.C. Cir. Jud. Council 2014). Therefore, it was certainly called for in the instant case when several Seventh Circuit judges are involved.

A review of the Memorandum and Order of The Judicial Council of the Seventh Circuit by Chief Judge Diane S. Sykes dated September 30, 2021, demonstrates the Seventh Circuit's interest of sweeping Kanne's criminal conduct of case fixing under the rug, and quite frankly, further demonstrates the complicity of Chief Judge Diane S. Sykes and her brethren members of that court. It is more than obvious that Chief Judge Sykes and the so called Judicial Council of the Seventh Circuit were more interested in covering for Kanne's criminal conduct of case fixing than dealing with the facts that clearly point to Kanne's case fixing, just as Judge Posner disclosed. So what did Sykes and her compadres do, they utilized a ridiculous rationale that because so much time has passed since the conduct alleged in the complaint, and because I didn't "immediately" didn't file the complaint exactly at the moment that I learned of Kanne's case fixing, that the complaint should be dismissed. Sykes and the so called Judicial Council of the Seventh Circuit took a play right out of Easterbrook's playbook by writing in its ridiculous order that "the complainant says he learned of the alleged events in 2018, but he waited three years to file this complaint and he did not identify anything that would have precluded him from filing it immediately after he learned of the alleged misconduct." Sykes and her minions on the so called Judicial Council of the Seventh Circuit either cannot read very well, or need to brush up on how Easterbrook has mastered the art of persistently presenting "wildly inaccurate, made-up statements as unquestionable statements of fact," because I did indeed identify my reasons for not "immediately" filing the complaint. As you can see, my reasons were explicitly stated at pages 5-10 of the judicial misconduct complaint, which constitutes six pages of the complaint, and yet the delusional Sykes and the so called Judicial Council of the Seventh Circuit had the audacity to state that I didn't identify my reasons for not filing the complaint "immediately." This further demonstrates just how corruptly this circuit operates as the "Easterbook Syndrome" is apparently rubbing off on this circuit as the Seventh Circuit quite obviously has no problem in doing exactly what has been reported about Frank Easterbrook, it apparently likewise is adopting Easterbrook's modus operandi of presenting "wildly inaccurate, made-up statements as unquestionable statements of fact."

In the obvious whitewashing of the complaint, Sykes and the so called Judicial Council of the Seventh Circuit stated that "[i]f the passage of time has made an accurate and fair investigation of the complaint impractical, the complaint must be dismissed" and adding for good taste in its whitewash "when a complaint is filed so long after an alleged event that memory loss, death, or changes to unknown residences prevent a proper investigation" even though there is no statute of limitations barring the filing of a judicial misconduct complaint. The problem with Sykes' and her Judicial Council compadres' position is that there is no evidence whatsoever of any of these factors. Where in the record is there evidence of "memory loss"? NOWHERE! Where in the record is there evidence of "death"? NOWHERE! Where in the record is there evidence of "changes to unknown residences" that would "prevent a proper investigation"? NOWHERE!

Judge Kanne is still a member of the Seventh Circuit, so there should be no problem with his "memory" as he would have to have a functioning memory to be able to function as a judge. And since Kanne is still a member of the Seventh Circuit, he obviously isn't dead, so that certainly isn't a factor. And since Kanne is still a member of the Seventh Circuit, there shouldn't be any problem in locating him for an interview as to the allegations against him.

And although Judge Posner is no longer a member of the Court, he still lives in Chicago and, thus, could very easily be interviewed with regard to the allegations. Interviewing Judges Kanne and Posner would seem to be a very easy and practical way for the Judicial Council to investigate the allegations in the Complaint. In asserting that any investigation would be "impractical" due to the passage of time, while the key players are available to be interviewed clearly shows that the Seventh Circuit's interest is not in getting to the bottom of what happened with Kanne's fixing of the decision, but rather shows the Seventh Circuit's interest in sweeping Kanne's corrupt activities under the rug.

It should not go unnoticed that Sykes and the Judicial Council did not give any reasons explaining why they did not interview Judges Kanne and Posner or why conducting such interviews would not be an acceptable way to investigate the allegations in the Complaint against Kanne. Clearly, interviewing the two judges involved in the Complaint *would* be a proper and practical way to investigate the allegations in the Complaint.

Why would interviewing Judge Kanne be "impractical" regarding the allegations in the Complaint since Judge Kanne is still a member of the Court? And in the face of the Seventh Circuit's decision to not interview Kanne, it is utter hogwash for the Seventh Circuit to say that a "proper investigation" is "impossible." Kanne could very easily be interviewed with regard to the allegations, and the fact that Sykes and her Judicial Council minions chose not to do so speaks volumes about what is happening in this very serious matter, which is an official judicial cover up of criminal activity of a federal judge of the circuit, namely Michael S. Kanne.

The bottom line is that there was no investigation of the complaint against Judge Kanne, and that is totally unacceptable. Instead, Sykes and her Judicial Council compadres ran with their tail between their legs and conjured up very false and very irresponsible reasons as a way to cover up the corrupt activities of their brethren (corrupt) judge Michael S. Kanne. So rather than interviewing Kanne, who was readily available to them, and rather than taking a statement from Kanne, on the record, Sykes and her Judicial Council compadres insulated him from lying and simply came up with nonsensical outmoded boilerplate reasons to cover and sweep under the rug Kanne's criminal conduct of case fixing a civil rights decision. And that is exactly what happened. This is a classic case of judicial corruption of the highest degree and lends credence to the saying *"The greater the power, the more dangerous the abuse."* - Edmund Burke.

I would suspect that you are aware of a very enlightening article that just recently came out by *Gallup* reporting that the peoples' approval of the United States Supreme Court is down to 40 percent, a new low. See *Approval of U.S. Supreme Court Down to 40%, a New Low (gallup.com)*. Based on the Seventh Circuit's apparent acceptance of case fixing of a civil rights decision by Judge Michael S. Kanne, and the 7th Circuit's slipshod handling of judicial misconduct complaints addressing such judicial corruptions, it is no wonder that the public has such a low approval rating of the federal judiciary.

I would suspect that you are aware of another enlightening article that just recently came out by CNN reporting that Justice Samuel Alito publicly stating that the Supreme Court is not a 'dangerous cabal.' See *Justice Samuel Alito says Supreme Court is not a 'dangerous cabal' - CNNPolitics*. In the article Alito said his goal of his lecture at the University of Notre Dame was to "dispel some imaginary shadows" and push back on a notion that he blamed on the media that the court was acting in a way, he said, that was "sneaky or dangerous." Alito said the recent criticism was geared to suggest "that a dangerous cabal is deciding important issues in a novel, secretive, improper way, hidden from public view." This is precisely what is going on in the Seventh Circuit with respect to Judge Michael S. Kanne's judicial corruption which is being protected by Chief Judge Diane Sykes and her Judicial Council compadres. By what the Seventh Circuit is doing to protect Kanne's criminal activities of case fixing, the Seventh Circuit is indeed a 'dangerous cabal' without question.

As Chief Justice of the United States you have an obligation to ensure that the federal judges across the country are conducting themselves on the up and up and not engaging in criminal conduct such as *ex parte* case fixing of civil rights decisions such as what Judge Michael S. Kanne clearly did as has been disclosed by the highly regarded judge, Richard A. Posner, a retired member of the Seventh Circuit and a member of the panel that Kanne corrupted in *ex parte* fashion, something that Kanne has not denied, as Sykes and her Judicial Council compadres protected him by choosing to not interview and take a statement from him on the record in order that Kanne be insulated for his corruption.

As Chief Justice of the United States you have an obligation to ensure that the investigatory process of judicial misconduct complaints are handled on the up and up with the highest degree of integrity, and not with the lowest level of integrity such as how Diane Sykes and her Judicial Council compadres of the Seventh Circuit go about their business of sweeping issues of judicial corruption under the rug and protecting criminal conduct of judges such as they are currently doing with Michael S. Kanne, a criminal judge of the highest degree who is guilty of fixing a civil rights decision that he himself hasn't denied on the record, nor does the record indicate that he was ever asked about his corrupt case fixing activities during the sham process by Diane Sykes and her Judicial Council compadres. This begs an answer to the question regarding the public statements from your *2019 Year-End Report on the Federal Judiciary* when you stated "I ask my judicial colleagues to continue their efforts to promote public confidence in the judiciary, both through their rulings and through civic outreach" and "We should reflect on our duty to judge without fear or favor, deciding each matter with humility, integrity, and dispatch." The questions now being, a) do you believe that a corrupt judge such as Michael S. Kanne who fixed a civil rights decision according to Judge Richard A. Posner's disclosure should remain on the federal judiciary?, b) and does such corruption promote public confidence in the judiciary?, c) and do you believe that an investigation such as what took place by Diane Sykes and her Judicial Council compadres of the Seventh Circuit in choosing to not interview the two judges, Judge Posner who disclosed Kanne's *ex parte* case fixing, and Judge Kanne whose case fixing has been disclosed by another federal judge who was on the panel promote confidence in the judiciary?, and, d) does such protectionism by a sham investigatory process during a judicial misconduct complaint process promote public confidence in the judiciary?

The actions of Chief Judge Diane Sykes and her compadres on the so called Judicial Council were essentially corrupt for they chose to not even ask Judge Kanne, who is still a sitting member of the court, if the allegations as stated in the judicial misconduct complaint were true or not, nor did

Chief Judge Diane Sykes and her compadres on the so called Judicial Council bother to ask Judge Posner, who lives in Chicago, if the allegations against Kanne as stated in the judicial misconduct complaint were true or not. Such deliberate indifference to the truth clearly renders the investigation by Sykes and her Judicial Council minions a complete sham. The question to you, Mr. Chief Justice, is, are you willing to accept such disgraceful conduct from a court that you oversee?

Mr. Chief Justice, as Chief Justice of the United States you are responsible for the goings on in the federal judiciary, and as I am sure you have heard the well known expression by President Harry Truman when he took responsibility for the goings on in government, "The Buck Stops Here." Mr. Chief Justice, do you agree, or disagree, that the goings on within the federal judiciary including the chicaneries that are taking place in the U.S. Court of Appeals for the Seventh Circuit in Chicago are your responsibility to correct and that the buck stops on your desk? When it comes to case fixing by federal judges such as has been done by Judge Michael S. Kanne at the Seventh Circuit in Chicago as disclosed by Judge Richard A. Posner, which has not been denied by Kanne, and the current sweeping of Kanne's criminal conduct under the rug by Chief Judge Diane Sykes and her Judicial Council minions, do you simply close your eyes and look the other way, or does the "buck" stop on your desk as Chief Justice of the United States? As Martin Luther King, Jr. once famously said *"The time is always right to do what is right."* The remaining question Mr. Chief Justice is, will you choose to do what is right here?

Respectfully submitted,
Brian Vukadinovich
Enclosure
cc: News Media

Not surprisingly, Roberts did nothing, but then again, Roberts is a chief justice who doesn't even believe in a code of ethics for the Supreme Court, so it stands to reason he doesn't have much interest in the lack of ethics of the judges in the lower courts. Roberts' ethical concerns are so lacking that he has consistently defended the Supreme Court's refusal to adopt a proposed bill which would have given protection to judicial employees subjected to sexual harassment by judges, or any other code for that matter, making it the only court in the United States without a formal set of ethics rules. Roberts says that "every justice seeks to follow high ethical standards" and therefore a code of ethics for the Supreme Court is unnecessary. Yeah, right! https://www.nbcnews.com/think/opinion/supreme-court-chief-justice-john-roberts-gives-incomplete-history-lesson-ncna1286943.

I found it interesting that The United States Courts, on September 23, 2022, cavalierly tweeted "The Judicial Conference of the United States has provided a century of service to the judiciary and to the public by setting policy and overseeing administrative needs." Along with this sound good tweet, it posted a self-serving article boasting how great a judicial agency it is and purported that "one of the greatest values of the Conference is that it brings judges together from across the country, with a shared goal of improving the delivery of justice," that "The independence of our courts is a hallmark of the federal judiciary," and that "The work of the Conference and its committees unify us in the administration of justice..." The Judicial Conference: A Century of Service to the Federal Judiciary | United States Courts (uscourts.gov). My, my, the kumbaya is enough to bring tears to one's eyes.

I found especially interesting the statement in the sound good article where it purported that "one of the greatest values" of the Judicial Conference of the United States was its "shared goal of improving the delivery of justice." I found this particular statement to be especially interesting because the Administrative Office of the United States Courts refuses to acknowledge the petition that I sent to the Judicial Conference of the United States where I addressed the case fixing and cover up going on at the U.S. Court of Appeals in Chicago. It is hard to understand how this nefarious governmental body could state with a straight face that it has a "goal" of "improving the delivery of justice," when in fact it has refused to deliver even a scintilla of justice as to the case fixing of my appellate decision that happened at the U.S. Court of Appeals in Chicago which this governmental body is trying to whitewash. The Administrative Office of the United States Courts is a prime example of what is wrong with the judiciary, and Roslynn R. Mauskopf, the director who runs this worthless agency, is a prime example of why we should be removing such unnecessary and dangerous miscreants from the judicial sector. The garbage that John Roberts and Roslynn Mauskopf spew under the letterhead of the U.S. Courts, with Roberts stating, "The judiciary's power to manage its internal affairs insulates courts from inappropriate political influence and is crucial to preserving public trust in its work as a separate and co-equal branch of government" and Mauskopf's bragging that "one of the greatest values of the Conference is .... improving the delivery of justice" are as laughable as can be. I found this statement to be quite interesting since Mauskopf doesn't want to address the petition that I filed with the Judicial Conference of the United States regarding the case fixing and cover up going on at the U.S. Court of Appeals in Chicago. The statements by John Roberts and Roslynn Mauskopf couldn't be more farcical. Retired Judge Richard A. Posner, the very judge who disclosed the case fixing of Judge Michael S. Kanne that John Roberts and Roslynn Mauskopf are working overtime to try to sweep under the rug in order to conceal from the public just how serious a problem there is with case fixing and cover up at the U.S. Court of Appeals in Chicago, let the cat out of the bag when he publicly stated that America has a "very bad" judicial system and that "we have a very crappy judicial system...that contaminates much of government." https://promarket.org/2017/03/28/richard-posner-real-corruption-ownership-congress-rich/.

Roberts and Mauskopf like to talk the talk, but neither likes to walk the walk when push comes to shove and they are taken to task. If Roberts and Mauskopf and the United States Courts, along with the Judicial Conference of the United States, want the public to believe that "improving the delivery of justice" is actually a "goal," as was purported in their recent publication, then they should have no problem in answering some very important questions.

Question number 1: Why is John Roberts afraid to respond to the letter I sent him on October 4, 2021, where I informed him of the case fixing and cover up going on at the U.S. Court of Appeals in Chicago that was disclosed by former judge Richard A. Posner when he came clean and disclosed that Judge Michael S. Kanne had a decision fixed from the appeal of a civil rights case I had against the Valparaiso Police Department from Indiana?

Question number 2: Why is John Roberts afraid to confront the U.S. Court of Appeals for the Seventh Circuit in Chicago for its refusal to follow Rule 26 of the Rules for Judicial-Conduct and Judicial-Disability Proceedings in refusing to request that the Chief Justice of the United States transfer my judicial misconduct complaint proceeding to the judicial council of another circuit rather than keeping the matter in house which was obviously done in order that it could sweep the information under the rug, even though the miscreant judge, Kanne, did not deny on the record that he had the appellate decision fixed—just as Judge Posner disclosed?

Question number 3: Since John Roberts as Chief Justice of the United States is the nation's highest ranking judicial official and speaks for the judicial branch of the federal government, serves as the chief administrative officer for the federal courts, heads the Judicial Conference of the United States, and appointed Roslynn Mauskopf as the Director of the Administrative Office of the United States Courts, Roberts should state on the record if he believes that the fact that the Administrative Office of the United States Courts, led by Roslynn Mauskopf, refuses to inform me of the status of my petition for review of the Seventh Circuit's dismissal of my judicial misconduct complaint against Kanne should be considered a "delivery of justice" and if the conduct of sweeping the petition under the rug should be considered a "delivery of justice" such as what the United States Courts bragged about in the article it tweeted out on September 23, 2022.

Question number 4: John Roberts should explain why he thinks it is okay and not an injustice for the Judicial Conference of the United States to sweep under the rug my petition for review of the Seventh Circuit's dismissal of my judicial misconduct complaint against Judge Michael S. Kanne for his case-fixing activities as was disclosed by Judge Richard A. Posner.

Question number 5: Roslynn Mauskopf should explain why her office, the Administrative Office of the United States Courts, refuses to inform me of the status of my petition for review of the Seventh Circuit's dismissal of my judicial misconduct complaint against Kanne, and if the conduct of sweeping the petition under the rug should be considered a "delivery of justice" such as what the United States Courts bragged about in its propaganda release.

Question number 6: John Roberts and Roslynn Mauskopf should each explain why they have not referred Chief Judge Diane S. Sykes of the U.S. Court of Appeals for the Seventh Circuit in Chicago, and her cohorts, to law enforcement authorities for their criminal activities of concealing Judge Michael S. Kanne's case-fixing conduct and for the cover-up activities by Sykes and her cohorts who were complicit in the cover-up which constituted criminal violations under 18 U.S. Code Sec. 2, 18 U.S. Code Sec. 3 and 18 U.S. Code Sec. 4.

The jig is up, and Roberts and Mauskopf are exposed. We don't need any further propaganda being spewed by either of them through the propaganda machine of the United States Courts. If Roberts and Mauskopf are afraid to answer the above questions, then they should do the public a big favor and stop putting out propaganda that has zero integrity and start doing some things that actually does deliver "justice," and they can start by explaining why they are so afraid of my petition to the Judicial Conference of the

United States where I addressed the case fixing and cover up going on at the U.S. Court of Appeals in Chicago. Are they nervous about it because I have exposed the judicial corruption of that court while they have been sitting back and looking the other way? The answer to the question is YES!

The fact that John Roberts and Roslynn Mauskopf are covering for the case fixing and cover up that is going on in the U.S. Court of Appeals for the Seventh Circuit in Chicago by trying to sweep it under the rug in order to keep the information about the judicial corruption away from the public speaks volumes. It is so sad that as a country we have to endure such a corrupt judiciary even at the highest levels, and Roberts' and Mauskopf's complicity in covering for the case fixing and cover up at the U.S. Court of Appeals in Chicago underscores just how serious a problem we have in this country with judicial corruption. Having corrupt judges in the federal judiciary who fix cases and having chief judges who cover up the case fixing with their brethren confederate judges, along with the Chief Justice of the United States and director of the Administrative Office of the United States Courts who play ball in acquiescing and accommodating the cover up of the case fixing and cover-up activities by complicity, such as what John Roberts and Roslynn Mauskopf are doing, are hardly acts of "administration of justice." Without question, the federal judiciary is a cabal of judicial miscreants. We as a country should be very concerned.

CHAPTER 8

THE STENCH ON THE 27TH FLOOR OF THE DIRKSEN FEDERAL BUILDING IN CHICAGO
CRIMINALS DISGUISED IN BLACK ROBES

"It is better to protest than to accept injustice."
~ Rosa Parks

The conduct of Judge Diane S. Sykes and her undisclosed judicial cohorts who participated in the infected so-called "Memorandum and Order" dismissing the complaint against Michael S. Kanne without either seeking a written response from him, interviewing him, or interviewing Judge Richard A. Posner who disclosed Kanne's case fixing misconduct, constituted clear evidence of a cover up by the Seventh Circuit of Kanne's criminal activities of having the decision fixed, as was disclosed by Judge Posner. It is noteworthy that Kanne didn't deny the allegations of his case-fixing activities that were clearly stated in the judicial misconduct complaint against him. The fact that Sykes and her undisclosed confederates didn't explain why they didn't take action on my request for the Judicial Council of the Seventh Circuit to request that the Chief Justice of the United States transfer the proceeding to the judicial council of another circuit, pursuant to Rule 26, and chose, instead, to keep the matter in-house where the corrupt actors could sweep it under the rug, speaks volumes as to the Seventh Circuit's corruption. To say that corruption is rife in the U.S. Court of Appeals for the Seventh Circuit in Chicago would be an understatement.

As a country, we have to face the fact that there is basically a Mafia type judiciary—the characteristics of it are uncanny. The American judiciary's covert type of operation, in secret society form, and the hierarchy's obvious modus operandi code of silence in its protectionism of its criminal judges in black robes, squarely places the American judiciary in "Mafia" category. Rather than referring to the American courts as a "judiciary," we would be better suited to call it "La Cosa Nostra" which means "our thing" or "this thing of ours" since the American judiciary enjoys such self-governance status with basically no oversight, which are similar characteristics of a mafia organization. In Mafia language, "Omerta" is a code of silence and a code of honor and conduct that places importance on silence in the face of questioning by authorities or outsiders; non-cooperation with authorities, the government, or outsiders.

The American versions of "Omerta" and "La Cosa Nostra" are on classic display with the actions of the Administrative Office of the United States Court's silence as to its reasons why it protected the case-fixing activities of Judge Michael S. Kanne and the cover up by the miscreants on the Seventh Circuit. And the American versions of "Omerta" and "La Cosa Nostra" were showcased by the corrupt actors, Chief Judge Diane Sykes and her cohorts at the U.S. Court of Appeals in Chicago, by their silence as to why they chose not to obtain an on-the-record statement from Kanne regarding Judge Posner's revelations about Kanne's case-fixing activities. It stands to reason that by not seeking a statement from Kanne—on the record—as to his alleged case-fixing activities, they spared him from a potential perjury crime if Kanne would have lied and denied his case-fixing activities that were disclosed by Judge Posner. All of these activities constituted criminal conduct, and it is more than evident that the United States Court system bent over backward to protect these criminal judges, and it is more than evident that if criminal charges would have been filed against these miscreant judges—as they should have been—these criminal judges would have been convicted. It was classic "La Cosa Nostra" American judicial style.

The chicanery exhibited by the Seventh Circuit and the stench of its corruption was very strong. Transfer to another judicial council of another circuit was certainly called for since several undisclosed judges from the Seventh Circuit were involved in the criminal activity of protecting Michael S. Kanne from his criminal conduct of having an appellate decision fixed—criminal conduct to which Michael S. Kanne has not denied on the record in the proceeding. The Seventh Circuit's conduct of refusing to transfer the proceeding to another judicial circuit speaks volumes and underscores the fact that it reeks of corruption. To say that the United States Court of Appeals for the Seventh Circuit in Chicago is a diabolically corrupt court would be putting it mildly.

If we had a Department of Justice that actually believed in "justice," there would be several black-robed criminals from the Seventh Circuit who would be in residence in federal penitentiaries. The law is such that when a judge acts as a trespasser of the law, when a judge does not follow the law, the judge *loses subject matter jurisdiction and the judge's orders are void, of no legal force or effect.* The U.S. Supreme Court, in *Scheurer v. Rhodes*, 416 U.S. 232, 94 S.Ct. 1683, 1687 (1974) stated that "when a state officer acts under a state law in a manner violative of the Federal Constitution," he "comes into conflict with the superior authority of that Constitution, and he is in that case stripped of his official or representative character and is subjected in his person to the consequences of his individual conduct. The State has no power to impart to him any immunity from responsibility to the supreme authority of the United States." By law, a judge is a state officer. The judge then acts not as a judge but as a private individual (in his person). The U.S. Supreme Court has made clear that "No state legislator or executive or judicial officer can war against the Constitution without violating his undertaking to support it." *Cooper v. Aaron*, 358 U.S. 1, 78 S.Ct. 1401 (1958). Any judge who does not comply with his oath to the Constitution of the United States wars against that Constitution and engages in acts in violation of the Supreme Law of the Land. The judge is engaged in an act of acts of treason. *S. v. Will*, 449 U.S. 200, 216, 101 S.Ct. 471, 66 L.Ed.2d 392, 406 (1980); *Cohens v. Virginia*, 19 U.S. (6 Wheat) 264, 404, 5 L.Ed. 257 (1821). This makes Sykes and her judicial confederates treasonous judges according to the Supreme Court's precedents.

Under federal law, which by the way is applicable to all states, the U.S. Supreme Court has made clear that if a court is "without authority, its judgments and orders are regarded as nullities. They are not voidable, but simply void; and form no bar to a recovery sought, even prior to a reversal in opposition to them. They constitute no justification; and all persons concerned in executing such judgments or sentences, are considered, in law, as trespassers." The Seventh Circuit's infected actions in keeping Kanne's criminal activities in house in the diseased Seventh Circuit in order to protect Kanne from appropriate punishment for his violation of the laws of the United States renders Diane S. Sykes and her unidentified judicial cohorts as "trespassers" under the law. *Elliot v. Piersol*, 1 Pet. 328, 340, 26 U.S. 328, 340 (1828).]

When judges act when they do not have jurisdiction to act, or they enforce a void order (an order issued by a judge without jurisdiction), they become trespassers of the law and are engaged in treason. The Court in *Yates v. Village of Hoffman Estates, Illinois*, 209 F.Supp. 757 (N.D. Ill. 1962) held that "not every action by a judge is in exercise of his judicial function. ...it is not a judicial function for a judge to commit an intentional tort even though the tort occurs in the courthouse."

The Seventh Circuit, in *U.S. v. Murphy*, 768 F.2d 1518, 1531 (7th Cir. 1985), held that the Circuit Court of Cook County was a criminal enterprise by virtue of the judges' failure to report the criminal activities of other judges, and thus the protective judges consequently became principals in the criminal activity. This Seventh Circuit decision determined that since judges who do not report the criminal activities of other judges become principals in the criminal activity and determined that since no judges reported the criminal activity of the convicted judges, the other judges are as guilty as the convicted judges under 18 U.S.C. Section 1. This is precisely the situation with the United Court of Appeals for the Seventh Circuit where the chief judge, Diane S. Sykes, failed to report the criminal activities of Michael S. Kanne's case fixing of the appellate decision done to protect the infected rulings of the trial court judge, James T. Moody, who protected the unlawful actions of the Valparaiso police at the civil rights trial—as Judge Richard A. Posner disclosed. It is clear that Sykes and her confederates at the Seventh Circuit were complicit in protecting and covering up the case-fixing activities of their brethren judge Michael S. Kanne as was disclosed by a former member of their very court, Judge Richard A. Posner. This renders the United States Court of Appeals for the Seventh Circuit as a criminal enterprise pursuant to the standards that the Seventh Circuit itself set in *U.S. v. Murphy*, 768 F.2d 1518, 1531 (7th Cir. 1985) when it held that the Circuit Court of Cook County was a criminal enterprise by virtue of the judges' failure to report the criminal activities of other judges, just as Chief Judge Diane S. Sykes and her undisclosed cohorts have likewise failed to report the criminal activities of Michael S. Kanne and were, in fact, involved in a cover-up of Michael S. Kanne's criminal activities. This is precisely what Sykes and her compadres did in choosing not to ask the Chief Justice of the United States to transfer the proceeding to the judicial council of another circuit pursuant to Rule 26 and instead chose to keep Kanne's criminal activities in-house where the Seventh Circuit could protect Kanne from the appropriate punishment. that he should have been subjected to for his criminal activities of having a decision fixed in violation of the United States laws—as disclosed by Judge Posner—which was not denied on the record by Kanne. The criminal activities of these judges has mafia written all over it as this is precisely how mafia organizations operate in committing crimes and then covering for one another. The judges on the Seventh Circuit who were involved in the illicit activities of the case fixing of the decision and their cover up of it may as well have been wearing pinstriped suits and fedora hats instead of the black robes they used to conceal their criminal activities.

It was utterly ridiculous for Sykes and her judicial compadres to imply that interviewing Michael S. Kanne was somehow "impractical" regarding the allegations in the complaint since Kanne was still a member of the Court when the judicial misconduct complaint was filed and when the infected orders were written protecting him. That defies all logic. How in the world could it be stated that it was somehow "impractical" to interview a judge who is the subject of a complaint when the subject judge is right there? That is ludicrous. And in the face of Sykes' and her unidentified judicial cohorts' decision to not interview Kanne or require him to submit a written response to the complaint, it is utter hogwash for Sykes and her unidentified confederates to have said that a "proper investigation" was "impossible" since Kanne could have very easily been interviewed with regard to the allegations as he was right there alongside them in his office on the 27th floor of the Dirksen Building in Chicago. The fact that Sykes and her unidentified judicial cohorts chose not to interview Kanne or require him to submit a written response to the complaint demonstrates evidence of the diseased nature of the Seventh Circuit's inherent inclination to cover up for judicial corruption as it clearly did in unlawfully protecting the criminal conduct of Michael S. Kanne. These were judicial criminals of the highest degree.

Sykes' conduct of submitting false statements in her memorandum and order dismissing the judicial misconduct complaint against Kanne demonstrates her willingness to falsify information on an official order of judicial business to which falsification of information was done to conceal and protect the criminal activities of

Judge Michael S. Kanne, along with the other matters of impropriety by Diane S. Sykes and her unidentified judicial cohorts in the sham proceeding, renders Diane S. Sykes and her unidentified judicial cohorts criminals under the laws of the United States as an accessory after the fact under 18 U.S. Code Sec. 3. And by Diane S. Sykes' and her judicial cohorts' knowledge of Michael S. Kanne's criminal activities in having a decision fixed, which Kanne has not denied on the record, and by Diane S. Sykes' and her unidentified judicial cohorts' concealment of Kanne's criminal activities by not making Kanne's felonious conduct known to some judge or other person in civil authority renders Diane S. Sykes and her unidentified judicial confederates who were complicit in the cover-up criminals under 18 U.S. Code Sec. 4. Sykes' failure to report the criminal case-fixing activities of Judge Michael S. Kanne as disclosed by Judge Posner and the associated aggregated actions of protectionism of the case-fixing activities in her court as disclosed by Judge Posner constitute criminal violations under 18 U.S. Code Sec. 2, 18 U.S. Code Sec. 3 and 18 U.S. Code Sec. 4. Indeed the blood of judicial corruption flowed freely through their veins. They belong in prison.

Courts violate laws under the RICO Act on a daily basis just as the Seventh Circuit did in my case with Judge Michael S. Kanne having the decision fixed and then Chief Judge Diane S. Sykes putting into operation the cover-up mechanisms to protect Kanne which was clearly an act of "obstruction of justice." Racketeering activity under 18 U.S.C.A. Section 1503 of the RICO Act relates to "obstruction of justice" and is considered an unlawful act of racketeering, but yet obstruction of justice happens on a daily basis in the courts every time a judge gives preferential treatment to a side in the case that the judge likes more so than the other side, which is exactly what happened in my case with Kanne's fixing of the decision and Sykes' cover up of it. Section 1503 contains an Omnibus Clause which states that a person who "corruptly" takes it upon himself or herself and influences, obstructs, or impedes, or endeavors to influence, obstruct, or impede, the due administration of justice" is guilty of the crime of obstruction of justice. Two types of cases arise under the Omnibus Clause: the concealment, alteration, or destruction of documents, and the encouraging or rendering of false testimony. Actual obstruction is not needed as an element of proof to sustain a conviction. The person's endeavor to obstruct justice is sufficient. What Kanne and Sykes and her confederates at the Seventh Circuit did falls squarely within the definition of obstruction of justice. Every time a judge looks the other way and bends or ignores a rule in a court case in order to benefit a certain side of the case, the judge participates in racketeering activity in violation of the RICO Act. Every time a lawyer encourages a witness or a client to give false testimony, the lawyer is guilty of obstruction of justice under the Racketeering Act. But because the judiciary and legal professions are such a close knit and protective society when it comes to lawyers and judges, such racketeering activities are sadly allowed, even though such violations are done at the expense of people who are entitled to fairness and justice in their cases but don't receive it because of allowed judicial improprieties that are taking place on a daily basis in the state and federal courts in the country, and as I have shown, certainly happened at the Seventh Circuit as disclosed by Judge Richard A. Posner, but swept under the rug by Chief Judge Diane S. Sykes and her cohorts at the Seventh Circuit. The U.S. Court of Appeals for the Seventh Circuit in Chicago is essentially the epicenter of injustice.

Unfortunately, the United States Department of Justice has no appetite to investigate criminal activities on the part of federal judges, for if it did, the U.S. Court of Appeals for the Seventh Circuit in Chicago would be one of its top customers. Unfortunately, we have an asleep-at-the-wheel attorney general in Merrick Garland who has a demonstrated propensity to protect judicial corruption, not only as attorney general, but also when he himself was a judge and looked the other way. [Merrick Garland Was Accused of Protecting a Judge Charged With Ethics Violations – Mother Jones]. That's not to say that his predecessors, Jeff Sessions and William

Barr and others before them, were any better—they weren't. Because of the lack of credibility in the Department of Justice, federal judges know they can get away with corruption such as the those taking place in the Seventh Circuit. Until such time that we have an attorney general who will have no problem with handcuffing and prosecuting the criminals wearing the black robes at the U.S. Court of Appeals in Chicago, the stench will continue on in the 27th floor of the Dirksen Federal Building on 219 S. Dearborn Street in Chicago.

The problem is that while the federal laws look great when you see them published, those laws are basically worthless unless you have law enforcement agencies that are willing to investigate and prosecute criminal judges in black robes who violate them; and in America, unfortunately, politics takes precedence over "right and wrong." For the most part, law enforcement officials aren't very interested in putting the black-robed criminal judges in prison where they belong. Those federal laws are basically window dressing when it comes to the criminals wearing the black robes. Law enforcement agencies in America are perfectly fine with judges putting regular people who violate the law in prison, and that is how it should be; but law enforcement agencies in America are not on board with putting corrupt judges who violate the law in prison, and that is not how it should be. That is the sad reality of it. Laws when not equally applied when it comes to influential persons—law-breaking judges—are useless. And let's be clear here, the laws are not at all equally applied when it comes to arresting and prosecuting corrupt judges—the case fixing and protectionism afforded to the criminal judges at the Seventh Circuit is Exhibit A. Had the United States Department of Justice had the integrity to enforce U.S. Codes, 18 U.S. Code Sec. 2(a)(b), 18 U.S. Code Sec. 3, and 18 U.S. Code Sec. 4 against Kanne and Sykes and her compadres on the Seventh Circuit, surely those judges would have been convicted and imprisoned for violating the laws of the United States; but the United States Department of Justice has no integrity when it comes to prosecuting corruption by federal judges in the United States—this shows just how much of a fallacy the old saying "nobody is above the law" really is. The U.S. Court of Appeals in Chicago is a cesspool of judicial poison. If dogs were trained to sniff out corrupt judges on the 27th floor of the Dirksen Building at the U.S. Court of Appeals in Chicago, they would have a field day.

CHAPTER 9
GOVERNMENT OFFICIALS ROUTINELY PROTECT CORRUPT ACTIVITIES BY GOVERNMENT PLAYERS
THE FLYING MONKEYS ARE MANY

"The greater the power, the more dangerous the abuse."
~Edmund Burke

In all honesty, I wasn't surprised when Indiana Senator Todd Young chose to play hide and seek when I asked him to request to the Senate Judiciary Committee that it hold public hearings on the case fixing and cover up going on at the U.S. Court of Appeals in Chicago which I addressed in my petition to the Judicial Conference of the United States. While I was hoping that perhaps he would actually do the right thing and make the request, which would have brought the judicial corruption to light, it was basically wishful thinking. There is something in the water that just won't allow elected officials to go out on a limb and actually do some good when they are called upon to assist with exposing governmental corruption. I knew it was a long shot for Senator Young to do the right thing and make the request, but I thought it was worth a try. I knew from personal experience how government officials steer clear of exposing governmental corruption and even get involved in whitewashing investigations when it comes to people of governmental power and influence.

The corruption that the U.S. Court of Appeals in Chicago was involved in with fixing the decision as to my appeal against the Valparaiso police years ago was an extension of what the feds did to protect the unlawful activities of that police department back in the day which led to the filing of the civil rights action from which Judge James Moody of the U.S. District Court for the Northern District of Indiana helped the Valparaiso police along. And then, to seal the deal, the judicial teamwork of corruption reared its ugly head when Judge Michael S. Kanne of the U.S. Court of Appeals in Chicago took care of things by having the appellate decision fixed. I am sure that the federal judiciary and Department of Justice thought everything was smooth sailing for all those years and that they were safe from their illicit and unlawful activities, but what they didn't count on was that at some point, one of their very own, Judge Richard A. Posner, would see the light and decide to come clean and expose what happened. This created a big problem for all of those governmental miscreants, and they had to circle the wagons and do what they do best, use their secret methods in protecting one another—and indeed they did just that. Unfortunately for the judicial hierarchy, what Kanne did in the dark has now come to light.

When "Round 1" happened, back in the day when I was fighting the various police harassments against me, I asked my congressman at the time, Jim Jontz, to help me get a review by the Department of Justice of the police activities that were taking place against me. And contrary to how Indiana Senator Todd Young has recently conducted himself when I asked him to request an investigation into the case-fixing and cover-up that is going on at the U.S. Court of Appeals in Chicago, Congressman Jontz had the integrity to actually ask for the federal investigation—Todd Young contrarily would not do so. And not only that, Congressman Jontz even sent me a copy of his request to the Department of Justice—something that Senator Todd Young refused to do. On August 3, 1987, Congressman Jontz wrote to John

Bolton and asked him to review my case. Yes, if you are wondering if this was the same one and only John Bolton who was Trump's national security adviser, you are correct. At the time, Bolton was the assistant attorney general who was directly involved in my case. On October 13, 1987, Bolton wrote to Congressman Jontz and stated that I had been arrested numerous times for traffic violations and stated that I "alleged" that I was beaten several times by police and that I "alleged" that police were arresting me as part of a conspiracy to harass me. Bolton then went on to state: *"We have carefully reviewed the reports of the FBI as well as documents submitted by Mr. Vukadinovich and have concluded that the facts presented do not support a prosecutable violation of federal civil rights laws."* The sad part of Bolton's letter was that he did not mention any evidence whatsoever. But that is how Bolton operated—always in a very shady manner.

It was very interesting that the "careful review"—as Bolton called it—was done without interviewing Jon Cooros, the former Valparaiso police officer who had direct knowledge of the Valparaiso Police Department's conspiracy to have me falsely arrested and vindictively prosecuted. Why wouldn't Bolton want to know what information former Valparaiso police officer Jon Cooros had about the situation? After all, one would think that a high-level official of the Department of Justice during a civil rights investigation would want to know about the information that a police officer had regarding schemes to falsely arrest and brutalize a citizen—but Bolton didn't want this information. Why wouldn't Bolton want this information you might ask? The answer is very simple; the information would have conclusively shown that the Valparaiso police were breaking the law, and Bolton then wouldn't have been able to clear them. This is what happens in our country when it comes to peoples' civil rights; unsavory officials from within the government have things taken care of. It is a big problem in our country. And just as in Bolton's infected decision to not interview Jon Cooros, Bolton's "careful review" also didn't include interviewing Linda Smith, who personally observed the several members of the Valparaiso Police

Department beat me in my yard on November 3, 1986. There were several other independent witnesses that Bolton could have interviewed that would have shown that the Valparaiso police were scheming to get me one way or the other, but Bolton's "careful review" did not involve interviewing any other people except the police who were the subject of the investigation.

The cover up by the FBI with Bolton's approval was a crime in itself. How in the world could John Bolton, with a straight face, conclude that the facts presented do not support a prosecution of federal civil rights laws when I provided a copy of the audio recording proving the false arrest against me on October 15, 1986, in which a Valparaiso police officer was caught on tape stating, "I'm goin' to get the son-of-a-bitch. F--- him"? It was interesting that Bolton's letter stating a so-called "careful review" didn't at all mention this tape recording. Bolton and his minions clearly were involved in a cover up since they refused to interview relevant witnesses who had important information about what had taken place—and they didn't want that information to be included in the so-called "investigation" which was a sham investigation, to put it lightly. What Bolton and his cohorts did in refusing to interview relevant witnesses who had important information was a disgrace. If the Department of Justice would have had any integrity, Bolton and his minions would have been prosecuted for the cover up—but a Department of Justice with integrity we unfortunately do not have.

On February 18, 1988, I wrote a letter to John Bolton regarding his so-called "careful review" of the FBI reports and the supporting documents I provided to the Justice Department. I asked how he could justify in a brief, one-page letter that did not contain any specific details as to evidence or witness statements of any kind his misguided conclusion that the Justice Department could determine that there were no prosecutable violations of civil rights laws from the several false arrests and beatings I took at the hands of the Valparaiso police, of which each and every arrest in the end did not stand. I asked Bolton to meet with me so we could discuss the facts in detail and go through the documented evidence that he chose to ignore during his whitewashing of the civil rights investigation. I received a letter from a Linda Davis, another assistant attorney general, stating, *"We must regrettably inform you that a meeting to discuss this matter would serve no useful purpose."* Bolton wasn't even man enough to write his own letter and depended on a minion to do so. He was a coward's coward to say the least.

Thus, when it was all said and done, John Bolton, on behalf of the United States Department of Justice, essentially tacitly approved of the corrupt activities of rogue police that took place in the effort to have my freedom taken from me. This shows that Bolton not only had a penchant to orchestrate coups against foreign governments that we all saw when he was Trump's national security adviser, but showed also that he liked to orchestrate coups against peoples' rights to be free from governmental oppression in this country, the good ol' USA, the land of the free and the home of the brave—so long as the person determining the freedoms and bravery was John Bolton. When Francis Scott Key wrote the words "the land of the free and the home of the brave" in 1814, he might have taken pause had John Bolton been around in those days. John Bolton is no patriot by any stretch of the imagination—he is a despot with a thirst for abuse of governmental power. The United States of America is worse off for John Bolton having been part of the government. A coward makes not a patriot, and the coward John Bolton is no patriot.

What this shows is that our federal government cannot be trusted to do the right thing to the point that the Department of Justice and the federal judiciary will work hand in hand to ensure that corrupt governmental actors are protected by the very system that is supposed to be protecting the people. Instead, it protects its own miscreants, against the people. The protectionism of the case fixing of my civil rights case at the U.S. Court of Appeals in Chicago in covering up the case fixing activities by the corrupt federal judges harkens back to Bolton's sham investigation of the unlawful police activities against me. The feds and the federal judiciary well know that they have a very serious problem here and that the only way they can survive their corruption from what they did is to circle the wagons and do whatever it takes to keep this information away from the public—and circle the wagons they have done. The graft in what took place here, and continues to take place, in the government's attempt to keep this information away from the public is mind boggling. One thing is for sure, as long as my petition sits in the Administrative Office of the United States Courts in Washington, D.C., it will serve as a constant reminder to the miscreant judges and court officials that they will never be let off the hook and that my eyes are upon them—with laser focus.

Indeed there has been a major effort by the federal judiciary to somehow refuse to follow the law and ignore my petition. The case has been credibly made and the federal judiciary knows it, and that is exactly why the judicial hierarchy is involved in these nefarious efforts to sweep my petition under the rug in order that the public won't know just how serious a problem we have in this country with case fixing and cover up at the federal judicial level. It is unfortunate that Indiana Senator Todd Young chose to acquiesce in the corruption by refusing to request a federal investigation by way of public hearings by the Senate Judiciary Committee where the evidence could be discussed in public view and appropriate measures could be taken. But Young did his part and refused to request a public Senate Judiciary Committee inquisition into the matter. We have many flying monkeys covering for judicial corruption, and Indiana Senator Todd Young's refusal to provide me with a copy of a letter he said he wrote on my behalf certainly raises a significant doubt that he, in fact, sent a letter; and Young's refusal to request to the Senate Judiciary Committee to hold public hearings as to the case fixing and cover up of the appellate decision of my civil rights case against the Valparaiso police renders him as a card-carrying member of the flying monkeys club that protects judicial corruption.

Chief Judge Diane S. Sykes and her compadres are making a big mistake if they think that I will be going away simply because they have such corrupt judicial protections in place. The chair of the Senate Judiciary Committee, Dick Durbin, and his minions on the committee, as well as the House Judiciary Committee minions, are stupid if they think I will be going away anytime soon simply by their cavalier choice of allowing judicial corruption to continue on as "business as usual" as if we, the people, don't know what is going on. They can all rest well assured that we, the people, know very well what is going on. The director of the Administrative Office of the United States Courts, Roslynn Mauskopf, is very stupid if she thinks she is going to be able to continue to hide the fact of my petition in favor of protecting the criminal judges who are violating the laws of the United States. And Senator Todd Young is very stupid if he thinks that by refusing my request to ask the Senate Judiciary Committee to hold public hearings as to the case fixing and cover up at the U.S. Court of Appeals in Chicago and the lack of action from the Judicial Conference of the United States as to my petition, that is required under federal statute 28 U.S. Code Sec. 355(a), is going to subside with the passage of time, that is not going to happen. In fact, the longer that these infected players continue protecting each other's complicit activities in this matter, the worse it will get—that is a given.

We are in trouble as a country when we have a federal judiciary that fixes cases, and we certainly have that in our country—the U.S. Court of Appeals in Chicago is Exhibit A. And we are in even deeper trouble as a country when we have federal judicial officials who protect federal judges who fix cases, and we certainly have that in our country—the U.S. Court of Appeals in Chicago is Exhibit A of that, as well. And we are in yet even deeper trouble in our country when we have United States Senators, such as Indiana Senator Todd Young, and the chair of the Senate Judiciary Committee, Illinois Senator Dick Durbin, and members of the Senate Judiciary Committee who are aware of the judicial corruption but sit back and allow the corruption to flourish while doing nothing about it—and we certainly have that in our country. Just as La Cosa Nostra has people in place to protect its criminal foot soldiers, the United States Judiciary has its foot soldiers in place to protect its criminals wearing the black robes. Omerta is alive and well in the American judiciary, to say the least.

A country with a federal judiciary that permits its federal judges to fix cases and allows brethren judges to cover up the case-fixing activities is akin to a banana republic. A country with a legislative system where United States senators are supposed to protect the Constitution and the interests of their constituents, but instead allows its senators to protect corrupt federal judges by not insisting that the government agency provide a status of a petition that has been filed that addresses corruption in the federal judiciary, is something one might expect to take place in countries such as China or Russia, but not in the United States. A governmental system that permits United States senators to purport to their constituents that letters have been sent to government agencies on their behalf regarding governmental nefariousness issues against the people but then refuses to provide a copy of the purported correspondence to those constituents is a very flawed system that reeks of malfeasance —and that is exactly what we have here. Judicial corruption certainly exists and thrives at a high level, and it is much more rampant than people may think. It is a very old paradigm of a system that has eliminated any sense of fairness to the common person. Back in the day, there was the Ku Klux Klan, a group of societal misfits which needs no introduction here, and now in our system of government we have the flying monkeys which is comprised of misfit judges and governmental enablers who protect the judicial miscreants in their routine lynching of peoples' rights in the peoples' cases against unsavory corporations and government agencies who break the laws. It is kabuki theater with lawyers dressed in costumes of black robes who do a stomp dance on the peoples' rights to justice. It is what it is.

CHAPTER 10

ROUTINE DISMISSALS OF JUDICIAL MISCONDUCT COMPLAINTS

"Our lives begin to end the day we become silent about things that matter."
~ Martin Luther King, Jr.

It has been reported that the federal judiciary is a rogue "secret society" that dismisses 99.82 percent of the complaints filed before it. https://www.truthcontrol.com/forum/dr-corderoitnj-us-federal-judiciary-rogue-secret-society-9982-complaints-dismissed-video.

It is entirely unreasonable for the judiciary to expect people to believe that a 99.82 dismissal rate of judicial misconduct complaints is equitable. In 2015, there were 1,214 complaints filed against federal judges, and not a single one of them resulted in remedial action against the judge. Merrick Garland Was Accused of Protecting a Judge Charged With Ethics Violations – Mother Jones. That is simply mind boggling, ridiculous, and borders on the ludicrous. A record of 0 for 1,214 hardly does much to preserve the public's trust. Not even one single case resulted in remedial action against a judge! That alone pretty much tells us what we need to know about the integrity of Roberts' insistence that the federal judiciary be allowed to manage its own internal affairs and "police itself" so it can maintain its "independence," as he has put it. This is a bright red flag, and people should be up in arms about it. But once people realize just how rigged the procedure is in terms of setting up safeguards to routinely exonerate federal judges from wrongdoing, it is easy to see why the dismissal rate is so unbelievably high. And because the process is so corrupt, it is easy to understand why the judiciary insists that it be a secret type process of perverse magnitude.

The discipline process against federal judges is initiated by the filing of a complaint by any person alleging that a judge has engaged in conduct "prejudicial to the effective and expeditious administration of the business of the courts, or alleging that such judge is unable to discharge all the duties of the office by reason of mental or physical disability." And then here is the kicker: if the chief judge of the circuit does not dismiss the complaint or conclude the proceedings, then he or she must promptly appoint himself or herself, along with equal numbers of circuit judges and district judges, to a "special committee" to investigate the facts and allegations in the complaint. Notice that the so-called "special committee" is comprised solely of judges. There is no independent citizen input, and there is no independent inspector general within the "special committee." Judges overseeing brethren judges is akin to "the fox guarding the henhouse." The so-called "special committee" supposedly must conduct such investigation as it finds "necessary" and then expeditiously file a so-called "comprehensive" report of its investigation with the "judicial council" of the circuit involved. Notice also that the "judicial council" is comprised only of judges and there are no independent citizens and no independent inspectors general within the "judicial council." And then upon receipt of such report, the "judicial council" of the circuit involved may conduct any additional investigation it deems necessary, and it may dismiss the complaint. Needless to say, almost all of the complaints are dismissed—to the tune of 99.82 percent.

A committee led by Supreme Court Justice Stephen Breyer warned us in 2006 about the potential dangers of a system in which judges are judging judges when it concluded that "A system that relies for investigation solely upon judges themselves risks a kind of undue 'guild favoritism' through inappropriate sympathy with the judge's point of view or de-emphasis of the misconduct problem." The Breyer committee found that complaints were not handled properly, and the main problem detected, in high visibility and other complaints, was chief judges' failure to conduct "adequate" inquiries before dismissing a complaint or to submit "clear factual discrepancies" to investigators to pursue. https://www.cnn.com/2018/01/25/politics/courts-judges-sexual-harassment/index.html. It is more than clear that the process is essentially a sham designed to protect inappropriate activities by judges. And we can be sure that as long as the people choose to not exercise their right to protest these inequitable processes taking place in the courts, and judges are allowed to continue to run roughshod in disrespecting the people who are trying to receive justice in the courts, we should just expect the status quo to continue on.

To put in perspective the sham process of how the federal judiciary protects its own, think about how ridiculous it is to have a system where judges judge other judges when complaints are filed against them—in many cases judges who are even personal friends with one another—but in the "real world" there are mechanisms put in place to prevent that very type of protectionism. For example, whenever trials take place, civil or criminal, in the "real world," jurors are selected with a process to keep out those who are biased. There is an intense procedure that takes place in the jury selection process called "voir dire" which is the part of a trial where a prospective jury panel is brought in and questioned by the lawyers—or pro se litigants—in the case. The purpose of the voir dire process is to evaluate whether or not any prospective jurors have any biases in the case as to the issues or to the parties. This is a very important aspect of a trial as this where the parties get an opportunity to try to select a jury that will be fair and give a just verdict based on the evidence without any biases or favoritism to anybody. However, the federal judiciary does the complete opposite when it comes to charges against one of its own—it has in place a process to do exactly the opposite of what it requires in trials against regular people where favoritism and biases are forbidden. It is disingenuous to treat corrupt judges any differently. How is it that in regular court procedures involving the citizenry there is a process to keep out biased jurors in civil or criminal court cases when charges are made against common people of society, but when it comes to charges against judges, they get to have their brethren judge them as to the charges against them? This pretty much tells us all we need to know in terms of how corrupt the judicial system is when it comes to protecting its own. We are in serious trouble when we let the criminals running things make the rules, and make no mistake about it, there are plenty of criminals out there who are wearing black robes—and they are making the rules.

Unless and until such time as the infected process is changed to a more meaningful and fair review process that includes civilian participation, with a process giving civilian panel members the power to make referrals of corrupt judges to a special grand jury, then we can only expect much the same. It will always be business as usual with rogue judges breaking rules and laws and violating peoples' rights to a fair judicial process so long as judges are allowed to keep protecting their brethren judges and able to do so without the public's input in the investigation and review process. But this is how the federal judiciary wants it, and this breeds corruption within the process which results in an infected judiciary. The complaint process of federal judges is a joke. The disciplinary process against state judges is not any better—secrecy and protectionism is the unwritten rule of the day there, as well.

This corrupt process could be cured by doing away with the outmoded "judicial council" which history has taught us is nothing more than a mechanism to protect and cover up illicit judicial activities. This infected process desperately needs to be replaced by a "citizen council" that has no allegiance to covering for brethren judges and a sole allegiance to conducting fair investigations and honest and equitable binding recommendations to judicial authorities for disciplinary actions against judges who conduct themselves in inappropriate ways. They also should have the authority to make criminal referrals to law enforcement authorities against judges who break the laws. History clearly demonstrates that chief judges and so-called "judicial councils" aren't willing to take disciplinary action or turn in judges to law enforcement authorities who act inappropriately or even break laws. For this very reason, the system needs to be changed to a more equitable one that is designed to meet the ends of justice and not designed to circumvent the ends of justice, which is exactly how the current system is designed. We need a "citizens council" to pass judgment on judges accused of improprieties.

In my work as executive director of the Posner Center of Justice for Pro Se's, I ran across many instances of misconduct by federal judges; and when the people file complaints against the judges, they get nowhere as the complaints are routinely dismissed without much of even a cursory review, let alone a meaningful review. This needs to change if we are to have a measure of fairness in our federal judiciary as there will never be so long as we have rogue federal judges who are allowed to violate the governing standards of conduct in abusing peoples' rights to a fair proceeding in the federal court in a system that not only looks the other way, but acquiesces in it by complicity. The shenanigans are many, and make no mistake about it, it is widespread. It mostly happens in cases where individuals are suing corporations or government agencies where judges like to bring the hammer down against the people while favoring the powerful. Time and time again, this has shown itself to be a culture in the federal judiciary, which in effect results in a diseased judiciary. There is no question about it, and it wouldn't take much to expose it **if** the House and Senate Judiciary Committees would be interested in doing so, and therein lies the problem—the House and Senate Judiciary Committees have no appetite to expose judicial corruption. It is a very broken-down system to say the least—and corrupt judges know it and take advantage of it.

Congress needs to take notice of this very serious situation, and there should be public hearings held by the House and Senate Judiciary Committees on this problem and steps put in place to ensure that all wrongdoing federal judges are held accountable and subject to appropriate disciplinary measures for their violations of the governing standards, and that the status quo of summarily dismissing peoples' complaints against the federal judges without a meaningful investigation be done away with. The time for covering up for federal judges who do not adhere to the governing standards should come to a halt. The time has come for the current illegitimate and outmoded system of judges covering for inept and corrupt judges to be cast by the wayside in favor of a system that is fair and non-protective of unfair and corrupt federal judges. I believe that there should be civilian input on committees in every federal judicial district so that civilians, and not solely judges, are investigating and reviewing misconduct complaints against federal judges. This should be an open process and not the "secret" process that is currently the status quo. Congress, particularly the House and Senate Judiciary Committees, should be taking action in this regard, for if no action is taken, then there is no justice.

It is completely unacceptable that the process is conveniently rigged so that brethren judges, many of whom work side by side on a daily basis, and in numerous cases judges who are personal friends with one another, should be the deciders of judicial misconduct complaints as to whether or not an accused judge should be disciplined. That makes no sense whatsoever. Think about it, in a regular court case when there is the possibility of a conflict of interest with the judge, the judge is obligated to recuse him or herself. But in situations when a judicial misconduct complaint is filed against a judge, the recusal standard does not apply. Judges who are professional acquaintances or even personal friends of the accused judge do not have to recuse themselves from the case. How does that make sense? In other words, judges must recuse themselves in conflict of interest situations in regular cases; but in cases involving judicial misconduct complaints, they do not have to recuse themselves, even when they are personal friends with an accused judge, and are then allowed to pass judgment in a judicial misconduct proceeding. That is ludicrous and as perverse as it gets. There should be civilians on review panels examining judicial misconduct complaints with authority to make referral of appropriate judicial misconduct findings to a special grand jury.

Something else that needs to be done away with is the present outmoded system of keeping judicial complaints confidential. All judicial misconduct complaints should be made public. It should be no different than when a police officer charges a regular person. The information is disseminated to the media and made public via local newspapers, radio and television news outlets, and on the internet. Formal complaints against judges who are accused of wrongdoing should also be made public. Insofar as state judges are concerned, by keeping complaints against state court judges a secret, the judiciary does a major disservice to the public as this secrecy protects its corrupt brethren judges from being voted off the bench in state retention elections. The electorate should not be kept in the dark about judges' backgrounds. The people of each state deserve to know about any judicial misconduct complaints that have been submitted against any of their judges so an informed decision can be made as to whether the people want to retain a particular judge or vote that judge out of office. Keeping judges' corrupt activities a "secret" results in the judiciary's ability to retain corrupt judges. It should not be forgotten that all judges are public employees, and their salaries are paid by the taxpayers; therefore, any situations of misconduct charges against them is the peoples' business.

Needless to say, the idea of judicial autonomy for the state and federal courts is a bad thing and needs to be eliminated. The state and federal courts have shown that they aren't capable, or interested, in policing themselves in a fair and just manner. This is the problem when courts enjoy unlimited autonomy; it has proven to be a disaster. The idea of judges reviewing other judges from the same jurisdiction, and in many instances when they are also personal friends, cannot be considered a fair and just process by any stretch of the imagination, especially in the secret manner in which they conduct such reviews where the public is kept completely in the dark. As Edmund Burke once famously said, "The greater the power, the more dangerous the abuse." And nowhere is there more power than in the state and federal judiciaries, and nowhere is there more dangerous abuse of that power than in the state and federal judiciaries.

The questions people should be asking is why are judges treated with such kid gloves when it comes to investigating allegations of corruption on their part, and why are they allowed to cover for each other in secret proceedings? Where is the integrity in such an infected process? There should be independent inspector generals in each state and in each federal judicial district. Complaints of wrongdoing against state and federal judges would be investigated by this inspector general with authority to recommend disciplinary and/or criminal charges upon a determination that a judge has engaged in wrongful and/or unlawful conduct. The present "good ol' boys" system simply doesn't work, and we all know it. Judges should never be involved in reviewing misconduct complaints against their brethren. That is ludicrous. Think about it, courts generally would never allow a personal friend of a defendant in a criminal case to sit on a jury and pass judgment on a personal friend who has been charged with a crime. So how is it okay for those same judges who would disallow such a thing to take place in a trial to be able to pass judgment on their associates, and even personal friends, when a friend of the judge is charged with wrongdoing? That is hypocrisy of the highest degree. It is no wonder that the courts keep such proceedings in secret and away from the public eye—the courts well know that what they are doing is very wrong. Unless and until such time that reforms are enacted and independent inspector generals are put in place, and unless and until such time that the public is involved in the investigation and review processes, there will always be judicial corruption by miscreant judges who know they have a free pass for corruption under the current system. This is the reality of where we are at as a country, and the major reason is that the state and federal judiciaries are infested with unbridled dishonest and corrupt judges. The miscreants on the state and federal judiciaries should be forever disrobed. As a country, we need to stand together and get the job done. Whether we want to admit it or not, many people don't want to face reality and admit that there is a very serious problem with how corrupt our courts are in the United States. Many people who realize it will talk about the problem behind closed doors but are afraid to publicly speak about it for obvious reasons, in fear of retaliation by the judiciary and government agencies. While that is understandable, it is unfortunate that there has to be such a fear factor involved. It shouldn't have to be that way.

CHAPTER II
SECRECY IN THE JUDICIARY

*"When the government fears the people, it is liberty.
When the people fear the government, it is tyranny."*
~ Thomas Paine

Secrecy in the American judiciary is a big problem. The judiciary operates under an arcane set of procedures designed to conceal its nefarious activities from the public. It breeds contempt for honesty and transparency and caters to a secret society type method of operation. All judges, state and federal, are public employees working off of the taxpayers' dime, and the taxpayers are entitled to know what is going on behind those "closed doors" of the courthouses. The very fact that the judges want to keep the public eye off of them speaks volumes. After all, if judges are operating on the up and up, then they should have nothing to worry about; but when they shut the public out of what is going on behind the judicially closed doors, then the public has good reason to be concerned and to demand openness in every respect. According to an article by "The Millennium Report," America is like a banana republic in that its legal system has become a "sink-well of secret proceedings" in how it is sullied with documented corruption, fake trials and court fraud. U.S. Criminal Injustice System: Crooked Judges, Corrupt Lawyers and Criminal Corporation – The Millennium Report. The article points out that secrecy, gag orders, and the court files you will never see is a judiciary that is an increasingly closed society, with much of its legal activity carried on in secret and hidden. This is very alarming. As a country, we should be very concerned with what is taking place with the people that are wearing the black robes who are basically card-carrying members of a very dark secret society.

There is a reason that the judiciary is so secretive, and the answer is very simple. It doesn't want the people to know just how corrupt it is. That is why, for the most part, the judiciary disallows cameras in the courtrooms and doesn't allow for civilians to be on investigatory boards that are reviewing allegations of judicial misconduct that have been submitted against judges. And that is also one of the reasons why the judiciary does everything it can to keep the facts of allegations against judges from being disclosed to the public. Think about it, when a person is arrested for anything, whether a misdemeanor or a felony, the fact of the arrest is considered public information, reported to the news media, and published for anybody to see; but when a judge is charged with allegations of misconduct, it is the complete opposite. The judiciary mechanism hides this information from the public to protect the dishonest judges. It is interesting that judges enjoy such protections in order to safeguard their reputations, but regular people, on the other hand, are subject to public scrutiny for what they are charged with, whether it has any validity or not.

As for courts not taking kindly to cameras in the courtroom, Judge Richard A. Posner of the Seventh Circuit Court of Appeals in Chicago wrote in his book *Reforming the Federal Judiciary: My Former Court Needs to Overhaul Its Staff Attorney Program and Begin Televising Its Oral Arguments* about how he argued in support of televising the oral arguments in the Seventh Circuit. He writes that the chief judge at the time, Diane Wood, resisted the notion of televising the

Seventh Circuit's oral arguments because she was fearful that the equipment would cost between $100,000 and $200,000, which the court couldn't afford. But when Chief Judge Wood told Judge Posner this, Judge Posner said that he would be glad to buy the equipment with his own money and give it to the court anonymously. Sounds like a great offer that remedied the purported concern that Wood had about not being able to afford it. And what do you think Wood did with Judge Posner's offer? She turned it down without giving a reason. Wood's action of rejecting such a generous offer made no sense as it would have been a great opportunity for the public to actually see the court in action. The fact that Wood said that televising the oral arguments was not doable because of the finances, and then when Judge Posner was willing to cure her concerns about financing the equipment, she did an about face and still said no, showed that Wood initially used a false excuse for not installing cameras in the Seventh Circuit, and when called on it, she showed her true colors, which were that she obviously wasn't interested in the public seeing any more of how the Seventh Circuit operates than is absolutely necessary. She should be ashamed of herself. But dishonest judges have no shame.

And in addition to Wood's preference to keep cameras out of the courtroom in the Seventh Circuit, she also had another preference against transparency in that she was against Judge Posner's desire to publish a book where he would enlighten the public about the Seventh Circuit's secret way of conducting business. Her disdain for the public's interest in the right to know was so strong that she apparently would have had no problem in utilizing unlawful prior restraint to stop the publication of Judge Posner's book. In it, he reprinted an email that Wood sent to all of the judges in the Seventh Circuit on August 8, 2017, which contained a diatribe attacking Judge Posner for writing his book and even stating that Judge Posner's book "...would do great damage to the court as an institution." Wood went on to state, "But it is not too late to take steps to ameliorate the problem" and that "there may be some way to recall those copies of the book." A chief judge's desire to recall a book that explains how a court operates behind the scenes is an undesirable trait for a chief judge, to say the least. Her penchant for secrecy is very unbecoming. Judge Posner discusses in his book a larger question of concern by the chief judge's reference to "internal deliberations of the court" as to whether the judges are too secretive—specifically, why judges' deliberations such as in post-argument conferences should not be concealed from the public. Judge Posner felt very strongly that there should be no internal deliberations and that such deliberations should be done in public rather than the Seventh Circuit's preferred policy of concealing the deliberations from the public. Why did the chief judge of the Seventh Circuit favor such secrecy? The answer to this question is rather evident. The Seventh Circuit essentially prefers to operate as a "secret society" in its "black-robed members only" club. To say that the Seventh Circuit operates in a very insidious way would be an understatement.

Chief judge at the time, Diane Wood should have been ashamed of herself. Had she looked at a world map, she would have learned that the U.S. Court of Appeals for the Seventh Circuit in Chicago is located in the United States of America, which happens to be a country where expression of free speech is not only allowed, but guaranteed as a fundamental right, and that people have a right to publish books about government corruption—and that includes corruption within the Seventh Circuit. As a federal judge, Chief Judge Wood knew, or she should have known, that prior restraint is an unlawful activity in our country. But unlawful activities in the United States Court of Appeals for the Seventh Circuit is the unwritten rule—not the exception to the rule. This is unfortunately what the citizens in our country have to put up with when judges are left unbridled to freely violate the laws of the land, laws that they, as judges, are actually supposed to be enforcing. And it will always be that way so long as the process continues in secrecy, allowing judges to protect their own brethren judges, with the citizenry excluded from the oversight process.

In addition to the judiciary's infected policies of keeping cameras out of the courtrooms, the judiciary even goes so far as to suppress peoples' free speech rights in how it protects itself from malfeasance issues when people file judicial misconduct complaints against judges. Case in point is how the federal judiciary tries to muzzle people who exercise their rights when they file misconduct complaints against corrupt judges, which people have the right to do under the Judicial Conduct and Disability Act that allows "any person alleging that a judge has engaged in conduct prejudicial to the effective and expeditious administration of the business of the courts" to file a complaint against the judge. [28 U.S. Code § 351 - Complaints; judge defined | U.S. Code | US Law | LII / Legal Information Institute (cornell.edu)](). And then when a complaint is filed, everything simply goes out the window in terms of transparency and accountability, and yes, even the ultimate goal of justice due to the judiciary's built-in rules systematically designed to muzzle the public and prevent an actual meaningful proceeding in order that the public be kept in the dark about the vast amount of miscreant judges that permeate the judiciary. It is akin to how police departments around the country conceal the identities of the rogue police officers who have records of violating peoples' rights in order that the public not know who the dangerous officers are who have a demonstrated propensity to violate the rights of the citizens of our country in so many different ways. Police departments around the country conceal this information not because there are laws against it, they do it simply because they know they can get away with it without much of a fight because they have been doing it for such a long time. The judiciary uses the same playbook but with much more force because it actually has the power to put rules in place to keep information about its corrupt judges secret, knowing that the only thing the public can do to fight back is to go to the very source of the problem, the judiciary, to complain about its infected rules. And it doesn't help that federal legislators cater to the judiciary by enacting statutes that give wholesale protections to federal judges who have become basically untouchable when it comes to oversight and accountability. We can thank our elected representatives in Congress for that. The flying monkeys are many.

A self-serving law was conveniently put on the books dictating that, with a few exceptions, all papers, documents, and records of proceedings relating to judicial misconduct complaints shall be confidential and shall not be disclosed by any person in any proceeding. https://www.law.cornell.edu/uscode/text/28/360. In other words, when someone has information regarding judicial corruption by a federal judge, once that person files a complaint, they cannot make any public statements about the judicial malfeasance. This law seems to be in substantial conflict with the First Amendment to the United States Constitution which expressly prevents the government from making laws which abridge the freedom of speech. You may be wondering then, since there is such a law apparently on the books, how I, as the author of this book, can discuss the judicial misconduct complaint that I filed with the U.S. Court of Appeals against Judge Michael S. Kanne for his case-fixing activities and also the Seventh Circuit's cover up of it? The answer is very simple. I believe I have a fundamental right under the First Amendment to the United States Constitution to publicly discuss judicial corruption as a matter of public concern, and I believe that the case fixing and cover-up activities at the U.S. Court of Appeals in Chicago is such a matter of public concern. If the government would like to prosecute me for publicly exercising my First Amendment rights in speaking out against the corruption in the U.S. Court of Appeals in Chicago, or any aspect of the federal judiciary, it knows how to find me. I believe the First Amendment gives me the right to do so and supersedes any infected law put in place to suppress the right of a citizen to publicly discuss judicial corruption.

The hierarchy of the federal judiciary is so hell bent on operating in secret as to the judicial misconduct complaints filed against federal judges that a watchdog group, "Citizens for Responsibility and Ethics in Washington," filed a lawsuit for injunctive and declaratory relief against the United States Department of Justice on October 6, 2022, seeking records showing how the Department of Justice responded to misconduct complaints against federal judges and U.S. Supreme Court justices spanning more than a decade. The lawsuit said the Department of Justice was "wrongfully withholding" records about alleged ethics matters involving federal judges. The complaint was submitted under the federal Freedom of Information Act seeking information from the Justice Department's professional responsibility office including seeking copies of complaints against any U.S. Supreme Court justice, U.S. Appeals Court judge, or federal district judge. According to the Reuters article reporting on the lawsuit, the Department of Justice's professional responsibility office said in its 2021 annual report that it had received nine complaints since 2019 alleging U.S. judicial misconduct and in four of those cases referred the matter to a judicial disciplinary authority. The annual report did not identify any judge by name. According to the Reuters article, a Justice Department spokesperson declined to comment, as did representatives from the Administrative Office of the U.S. Courts. <u>U.S. Justice Dept sued over records about complaints against federal judges | Reuters</u>. I found it very interesting that the Administrative Office of the U.S. Courts declined to comment as this is the very office that refuses to acknowledge that I filed a petition with the Judicial Conference of the United States for a review of the infected decision by Chief Judge Diane S. Sykes and her confederates as to the judicial misconduct complaint I filed against Judge Michael S. Kanne of the U.S. Court of Appeals for the Seventh Circuit in Chicago for his case-fixing activities and where I also addressed the Seventh Circuit's protectionism and cover up of it. It goes without saying that we have a very serious problem with judicial perversion in our country. The fact that the Administrative Office of the United States Courts refuses to answer questions about it is proof positive that the judicial perversion is of a very seriously high magnitude.

It is bad public policy for federal lawmakers to be so influenced as to enact unconstitutional laws to protect bad behavior of federal judges by muzzling people by impermissibly suppressing their free speech rights to speak about secret processes that are calculated to insulate misbehaving federal judges from public scrutiny—there is nothing in the Constitution that affords unlawful secrecy protections to the persons wearing the black robes who violate their oaths of office. Public policy is served best by allowing people to exercise their free speech rights by allowing public denouncement of a poisoned process of protectionism of judicial corruption; public policy is not well served by an unconstitutional law that suppresses that right. And public policy is served best by allowing people to exercise their fundamental right to seek redress of their grievances against infected decisions by chief judges, and that right includes the right to seek redress of corrupt decisions from judicial councils who unlawfully protect criminal activities by federal judges. It is bad public policy to impermissibly prevent aggrieved people from seeking a judicial review of infected decisions by judicial councils given by the brethren of misbehaving judges. After all, the right of people to petition for redress of grievances is the First Amendment's capstone. What the Seventh Circuit did in protecting Kanne's case-fixing activities constituted criminal conduct, and it is more than evident that the United States Court system is bending over backwards to continue protecting that judicial corruption. I am sure such protectionism is going on with many other peoples' cases, as well.

It is ever so evident that the judiciary and legislators share the same beds when it comes to protecting wrongful and unlawful activities of judges in how the judiciary and legislators enact rules and laws that are designed to keep the facts of wrongful and unlawful activities by judges away from the public's knowledge. Corruption by judges is *de rigueur* these days and has been for a very long time. The judiciary and its enabling legislators well know that if the public had access to the information regarding the miscreant judges that not only would there be a public outcry for the removal of those miscreant judges, but there would also be a public outcry for the prosecution and imprisonment of those miscreant judges for their criminal conduct. It is for these reasons that the United States judiciary has been bending over backwards, and will continue to bend over backwards, in flexing its judicial and political muscle in protecting the criminal judges that permeate the judiciary. And make no mistake about it, the judiciary is indeed infested with many criminal judges. It is a very perverse system.

For there to be any credibility in the American justice system, federal grand juries must be empaneled when information is brought forward against corrupt judges, and all judges who were involved in any judicial shenanigans would then be prosecuted and sent to prison for the common criminals that they are; but instead, they are protected by the very system that they have infected. Until such time that we as a society demand and see to it that the outmoded protections given to criminal judges are cast by the wayside, and that our government takes steps to hold grand juries and indict, prosecute, and imprison corrupt judges to the fullest extent of the law, rather than protecting the criminals who wear black robes and allow them to skate free, then the words "nobody is above the law" should ever be uttered.

CHAPTER 12

THE FEDERAL JUDICIARY IS A WEAPON OF MASS DESTRUCTION!

THE NUCLEAR BOMB IS "SUMMARY JUDGMENT"

"When tyranny becomes law, rebellion becomes duty."
~ Thomas Jefferson

I know this sounds harsh, but I strongly feel that basically the judiciary is a weapon of mass destruction insofar as the rights of the people are concerned. The extermination of the peoples' rights by the federal courts is well documented. The vast number of the peoples' cases that the courts are dismissing is alarming. And the courts have a nuclear bomb at their disposal designed for the express purpose of denying people their fundamental right to a jury trial as to their grievances. The nuclear bomb is what is referred to in the legal world as "summary judgment." A motion for summary judgment is a procedure that corporate and government agency lawyers use to have the judge dismiss the case so that it will not be decided by a jury, in other words, a premeditated action to deny people of their so-called fundamental right to a jury trial. Courts are infamous for granting motions for summary judgments brought by corporations and government agencies in order to keep the allegations against them from being decided by a jury, and in effect, escape liability for their wrongful actions. Federal judges across the country are passing out favorable summary judgment rulings to corporations and government agencies as if they were giving candy to a baby. Make no mistake about it, the judiciary has made this a very convenient way for corporations and government agencies to escape liability for their wrongful actions. The modus operandi is that once a corporation or government agency files a motion for summary judgment, infected judges then do their thing and view the evidence and the case laws in the way they would like, many times ignoring evidence and twisting the rules and case laws in order to grant a summary judgment in favor of corporations and government agencies. (Case law is law established by following judicial decisions given in earlier cases). It happens routinely, and it is plain wrong. It is not hard to figure out that the reason for this problem is that the federal judiciary is overwhelmingly comprised of extremist judges who are there to protect the interest of corporations and government agencies rather than protecting the interests of the constitutional rights of the citizens. And that is no accident; it is by design.

When I asked the Administrative Office of the United States Courts to tell me how many cases were dismissed without a trial, the Administrative Office responded that they didn't keep track of that information. That is essentially unbelievable in this day and age of technology as all federal court systems operate under an electronic data-based system. There is no way that the Administrative Office of the United States Courts and the judiciary hierarchy doesn't know the numbers of cases that are dismissed in the federal judiciary year by year. All of the cases are docketed in each judicial division in the country, and every docket shows the developments and status of all of the cases, from beginning to end. It is ludicrous to even suggest, let alone state, that the judiciary doesn't maintain such information. The judiciary doesn't want the people to know that the federal judges across the country are dismissing peoples' cases at an alarmingly high rate. And even though the Administrative Office of the United States Courts doesn't want the people to know of the alarmingly high rate of dismissal of cases, which thereby results in depriving people of their "day in court"—a phrase that we hear so much about but hardly ever see—we do have some very interesting information that sheds some light as to why the judiciary doesn't want the people to know. The reason is, in the vast majority of cases, the judges side with corporations and government agencies and grant dismissals so that the peoples' cases never make it to a trial. https://www.theatlantic.com/ideas/archive/2018/07/big-business-keeps-winning-at-the-supreme court/564260/, https://www.washingtonpost.com/news/posteverything/wp/2017/06/26/why-big-business-keeps-winning-at-the-supreme-court/, https://www.findlaw.com/legalblogs/in-house/do-federal-courts-favor-big-business-corporations/. The courts are mobbing and robbing people of justice, there is no question about it, and this is why the judiciary doesn't want the people to know about the alarmingly high dismissal rate of peoples' cases. Corporations and government agencies have the judges in their back pockets.

So in the end, the sad truth and the sad reality is that the vast majority of the people in our country are not at all seeing their "day in court" as most of the cases are being dismissed by the federal judges. Federal judges enjoy lifetime appointments and enjoy the luxury of controlling their own calendars. Routinely at will, they simply dismiss cases rather than hold trials despite the peoples' right to a trial by jury, a right actually guaranteed by the Seventh Amendment to the Constitution of the United States. To fully appreciate what the Seventh Amendment means to us, the people, we need to know a bit of the history of the Seventh Amendment to put it in its proper perspective and to understand why it is such a sacred right—albeit a right that judges routinely deny to the people.

Before 1688, English judges were servants under the king of England. These judges were often biased toward the King, and because of this, their rulings were not always fair. Does this sound familiar? You bet it does. It happens every day in our American court system with judges who are overwhelmingly biased in favor of corporations and government agencies just as the English judges were biased toward the king. During the Act of Settlement of 1701, English judges won their independence from the king, but judges in the American colonies were still biased toward the king. King George III got rid of trials by juries in the Colonies, which made colonists very upset and fueled the fire that led to the American Revolution. When the Framers wrote the Bill of Rights, they understood how important it was to have a fair court system, so they made sure that the right to have a trial by jury was a fundamental law of the country. In the state ratifying conventions for the federal Constitution, Anti-Federalists strongly protested the lack of a right to a civil jury trial. They argued that juries could protect litigants from bad laws passed by the legislature, tyrannical actions by the executive, and corrupt or biased judges. Fearing that a second constitutional convention might be called if a right to a civil jury trial were not included in a federal Bill of Rights, James Madison drafted what became the Seventh Amendment. Sadly, judges routinely disregard the essence of the Seventh Amendment requirement of a civil jury trial in order to help along influential corporations and government agencies by dismissing peoples' cases by way of "summary judgment" rather than letting a jury decide the outcome. This is not what the Framers had in mind. James Madison must be rolling over in his grave.

It is interesting that after our forefathers drafted the Seventh Amendment right to a jury trial in civil cases, and embodied this fundamental right into our Constitution, federal judges have since connived to actually deprive the peoples' right to a civil jury trial by conjuring up a way to do it by way of "summary judgment." Yet we never hear discussions from anybody in the legal universe as to why the judiciary created the summary judgment procedure, which in essence is a built-in mechanism contrived by the judiciary as a way to prevent people from getting their cases decided by a jury, notwithstanding that the "right of trial by jury shall be preserved" under the Seventh Amendment. The Seventh Amendment is generally considered one of the more straightforward amendments of the Bill of Rights.

In my opinion, the use of a summary judgment procedure is an impermissible and unconstitutional intrusion against citizens' rights to a trial by jury guaranteed by the Seventh Amendment, and judges violate the Seventh Amendment to the United States Constitution every time they dismiss a person's case. The Seventh Amendment to the United States Constitution is part of the Bill of Rights. This amendment codifies the right to a jury trial. Because of the extremism of the judges on the federal judiciary, summary judgment procedures were put in place in order to protect corporations and government agencies who benefit greatly by a system that prevents citizens from exposing corporations and government agencies of their wrongdoings and unlawful conducts. For example, in a case involving wrongful discharge of public employment, or a case involving false arrest, the people would overwhelmingly prefer that juries make the ultimate decision about their grievances as such governmental abuses implicate the peoples' fundamental right to the "pursuit of happiness" as to their employment and liberty interests, but then federal judges come running to the rescue of corporations and government agencies by trampling on the peoples' fundamental rights by arbitrarily taking away their right to a trial by jury. Consequently, the people end up not getting their fundamentally entitled "day in court" thanks to a nefariously conjured-up system by the judiciary. The Constitution explicitly states that all people in the United States of America have a fundamental right to a trial by jury in redress of their grievances; the Constitution doesn't empower judges, or anybody for that matter, to put any rules in place that in any way interfere with a person's right to a trial by jury which is guaranteed under the Seventh Amendment. And yet, we never see or hear any of the so-called "legal geniuses" ever discuss this very important point. And that, in and of itself, should tell us something. In essence, the federal judiciary is much more interested in helping along unsavory corporations and government agencies more than it is interested in dispensing justice to the people.

The Millennium Report in April 2019 characterized U.S. judges as "goons" for the big corporations. The article wrote that the corporations own the U.S. lawyers and judges in America by way of the corporate money and bribes that flow in the billions of dollars through U.S. law firms, which is why they rarely lose cases among the "pro-business" U.S. judges. The article points out that the judges enforce the "law," which in the United States means the "law" of the "big corporations." According to the article, in exchange for controlling things for the benefit of the big corporations, U.S. judges and lawyers are allowed to act like perverts with regard to the average person where they lie, rob, cheat, steal, kill, and destroy any mere average person who doesn't have the monetary means to fight back. <u>U.S. Criminal Injustice System: Crooked Judges, Corrupt Lawyers and Criminal Corporation – The Millennium Report</u>. It is quite sad that a big problem within the federal judiciary is that it is overwhelmingly comprised of extremist judges who are there to protect the interest of corporations and government agencies rather than protecting the interests of the constitutional rights of the citizens. As they say, "money talks" and that certainly seems to be the case when it comes to the federal judiciary. Yes, indeed, "summary judgment" is a friend to the big corporations—and the judges know how to use it against the people to protect their money friends in corporate America.

Another elephant in the room is when people or corporations are being defended by insurance companies in state or federal courts. In the vast majority of civil cases, there is usually an insurance company involved, and what usually comes with that are unscrupulous insurance lawyers who will stoop to the lowest of all lows to protect the insurance company from paying any money to a person who has been injured or damaged by their insured. So, in essence, what is generally involved is a rich and powerful insurance company on one side of the case going up against a usually not so rich and not so powerful regular person who is simply trying to be made whole for an injustice that took place against him or her, but faces many obstacles by the opposing insurance lawyers. And unfortunately there will be a judge who, more often than not, tends to be friendly to insurance companies and insurance lawyers and not willing to let a jury decide the person's case. This is especially so in civil rights cases, even though the Seventh Amendment requires it. This is a big reason why so many of the peoples' cases against corporations and government agencies are dismissed by courts without a trial, and also in cases between civilians where one of the parties' cases is being financed by an insurance company. Many times judges are in the back pockets of insurance companies and become puppets for the insurance lawyers who are the puppeteers. What we have is the "almighty" judge in the "black robe" making the critical decisions that have a far-reaching impact on how the case will be decided in the end, and in most cases, to the benefit of the rich and powerful insurance company and against the regular person who is simply trying to have his or her supposed entitled day in court, but doesn't get it. While The Millennium Report in April 2019 characterized U.S. judges as "goons" for the big corporations, I would add in particular that there are many state and federal judges who are "goons" for insurance companies. Judges have a keen sense for the smell of money, and make no mistake about it, insurance lawyers know how to get that smell of money to the judges' noses.

Many people wonder what goes on behind the scenes in these types of cases where money is in play. Many people believe that unscrupulous insurance lawyers pay bribes to unsavory judges to receive favorable outcomes such as in motions for summary judgment when the judge is asked by insurance lawyers to dismiss cases brought by the people. Not only is this distasteful conduct reprehensible, but it further serves to show how judges are routinely violating the essence of the Seventh Amendment to the United States Constitution where it explicitly states, "In suits at common law, where the value in controversy shall exceed twenty dollars, **the right of trial by** jury shall be preserved." Dismissing peoples' cases without their constitutionally-entitled right to trial by jury flies in the face of the federal constitution, and let's be clear and honest here, judges across the country are rampantly dismissing cases in favor of influential corporations, government agencies, and rich and powerful insurance companies. This gives rise to a very serious question about the integrity of the judiciary.

It is very important for people to understand that the federal constitution is the supreme law of the land, and the Seventh Amendment explicitly states, "In suits at common law, where the value in controversy shall exceed twenty dollars, the right of trial by jury shall be preserved, and no fact tried by a jury, shall be otherwise reexamined in any Court of the United States, than according to the rules of common law." We seem to have lost sight of the fact that the purpose of the Constitution was to limit the power of the federal government and to protect the natural rights of life, liberty, and the pursuit of happiness as enunciated in the Declaration of Independence. This is the law of the land. The Preamble to the United States Constitution, beginning with the words "We the People," is an introductory statement of the Constitution's fundamental purposes and guiding principles, one of which is the explicitly stated principle of its fundamental purpose being to "establish justice." Yet, the federal judiciary has no problem in ignoring the peoples' fundamental right to a jury trial in their civil cases so, in essence, what that really means is that the federal judiciary does not consider a person's fundamental right to a jury trial as a form of "justice." Let's not sugar coat this. Every time a federal judge dismisses a person's lawsuit and denies that person his or her Seventh Amendment fundamental right to a jury trial, that judge might as well be spitting on the Constitution.

If the Seventh Amendment to our Constitution is to have any meaning, then we need to have a serious discussion about this issue, and corrective measures need to be taken to remedy this governmental injustice in order that the peoples' rights to a trial by jury under the Seventh Amendment are preserved and not abused as is currently happening with the unconstitutional process of summary judgments, which is disallowed under the spirit of the Seventh Amendment. Federal judges should no longer be permitted to ignore the peoples' rights to a trial by jury under the Seventh Amendment in order to protect corporations and government agencies who are abusing peoples' rights—the Constitution forbids it!

It doesn't help that we have a chief justice of the United States, John Roberts, who chooses to throw out propaganda that makes it sound as though we have an honest and above-board judiciary when that is hardly the case. Chief Justice John Roberts issued a so-called "2019 Year-End Report on the Federal Judiciary" that was laughable at best. While the words sounded well and good, the reality is that the piece was nothing more than sound good propaganda coming from a chief justice of a very infected federal judiciary, of which words were obviously calculated to brainwash the public from the realities that are actually taking place in the federal judiciary. Roberts stated, "I ask my judicial colleagues to continue their efforts to promote public confidence in the judiciary, both through their rulings and through civic outreach. We should celebrate our strong and independent judiciary, a key source of national unity and stability. But we should also remember that justice is not inevitable. We should reflect on our duty to judge without fear or favor, deciding each matter with humility, integrity, and dispatch. As the New Year begins, and we turn to the tasks before us, we should each resolve to do our best to maintain the public's trust that we are faithfully discharging our solemn obligation to equal justice under law." 2019year-endreport.pdf (supremecourt.gov). And yet most people in the country who have had dealings in the federal judiciary have serious questions about the integrity of the "rulings" by the federal judges since most of their rulings go in favor of corporations and government agencies, and against the people, as in the vast majority of cases, judges side with corporations and government agencies and grant summary judgment dismissals so that the peoples' cases never even make it to a trial. Arbitrarily preventing peoples' cases from getting to a trial by jury hardly breeds "public confidence" in the judiciary.

Roberts also spewed out in his so-called report that "…In our age, when social media can instantly spread rumor and false information on a grand scale, the public's need to understand our government, and the protections it provides, is ever more vital. The judiciary has an important role to play in civic education, and I am pleased to report that the judges and staff of our federal courts are taking up the challenge." I would remind Chief Justice Roberts that while it is true that social media can instantly spread rumor and false information on a grand scale, that it is equally as abhorrent when the chief justice of the United States spreads rumor and false information on a grand scale by way of public reports that are nothing more than mere propaganda designed to mislead the public. And that is exactly what Roberts did in his so-called "report" which wasn't worth the paper it was printed on. Roberts might as well put up a sign on his door saying "Chief Justice of Corporate America."

The last thing that Roberts should be doing is thumping his chest in a public writing and invoking the phrase "equal justice under the law." For if there was actually "equal justice under the law," the federal judges wouldn't be so predetermined to issue overwhelmingly favorable rulings to corporations and government agencies while ruling against the people on a grand scale, and the majority of the peoples' cases would make it to a jury trial. But the federal judges don't allow that to happen for the most part—and Roberts knows it. Simply put, Roberts' "2019 Year-End Report on the Federal Judiciary" was a farce. He would never admit it, but Roberts knows that judges do pretty much whatever they want, which includes routinely stepping on the people's constitutional rights in an unfettered manner. Roberts spewed all of this with a straight face and fake smile, all while knowing that the federal judges in this country shamefully and overwhelmingly foam at the mouth to utilize summary judgment as a way to rule in favor of rich and influential corporations and government agencies and against the people. Former Justice Charles Evans Hughes was up front and honest when he said, "We are under a Constitution, but the Constitution is what the judges say it is." The short and simple of it is that the judiciary is inundated with cockroach judges who have no respect for the rules or the laws or peoples' rights. There are many cockroach judges infested in the judiciary who demonstrate their indifference to what is right and routinely go out of their way to screw the common people over in their cases in order that corporations and government agencies prevail. It's very sad, but that is the reality of it. In essence, what is happening is the extermination of the rights of the people to get justice. It is the quietest genocide to ever happen. In the former Nazi Germany, there was genocide against the Jews; in South Africa, there was Apartheid; and in the United States, there is systematic genocide against the peoples' constitutional rights to justice with the state and federal judges running the lynching parties. Every time a judge grants a summary judgment in favor of a corporation or government agency, thereby depriving a person of his or her right to a jury trial, that judge has, in essence, wrapped a noose around the Constitution and hung it from a tree.

It would be great if our courts could be considered a friend of the people when it comes to dispensing justice when they are wronged by powerful corporations or government agencies, but sadly the courts fail the test in a big way. To have a well-working federal judiciary that the American people have confidence in, we must have federal judges who are honest and do not have a baked-in bias in favor of corporations and government agencies, and that certainly is a major problem. Judges take an oath of office solemnly swearing to "administer justice without respect to persons, and do equal right to the poor and to the rich, and that I will faithfully and impartially discharge and perform all the duties incumbent upon me as under the Constitution and laws of the United States." Unfortunately, there has been a major breach of this oath across the federal judiciary in many different very troubling ways.

The time has come for the people to wake up and start realizing what is taking place in the federal judiciary. And the time has come for the people to stand up and say enough is enough. We as a people of a democracy are fools if we continue to sit back and say and do nothing and continue to subsidize our infected judiciaries by accepting what the judiciary has been doing when the people try to assert their rights in cases against corporations and government agencies, but get gunned down at every turn by pro-corporation and pro-government-type judges when people seek redress for their grievances in the judiciaries around the country. Federal judges are completely out of control in routinely granting summary judgments in favor of corporations and government agencies in order to prevent the peoples' cases to be decided by a jury and, in essence, acquiescently letting the unsavory corporations and government agencies off the hook for the wrongs they committed. This is very wrong and goes completely against what the Seventh Amendment to the Constitution of the United States requires—a trial by jury.

During controversies regarding the appointment of federal judges, we so often hear the politicians of the right wing constantly say that they want judges who "follow the constitution," and yet they strive to appoint judges who do the very opposite as a matter of routine. Think about it, when is the last time you have ever heard a politician on the right publicly say that we need judges to be appointed who will protect the peoples' right to a trial by jury as preserved by the Seventh Amendment and that there should be no judges appointed who are not willing to follow the Seventh Amendment? I would venture to say that the answer to that question is zero, that you have never heard a single right wing politician publicly say that. People need to be smarter when they are listening to these political monkeys and not be so hoodwinked by buzz words that sound good but are nothing more than political propaganda in order to mislead the public. There should be jury trials taking place in every courtroom in the country on an almost daily basis, but the reality is that there aren't very many jury trials at all because the judges across the country so blatantly disregard the Seventh Amendment and routinely dismiss peoples' cases against corporations and government agencies by summary judgment. These types of serpent judges permeate the federal judiciary. This has been tolerated for far too long and must be stopped. Make no mistake about it, the federal judiciary is basically a cabal designed to protect corporations and governmental agencies—and the people have tolerated it for far too long.

In looking at the seriousness of what the miscreant judges have been doing by refusing to respect the Seventh Amendment in order to pacify corporations, government agencies, and insurance companies in dismissing cases against them, and thereby depriving the common people of their right to a trial by jury, it would behoove every state and federal judge in this country, including the justices on the Supreme Court, to study what Justice Owen Roberts admonished in the decision of *Hazel-Atlas Class Co. v. Hartford-Empire Co.*, 322 U.S. 238 (1944) when he noted that "No fraud is more odious than an attempt to subvert the administration of justice." And further that "The resources of the law are ample to undo the wrong and to pursue the wrongdoer, and to do both effectively with due regard to the established modes of procedure." Justice Owen Roberts went on to admonish that when members of the bar have knowingly participated in the fraud that "Remedies are available to purge recreant officers from the tribunals on whom the fraud was practiced." All judges are officers of the tribunal on whomever fraud was practiced, and whenever judges take part in issuing infected decisions or are involved in any type of activities calculated to thwart the effective administration of justice in order that undeserving parties receive preferential treatment and undeserved rulings, that constitutes fraud. Now, what the country needs is for the chief justice of the United States, and the justices on the Supreme Court, and all federal district court and appellate court judges, to read what Justice Owen Roberts said—and they should start following it!

CHAPTER 13

JUDGES SHOULD BE REQUIRED TO TAKE A YEARLY POLYGRAPH TEST

"A well informed citizenry is the best defense against tyranny."
~ Thomas Jefferson

In the 1980's, the feds conducted a sting operation in Cook County, Illinois, courts that revealed serious evidence of rampant judicial bribery in that court system. It was called "Operation Greylord." Numerous crooked judges and crooked lawyers were arrested and served jail time. Nine judges, 37 lawyers, and 19 court personnel including deputy sheriffs, deputy clerks, and police officers were convicted and sentenced as of June 1, 1988. Greylord should have taught us that there are many judges and lawyers who are on the take and that there is a great need for ongoing checks and balances when it comes to investigating the goings on in the judiciary with lawyers and judges. I am sure that Greylord was just the tip of the iceberg. There can be no question about that. It took a federal sting operation in the Cook County, Illinois, Chicago-area courts, to prove that there are many corrupt lawyers and judges who are on the take, which was in fact proved in Operation Greylord. But yet today, we act as though everything is perfectly fine in the courts and that everything is on the up and up, which is hardly the case by any stretch of the imagination.

It goes without saying that corruption in the judiciary is particularly insidious, and for that reason, there should be more Greylord-like stings. Sting operations of corrupt courts are very few and far between, and that is very concerning. It makes no sense that federal law enforcement agencies have no problem with going after so called "illegal immigrants" and drug dealers and the like, but when it comes to corrupt judges selling out their offices in order to take the almighty dollar under the table, well then that type of criminal activity is off limits for the most part—at least as far as state and federal law enforcement is concerned. It certainly cannot be said that corrupt judges can't be caught, convicted, and put in prison; Greylord proved that it can be done. The basic method in Greylord was that while wearing a recording device, FBI agents and those cooperating with the FBI would bribe clerks, and later judges, to fix the outcome of cases. The tape recording would provide evidence of the transaction independent of the agents' testimony. With both the testimony and a recording to back it up, conviction would be certain.

Greylord proved that these methods are ways to develop evidence sufficient to prove judicial corruption, but for some reason, state and federal law enforcement officials simply don't have an appetite to go after corrupt judges who partake in criminal activities in accepting bribes these days. Greylord was triggered by the Watergate scandal or, more accurately, the Department of Justice's response to Watergate. The Department of Justice had always been responsible for prosecuting corruption cases involving federal government employees and had occasionally prosecuted state and local officials for corruption, as well. But until Watergate, neither federal nor state and local public corruption had been a major concern. Watergate revealed an astonishing degree of corruption at the heart of the American system of government, but for some reason, the feds don't conduct very many sting operations into corrupt courts, at least not nearly as many as they should be as judicial corruption is a very serious problem across the country, and will continue to be, until such time as the state and federal law enforcement agencies decide to place judicial corruption as a high priority. Unfortunately, that day may never come. For the most part, after the Greylord sting operation was over, it was business as usual again. If the feds were truly interested in judicial integrity, they would conduct more sting operations like Greylord, but they are not. I am sure there is a reason for that. I will leave it up to you to come to your own conclusion as to why there are no sting operations in the judiciary these days. I think we all pretty much know the answer to that question. We know from Greylord that a well-planned undercover operation can catch corrupt judges, court staff, and lawyers and successfully prosecute them, convict them, and send them to prison where they belong. After all, if it could be done in Chicago, it can be done anywhere, and should be—but isn't. In essence, the judiciary has been given carte blanche to do whatever it wants, including taking bribes, to give favorable decisions in cases. This is a consequence of giving a particular branch of government too much unbridled power.

It is sad to think about how our governmental leaders criticize corruption that goes on in other countries around the world, but when it comes to corruption going on in our country's judiciary, those same leaders are noticeably silent. And it is sad that the people of our country are expected to accept the judicial corruption that take place on a daily basis right here in our own backyards. The judicial thievery is mind boggling. My advice to anybody who has hired a lawyer is keep an eye on them—and don't blink. And if you are in court on any matter, keep an eye on the judge as well—and don't blink. If there is a profession in this country that warrants the taking of a yearly polygraph (lie detector) exam, it is the legal profession. Every lawyer and every judge in the United States should be required to take a yearly polygraph exam in order to safeguard the public from malfeasance within the legal profession. One need only look to Operation Greylord for convincing evidence of the need of yearly polygraph exams for judges and lawyers. It is a crime against the people when lawyers and judges are allowed to operate in an unfettered system that allows them to line their pockets with money in court-related shenanigans. Corrupt judges who are willing to violate their sworn oaths to do justice and use their offices for personal financial gain by way of sinfully accepting bribes for favorable decisions desecrate what is supposed to be a system of fairness and are a disgrace to the judiciary and a disgrace to themselves as human beings. It is a very serious problem in our country's judiciary. It is a problem of epidemic proportion that needs to be completely eradicated.

Judicial bribery-type corruption has been going on for a very long time. It isn't going to end anytime soon, and probably never will, as it is increasingly apparent that law enforcement authorities don't seem to have much of an appetite to stop it. According to the Association of Certified Fraud Examiners (ACFE), the two most common types of judicial corruption are "political interference" and "bribery." Political interference is when politicians or staff from the legislative or executive branch meddle in judicial affairs or collide with judges in fraudulent schemes. The ACFE maintains that despite efforts to isolate the judiciary from politics, judges and other court personnel still face significant pressure to rule in favor of powerful political or business entities rather than in accordance with the law. I would add that there are also significant pressures for judges to corruptly rule in favor of government agencies such as police departments and public employers rather than in accordance with the law. A malleable judiciary can and is used by those in power to provide protection for and lend legitimacy to fraudulent acts. Judges also collude with politicians in a variety of different white-collar crimes such as extortion, money laundering, and embezzlement.

According to ACFE, bribery is a common form of judicial corruption where judges or other court officials accept bribes to exercise their influence over a case in a way that benefits the briber. As an example, a judge might delay or accelerate cases, accept or deny appeals, or simply rule in a particular way in exchange for kickbacks;

and it doesn't always have to be for money. In June, 2016, New York Supreme Court Judge John A. Michaelek pleaded guilty to receiving bribes and offering a false instrument for filing in a court case involving a politician operative named G. Steven Pigeon (who was also indicted for nine charges including bribery, extortion, and grand larceny). As the old saying goes, "Politics certainly makes strange bedfellows." Prosecutors in the case alleged that Michaelek reached an understanding with Pigeon that the judge would engage in "official misconduct which advanced Pigeon's interests." As part of the arrangement, Pigeon helped relatives of Michaelek find employment and provided Michaelek with tickets to hockey games and a political fundraiser. The Michaelek ordeal is only a drop in the bucket, a tiny drop in a very large bucket unfortunately. Our country has a multitude of corrupt judges, but what we don't have is a multitude of law enforcement agencies and prosecutors who are willing to drain the judicial swamp. It is sad that corrupt judges have weaponized the judicial system and made whores of themselves. Until the toilet is flushed of these greedy and law breaking judges, we as a society will continue to suffer, and we should not be at all surprised at the high price of justice being bought and sold. Make no mistake about it, justice is for sale in courtrooms all across the country in the state and federal courts.

History gives us a strong roadmap as to how serious the problem of judicial bribery has been going on. For example, Judge Robert W. Archbald, a judge of the United States District Court for the Middle District of Pennsylvania and United States Court of Appeals for the Third Circuit, was impeached by the U.S. House of Representatives on July 13, 1912, for improperly soliciting and accepting gifts from litigants and attorneys. He was convicted by the Senate on January 13, 1913, for several articles of impeachment.

In 1981, a federal grand jury indicted Judge Alcee L. Hastings along with his friend, William A. Borders, a Washington, D.C., lawyer. Hastings was charged with conspiracy and obstruction of justice for soliciting a $150,000 bribe in return for reducing the sentences of two mob-connected felons convicted in Hastings' court. A year after Borders was convicted of conspiracy, the result of an FBI sting effort, Hastings' case came before the criminal court. Despite Borders' conviction and the fact that Hastings had indeed reduced the sentences of the two felons, he was acquitted in a criminal court in 1983 and returned to his judicial post. Subsequently, suspicions arose that Hastings had lied and falsified evidence during the trial in order to obtain an acquittal. A special committee of the 11th Circuit Court of Appeals began a new probe into the Hastings case. The resulting three-year investigation ended with the panel concluding that Hastings did indeed commit perjury, tamper with evidence, and conspire to gain financially by accepting bribes. The panel recommended further action to the U.S. Judicial Conference which, in turn, informed the House of Representatives on March 17, 1987, that Judge Hastings should be impeached and removed from office. The trial committee presented its report on October 2, 1989. Sixteen days later, the trial began in the U.S. Senate. The Senate deliberated in closed session on October 19, 1989. The following day, the Senate voted on 11 of the 17 articles of impeachment and convicted Hastings, by the necessary two-thirds vote, on 8 articles. Having achieved the necessary majority vote to convict on 8 articles, the Senate's president pro tempore (Robert C. Byrd) ordered Hastings removed from office. However, the Senate did not vote to disqualify him from holding future office. Hastings was elected to the United States House of Representatives in 1992, representing Florida's 23rd district. So because of the Senate's incompetence in failing to vote to disqualify Hastings from holding future office, the country consequently ended up with an evidence-tampering, bribery-accepting judge in the House of Representatives.

Robert Frederick Collins was a judge of the United States District Court for the Eastern District of Louisiana, and in 1991, Collins was convicted of accepting money to influence his sentencing of a marijuana smuggler. He served five years in the Federal Prison Camp in Montgomery, Alabama, and in other federal prisons.

Judge Abel Corral Limas of Brownsville, Texas, was convicted of racketeering and sentenced to 72 months in federal prison. At the time of his guilty plea, Limas admitted his part in the use of the office of judge of the 404th District Court as a criminal enterprise to enrich himself and others through extortion. Limas accepted money and other consideration from attorneys in civil cases pending in his court in return for favorable pre-trial rulings in certain cases, including a case involving a helicopter crash at South Padre Island in February, 2008. Evidence showed Limas participated in a series of meetings with attorneys Marc Garrett Rosenthal and Jim Solis in the summer of 2008 during which they planned and negotiated the terms of Limas' employment as an "of counsel" attorney with the firm. During those meetings, Rosenthal promised Limas an advance of at least $100,000, as well as a percentage of attorneys' fees earned in the helicopter crash case, in return for favorable rulings on the case. Limas' employment arrangements were confirmed in calls on August 28, 2008, between Limas and his wife and son. Limas was expecting to be "cut in" on 10 percent of the settlement/judgment of the helicopter crash case pending in his court along with the $100,000 advance. On December 31, 2008, Limas received a check for $50,000 payable from the Rosenthal & Watson Law Firm. On January 2, 2009, Limas received a check for $50,000 from Solis. In October, 2009, the helicopter case settled for approximately $14 million, and Limas received approximately $85,000 from the Rosenthal & Watson Law Firm approximately two months later.

In February of 2011, a Pennsylvania judge, former Luzerne County Judge Mark Ciavarella, Jr., was found guilty of racketeering for taking a $1 million kickback from the builder of for-profit prisons for juveniles. In August, 2011, he was also convicted in connection to a bribery scandal that roiled the state's juvenile justice system. This corrupt judge, nicknamed "Mr. Zero Tolerance" was known for harsh sentences for kids and presided over cases that would send juveniles to those same centers that he had a hand in building. The case came to be known as "kids-for-cash." According to news accounts,

Ciavarella, who presided over juvenile court, sent kids to juvenile detention for crimes such as possession of drug paraphernalia, stealing a jar of nutmeg, and posting web page spoofs about an assistant principal (three months of hard time). Some of those sentenced were as young as 8 years old. In one of the cases, he sentenced a 17-year-old promising high-school athlete with no prior convictions to months in private prisons and a wilderness camp. He missed his entire senior year of high school and never recovered from the experience, according to his mother. In June, 2010, he took his own life at the age of 23. It took a while but this criminal judge, "Mr. Zero Tolerance," was finally figured out and eventually convicted and sentenced to 28 years in prison. Following his sentencing, nearly 4,000 of Ciavarella's previous convictions were overturned.

A district court judge in Texas, Judge Rodolfo "Rudy" Delgado, who presides over Texas' 93rd District Court in Hidalgo County, was arrested on bribery charges and accused of accepting more than $6,000 in bribes in exchange for favorable rulings on criminal cases in his courtroom as reported on February 2, 2018, by *The Washington Times*.

This is proof positive evidence that there is a very significant problem in our country with bribery of judges. These were just a few examples of many and underscores just how serious the problem is and that we need more safeguards put in place such as a yearly polygraph exam for all judges in the United States, state and federal, as a condition to remain employed in the judiciary. We should not mistakenly believe that "buying judges" is not a problem in real life and that it only happens in the movies. Make no mistake about it, the buying and selling of judges in court cases is a common practice that is indeed alive and thriving, particularly in court cases involving insurance companies. Big insurance companies indeed fix elections and indeed bribe judges. The *ABA Journal* reported in November, 2018, that State Farm Insurance paid $250 million to settle a class action lawsuit claiming the insurer created a RICO enterprise to secretly fund the election of Illinois Supreme Court Justice Lloyd

Karmeier, who later voted to overturn a $1.05 billion verdict against the Bloomington, Illinois-based company. The suit had alleged State Farm used nonprofits to secretly fund and orchestrate Karmeier's election. The plaintiffs' amended complaint had alleged State Farm supported the election of Karmeier in 2003 and 2004 through the Illinois Civil Justice League and the U.S. Chamber of Commerce. State Farm orchestrated as much as $4 million of Karmeier's $4.8 million in campaign contributions, the amended complaint had claimed. U.S. District Judge David Herndon gave preliminary approval to the settlement on September 5 and scheduled a hearing on final approval for December 13. A trial was scheduled and Karmeier was scheduled to testify. The lawsuit claimed that State Farm and its in-house lawyers recruited a specific candidate for the election of a new Justice to the Illinois Supreme Court. According to the *ABA Journal* report, State Farm picked its man, got him on the ballot, and then used political action committees to send their candidate lots of "dark money," or political contributions that do not reveal the origin of the money. In point of fact, so much money was involved that it was the most expensive election of any judge in Illinois history.

One might wonder what kind of a particular motive would there be for State Farm to pick and back the campaign to elect this judge, Lloyd Karmeier. But as facts are revealed in the *ABA Journal* report, it turns out that the $250 million that State Farm paid was just a drop in the bucket for what it got in return. The financial support of State Farm enabled its chosen candidate to win the election and become a member of the Illinois Supreme Court. And then when he (Karmeier) got there, he voted to overturn a $1 billion judgment against State Farm that was being reviewed on appeal in the Illinois Supreme Court. A lawyer for the plaintiffs, Robert Clifford, told Reuters that the litigation helped expose truths about hidden corporate influence in judicial elections. "We learned a lot about dark money in America," Clifford told the wire service. "The problem isn't confined to Illinois," he said, "and it's not going to change unless there's campaign finance reform." At the time, Clifford said Karmeier's deposition testimony would likely be released after final approval of the settlement. It would have been a great thing if Karmeier's deposition would have been published in order that the public could have seen just how corrupt the process is when money is used to put certain judges on the bench who will repay the favor by giving favorable rulings to certain parties. In this case, State Farm Insurance, a very wealthy insurance company, spent every dollar necessary to get its man, and get its man it did when it used nonprofits to secretly fund and orchestrate Karmeier's election according to the suit, to which Karmeier later voted to overturn a $1.05 billion verdict against State Farm. This case underscores how money talks when it comes to the judiciary.

These cases are just the tip of the iceberg. Had these corrupt judges been required to take a yearly polygraph exam, the system would have been cleansed of their dirty hands, and many people could have been spared a lot of suffering. The infestation of corrupt people in the courts and in the legal profession is a very serious problem. It is widespread without question. Because of the lack of investigation into case fixing involving unsavory insurance companies and unsavory businesses looking for judicial favors by putting dirty money in judges' pockets, one can only imagine how many corrupt judges are out there taking bribes from corrupt insurance companies and corrupt businesses looking to pay for favorable rulings. I am sure the number would be mind boggling. But until such time that state and federal law enforcement authorities cast politics aside and decide to do the right thing and investigate and prosecute corrupt judges, these types of horror stories will continue on, and many innocent people will be unfairly sent to prison in criminal cases. And many unsavory insurance companies and unsavory businesses in civil cases will receive favorable rulings, while the corrupt judges get rich from the dirty money. It's going on every day and will continue to go on so long as the state and federal law enforcement authorities continue to look the other way. Make no mistake about it, there are plenty of judges out there who like the smell of money, and their noses have a very keen sense of smell for it.

Generally, the courts are more inclined to be favorable to unsavory insurance companies than they are to the regular people. And you might ask, "Why is that?" The answer is very simple: the insurance companies control the courts with their money! And make no mistake about it, money does talk, even in court. That is why it is so difficult to prevail in court cases involving insurance companies. Judges routinely abuse the rules and laws that they are supposed to be following in order to prevent the common people in cases involving insurance companies from having a fighting chance when going up against people or corporations whose cases are being financed by wealthy insurance companies. Corrupt judges should be *persona non grata*, but that is certainly not the case. The American courts are infested with greedy and money-hungry judges who hold their hands out for money, which insurance lawyers and corporation lawyers gladly accommodate for favorable rulings. Operation Greylord taught us about this very serious problem, but the lessons from Greylord are all but forgotten. State and federal law enforcement authorities have basically adopted the attitude "don't ask, don't tell." Remember, as long as there are no meaningful investigations and sting operations such as Operation Greylord from back in the day, then the fake persona that the government wants the public to believe about the judiciary is a much easier sell. It is basically kabuki theater—black robe costume and all.

All of this underscores the point that every state and federal judge and every lawyer in our country should be required to take a yearly polygraph exam in order to safeguard the public from malfeasance within the legal profession and judiciary. The American Polygraph Association sets the standards for testing and maintains that polygraphs are "highly accurate," citing an accuracy rate above 90 percent. Polygraph exams are used by law enforcement in criminal investigations, by federal agencies to screen potential employees, and by probation officers to supervise sex offenders. And yet while government agencies employ polygraph exams, it is mind boggling that the judicial system won't allow them to be submitted into evidence. Think about it, the judiciary routinely allows false information on documents to be admitted into evidence in civil and criminal cases and allows for people who have histories of lying and doing very bad things, including felons convicted of heinous crimes, to testify in criminal proceedings at the request of prosecutors. Also, the judiciary allows so called "expert" testimony by lawyers, doctors, forensic professionals, the list goes on, and all of these types of evidentiary testimonies are based on "opinions" of these so called "experts." Very often their "expert" testimony is called into question during trials, but yet in the face of all of those highly questionable sources of information, the judiciary disallows polygraph exam results into evidence despite an accuracy rate of above 90 percent. Polygraph tests should be treated the same way as any other form of questionable evidence that is allowed into a trial of which evidence may be called into question. It makes no sense to forbid an aspect of evidence that has a 90 percent accuracy rate but yet allows evidence that many times has an even zero percent of accuracy. That makes no sense. Polygraph exam results can be challenged just like any other piece of questionable information, but the system is set up to keep information that could be helpful in getting to the bottom of the truth out of the proceedings. Polygraph exams have a very high rate of accuracy, and in most cases, are more accurate than information being allowed into evidence. This would seem to be a no-brainer.

Currently, there are 23 states that are open to polygraph exams being used in court, mostly in civil cases but not in criminal cases; and they require the approval of both parties before they can be submitted. In Florida, California, Georgia, and Nevada, polygraph exams can be used if everyone agrees to it. In California, lawyers can present the results to the jurors and allow them to make up their minds. So if polygraph tests are good enough for the Florida, California, Georgia, and Nevada courts, it stands to reason that they should be good enough for all courts in all of the states. Because there is such a major concern with judges accepting bribes in court cases, which was proven to be the case in Greylord, common sense dictates the need for a yearly polygraph testing requirement of judges and lawyers, and a need for every judge who has been accused of wrongdoing in a case to be required to submit to a polygraph exam whenever there is an issue of corruption submitted against a judge. It is a crime against the people when lawyers and judges are allowed to operate in an unmonitored and unfettered system that allows them to line their pockets with money in court-related shenanigans. The infestation of corrupt judges and other corrupt court personnel is a very serious problem without question. Polygraph testing of judges can help cure that problem, and it should be done.

Anybody who isn't willing to consider the very real possibility that state and federal judges are being bought off for favorable decisions, or that they aren't fixing decisions in certain cases as personal or political favors, isn't being realistic. Judges have the perfect situation for it. They are basically unmonitored and come and go as they please. They are insulated from public scrutiny to a very high degree, and even when they are suspected of wrongdoing, there are mechanisms in place to protect them such as their own brethren judges who make the decisions about any judicial misconduct complaints that are filed against them. Even then, the proceedings are done in secret. Think about it, when was the last time that you read or heard about any state or federal judge who went through a public court trial regarding malfeasance issues? The reason you never hear of public court proceedings against any judges is because public trials against corrupt judges are basically nonexistent. Even in the few cases when they are caught with the goods, they are treated with kid gloves and given sweetheart deals that regular people don't get. Law enforcement agencies and courts routinely bring the hammer down against the regular people of society, but when it comes to judges who violate the laws, the "system" simply will not do it—and that is very sad.

CHAPTER 14
HOW THE COURTS FLEECE THE PUBLIC

"A body of men holding themselves accountable to nobody ought not to be trusted by anybody."
~ Thomas Paine

Ka-ching, ka-ching $$! This is what courts are all about. MONEY! Collecting peoples' money! Make no mistake about it, the judiciary is basically a **cabal** devoted to fleecing people out of their money. The proof is in the pudding. The moment a person walks into a court clerk's office to file a case, the clerk will demand payment for a filing fee—and court filing fees are very hefty. People currently have to pay $402 to file a federal lawsuit. State court filing fees vary depending on the location, but they are generally in the hundreds of dollars. Some state courts even charge a certain fee each time a motion is filed in the case. And how about the costs for depositions—this is a big cash cow for court reporters. Court reporters charge mega bucks for depositions such as an appearance fee, an hourly rate, and usually a charge of several dollars per page if you want a copy of the transcript of the proceeding. Depending on how many witnesses are deposed and how long the depositions are, it very easily runs into several thousands of dollars. And whenever a person loses a court case, whether the case is dismissed by the judge or a losing verdict at trial, and the person would like to appeal, there is a very hefty filing fee—currently $505 for a notice of appeal in the federal appellate courts, and into the hundreds in the various state courts whose appellate filing fees vary from state to state. And when there is an appeal—whether in state or federal court—the person will require a transcript of the court proceedings. That person almost needs to be prepared to take a second loan out on their mortgage because it often involves many thousands of dollars. And there are many other ridiculously high fees that state and federal courts charge for copies of documents and a plethora of other things. With the exception of South Dakota, which charges a reasonable fee of $70 for a filing fee and related costs including a jury trial, the rest of the state courts and the federal judiciary choose to fleece the public; and make no mistake about it, fleece the public they do.

And once a litigant loses his or her case in a federal appellate court, they must then resort to the Supreme Court of the United States, which fleeces the people out of their money to an immorally high level. And the kicker is that the Supreme Court of the United States doesn't have to review peoples' cases as a matter of right, and in fact only reviews a very small handful of cases filed, approximately 3 percent, but doesn't mind at all collecting a filing fee of $300 from people for filing cases that it essentially will refuse to review. And after the Supreme Court collects the $300 from a litigant, it then has a very expensive policy requiring the litigants to file a booklet with a certain opaque unglazed typeset, 6 1/8 by 9 1/4 inches in size, and not less than 60 pounds in weight. And the booklet must be bound with saddle stitch or perfect binding preferred, and on top of all of that, 40 copies of the booklet must be filed. Most people obviously don't have the capability to do all of these stringent requirements and must have a specialty printer do this work, which is very expensive to say the least. It is absolutely ridiculous and essentially immoral for the Supreme Court to require people to have to spend so much money to file their cases and then force them to have to pay for such elaborate booklets for cases that essentially are not even going to be reviewed. This is unnecessary nonsense as all of this could be done by electronic filing, which all of the state and federal courts not only utilize, but prefer, as it is a much more efficient and less costly process—but not the Supreme Court. The Supreme Court prefers that people should have to pay thousands of dollars to prepare the petitions and briefs, which of course keeps the cash flow running. One must wonder what the real goal is? One could certainly come to a conclusion that the primary goal isn't about "justice" but more so to make money off of the people to enrich the financial coffers of the judiciary and law-related businesses that are very happy to take the peoples' money. That is very sad and very unfortunate, to say the least. The court system is using the people as a cash cow with little to no regard for justice. Let's call a spade a spade here.

Courts charge people all of this money even though they are funded by taxpayer money in the first place—in effect courts receive a double windfall, first from the taxpayers, and then from the litigants. Court fees are outrageous and essentially cost-prohibitive against many people who are in need of justice and depend on the courts to obtain it. And this is exactly why the courts know they are able to get away with the exorbitant fees. The courts know that the people are desperate for justice and are willing to pay the excessive fees for a chance at it—but have very little chance of receiving it. It's all about the money and very little about justice.

The pro se's (litigants who represent themselves without a lawyer) are a major windfall for the courts. Almost all pro se cases are dismissed at very early stages. It doesn't matter that the people who represent themselves have a right to their day in court, the courts have little to no respect for the rights of unrepresented litigants. When Judge Richard A. Posner retired from the U.S. Court of Appeals for the Seventh Circuit in Chicago, he made that point very clear when he publicly revealed that the judges on the Seventh

Circuit Court of Appeals in Chicago viewed pro se litigants as "trash." He said, "None of the judges paid any attention to the pro se's..." and "The basic thing is that most judges regard these people a kind of trash not worth the time of a federal judge." But the Seventh Circuit Court of Appeals in Chicago, as well as all of the state and federal district courts and appellate courts all across the country, certainly have no problem in taking the money from the pro se's even though the vast majority of the cases for which they accept a hefty filing fee are pretty much already predisposed and will never get a meaningful review. Judge Posner certainly underscored the fact that the courts are very hostile to pro se litigants and that the courts have a bad habit of routinely dismissing pro se lawsuits—which is a serious problem in the country—but the courts don't mind collecting the hefty filing fees and other court fees from the pro se's, and then after taking their money, they essentially prefer not to hear from them, and for the most part, throw their cases into a garbage can. If a regular business did the same thing in collecting money from people under false pretenses, it would be in trouble and risk losing its business license, or even be prosecuted, but when courts do it, it is perfectly fine, even though it is essentially a racketeering operation designed to fleece people out of their money under false pretenses. That is exactly what is going on in the state and federal court systems in the United States, including the Supreme Court. When the common criminal bilks people out of their money under false pretenses, it's considered a crime, but when courts do it, it's considered a service. Something is very wrong with that picture.

When it is all said and done, let's face it, courts are essentially a criminal enterprise based on making money through their illicit actions—basically a RICO-type operation. Merriam-Webster dictionary defines racketeering as "a patten of illegal activity that is carried out in furtherance of an enterprise which is owned or controlled by those engaged in such activity." It stands to reason that since courts are taking exorbitant amounts of money from people for so-called "filing fees" while at the same time having predisposed notions about their cases and not giving them their entitled "day in court" by way of their routine dismissal of peoples' cases, of which conduct is controlled by the judges of the courts, then a plausible argument can be made that the courts are thereby involved in racketeering. Let's call it what it actually is.

American courts are the white-collar version of the Mafia, just using different tactics to achieve the same objectives in terms of profiteering. Fraud is fraud, and what the courts are doing is committing fraud under the guise of "justice." Fraud is a crime such as with Ponzi schemes or when people or companies swindle people out of their money. It is just as equally a crime when courts swindle people out of their money by charging hefty filing fees for the promise of "justice" in their cases but instead cater to influential parties such as wealthy and powerful corporations, insurance companies, and government agencies, and throw favorable decisions their way. It happens all the time, especially with summary judgments when courts issue rulings determining that peoples' cases should be dismissed rather than having a jury see the evidence and make a determination.

Without question, people are used as a cash cow for the courts. Courts depend on revenues for them to exist, so every time a person files a case and pays several hundreds of dollars for the filing fee, the courts profit. This money keeps judges, bailiffs, and many other court personnel employed. Many times, the court personnel are family members or close friends of the judges, and the money that people pay into the court system keeps these people employed. It's basically a shell game that the judiciary plays with the public to fleece people out of their money for filing fees and other court-related costs under the guise of a court proceeding that is supposed to be a fair process but is really nothing more than a predetermined façade designed to extract money from people in order to keep the judiciary's coffers filled. So when the judge walks into the courtroom wearing the "black robe" and the courts require everybody to stand up in reverence to the person wearing the "black robe," in essence genuflecting, people are essentially being required to stand up in respect of a criminal enterprise. It is tantamount to a burglar requiring everybody to stand in respect of his face mask, the only difference between the two are the attire—one type of thief wearing a face mask, and the other type of thief wearing a black robe.

CHAPTER 15
WHO DIED AND MADE JUDGES KINGS?
THE GRAND LIFESTYLE OF THE JUDICIARY

"The law is king."
~ Thomas Paine

We have a very serious problem in our state and federal judiciaries with judges acting as though they are kings and treating the litigants before them as though they are their subjects. Many judges let the power of being a judge go to their heads and act as though they are royalty with unlimited power, forgetting that they have a set of canons that they are supposed to be following requiring them to be cordial to all litigants and participants in a court case. To be fair, not all judges are like that, but it is a very significant widespread problem all across the country at every level of the judiciary. Many judges feel that once they put on the black robe that they somehow are allowed to abdicate their obligations to treat litigants fairly and that they have a license to bully people appearing before them just as kings did back in medieval times. It apparently makes them feel big and powerful when, in reality, it makes them very small and very puny. They are drunk with power—a "black robe disease." Think about it, when a king enters the room, he wears a robe, and the subjects must bow. When a judge enters the room, he or she also wears a robe, and the people (the subjects), are directed to stand—and are expected to stand until given permission to sit. A king's throne is elevated above his subjects, and he looks down on his subjects when he addresses them. A judge's large padded chair (throne) is elevated above the commoners (the subjects), and the judge looks down on them when he or she addresses them. When a king's subjects address him, they address the king as "Your Majesty;" when commoners in the American courts address a judge, they address the judge as "Your Honor." The judicial charade couldn't be more pretentious. To say that it is all a big charade would be an understatement. The charade gives new meaning to kabuki theater.

The last I checked, the United States is not a monarchy, and judges are not royalty—although there probably are some judges who think they are. But in reality, judges are nothing more than lawyers who were politically connected enough that they were able to get a judicial appointment. Judges are simply lawyers wearing a costume—a black robe. We should be spared the charade and move into reality mode. As for people having to stand up when a judge enters a courtroom and being required to address the judge as "Your Honor" when "Mr." or "Ms." would suffice just fine, I think is a farce and overkill—judges are not royalty. To put it bluntly, this part of the charade is essentially akin to having to stand and show reverence to a lawyer and address that person as "Your Honor," someone who is basically just a politically-connected cockroach lawyer feeding from the public trough while wearing a black robe, which is nothing more than a costume, who then becomes emboldened to act as though he or she is a super being of some sort and superior to the general population. And if the truth were told, many of the lawyers who have become judges in one way or another actually lacked qualifications to be a judge, and many had questionable backgrounds and were appointed to the bench without proper vetting and are there because of one reason, and one reason only—political connections. Some people call them public parasites living off of the taxpayers' dime. I fail to see the royalty of it. There should be no requirement for a citizen to have to address a public employee—make no mistake about it, judges are nothing more than public employees, nothing more, nothing less—as "Your Honor." And let's not forget that many of the lawyers who became judges had plenty of "dishonor" in their wheeling and dealings as a lawyer. Lawyers who become judges should always keep in mind that should they choose to conduct themselves in a dishonorable manner, that that is exactly how they will be perceived by the public. There is no "honor" in "dishonor," especially so with judges.

And when you think about it, it's not like judges own the courtroom and the courthouse and the office equipment, or even the black robes they wear. They don't own any of it, yet act as though the courtroom is their personal kingdom when, in fact, the courtroom actually belongs to the people as we pay for the lights and the existence of the very courtroom over which the judge presides. The judge is simply a public employee, nothing more and nothing less—and certainly not a king. The courthouse is not a judge's personal kingdom, it is the property of the people; as such, the people are the masters and the judges are the servants—not the other way around. To be clear, the judges do not own the courthouses or courtrooms—the taxpayers do; the judges do not pay the light bills—the taxpayers do; the judges don't even pay for the black robes they wear—the taxpayers do. So in reality, the judges are operating in rent-free facilities and even the black robes they wear are basically clothes furnished to them free of charge on the taxpayers' dime. So it stands to reason that we, the people, are the landlords, and the judges are the tenants, and yet judges expect the public to kiss their rings and be mesmerized by them. Society needs a rethinking on this point.

Unfortunately, we have far too many misfit politically-connected lawyers dressed up in black robes. The people have put up with this judicial nonsense for far too long and need to take a stand. The brainwashing and kabuki theater has gone on long enough, and it is now time to remove the illusional masks of "grandeur" and put on the masks of "reality." The black robes do not make the judges our masters—as the judges think. The judges are actually our servants who are supposed to be serving the citizenry by dispensing justice in a fair and even-handed manner whether they like it or not—and most don't like it. The federal judges are part of the federal government, meaning they work for the citizenry. We need to take heed to what Thomas Jefferson admonished long ago when he said, "Does the government fear us? Or do we fear the government? When the people fear the government, tyranny has found victory. The federal government is our servant, not our master!" This holds true for federal judges, who we should not fear. And because Thomas Jefferson answered his rhetorical question by emphasizing that the federal government is our servant and not our master, he made it crystal clear by that statement that the federal government is our servant, and, we, the people, are the master, and not the other way around. As a society, we need to educate the federal judiciary of this important fact and that it needs to clean up its act or we, the people, the masters of the federal government, will use our free speech power under the First Amendment, as well as our voting power, to pressure the recreant politicians responsible for serving up misfit judges to have those misfit gargoyles purged from the judiciary.

As a society, we are conditioned to believe that we should always trust our state and federal judiciaries to be honest and believe that they always do justice. There are many different ways that we are conditioned to hold such a belief. Etched onto the exterior and interior walls of the state and federal courthouses are phrases that are designed to make us feel safe and secure and that we should trust the judiciary in every way. For example, the phrase "Equal Justice Under Law" is engraved above the front entrance of the United States Supreme Court building in Washington, D.C. Judges wear black robes creating an impression of dominance, and courts insist that people stand up in reverence to judges when they enter the courtroom as if they are gods. They even have a special term for their offices, namely, "chambers." And judges of state supreme courts and the United States Supreme Court insist that they be addressed as "Justice." And when trying to display their power when addressing a person with whom they are having an issue, the judge will loudly blurt out "My Courtroom" as if it were the personal property of the judge, when in point of fact the courtroom is the property of the taxpayers and not the personal property of the judge. If a person didn't know any better, he or she would think that the judiciary is a certain form of royalty.

The only thing "royal" about federal judges is that they receive "royal" salaries which, in effect, results in a "royal" screw job against the public—the taxpayers—who get tapped to pay the enormous lifetime salaries of the federal judges. As of 2022, federal district court judges currently are paid $223,400 a year, circuit judges are paid $236,900 a year; associate supreme court justices are paid $274,200 a year; and the chief justice of the United States is paid $286,700. And as if these six-figure salaries are meager wages, Chief Justice John Roberts has pleaded for an increase in judicial pay, calling the situation "a constitutional crisis that threatens to undermine the strength and independence of the federal judiciary," suggesting that unless the pay is raised, there will be a pool of lesser talent. Roberts warned that unless judicial pay is significantly raised, that "the Framers' goal of a truly independent judiciary will be placed in serious jeopardy." What happened to the concept of "public service" that we often hear about? By Roberts' statement in pushing for more money for the federal judges, he is essentially saying if the judges are paid more, we will then have an "independent judiciary;" but if they aren't paid more, then we will not have a "truly independent judiciary." That is a very scary thought. When we get to the point that the independence of the federal judiciary is based on monetization, then we are in serious trouble—and that is exactly what Roberts unwittingly spewed.

It is very interesting, actually disheartening, that the Chief Judge of the United States has essentially declared that money is tied to whether or not we will or will not have a "truly independent judiciary." As for the issue of federal judges getting even higher pay as pushed by Chief Justice John Roberts, perhaps the judges should work harder if they want higher pay. And by working harder, for one thing, I mean perhaps they should actually do their jobs and write their own opinions rather than leaving the drafting of opinions to their law clerks—which is, in essence, the law clerks doing their jobs for them. When Judge Richard A. Posner was asked if we were to demand that judges should write their own opinions, he said, "Oh, it'd be great! Half of them would resign immediately." <u>Judge Richard Posner On SCOTUS: 'The Supreme Court Is Awful' - Above the LawAbove the Law</u>. Somehow, I have a hard time buying what Chief Justice Roberts is selling when he said that unless the judges are paid more money that it could result in a "constitutional crisis" that "threatens to undermine the strength and independence of the judiciary." Making well over $200K a year with a lifetime job sounds like a pretty good gig and does not sound much like a "constitutional crisis" as spewed by Chief Justice Roberts who embarrassed himself by spitting out such nonsense. With judges pocketing this much money off of the taxpayers' dime, perhaps it should be the judges standing up in reverence to the people when people enter the courtroom, and not the other way around.

And how big of John Roberts to bring the "Framers" into his sales pitch spewing that unless judicial pay is significantly raised, that "the Framers' goal of a truly independent judiciary would be placed in serious jeopardy." Somehow I don't believe that the Framers would agree with him. And what does Roberts mean by suggesting that unless the judges are paid more money that the judiciary's "independence" would be undermined? Reading between the lines of that statement, it sounds like unless judges are paid more money, then they will make up the difference in other ways, which would, of course, undermine the so called "strength and independence" of the judiciary when judges accept bribes if they don't receive the amount of pay that they want. Invoking "constitutional crises" if federal judges aren't paid more money is very unbecoming—especially when invoked by the Chief Justice of the United States.

And let's not forget that in addition to making well over $200K a year, another perk of the job is the great job security that federal judges enjoy, as it is essentially a lifetime job that they get to keep under the rule "during good behavior"—whatever that means. Article III, Section 1, of the federal constitution states that "The Judges, both of the supreme and inferior Courts, shall hold their Offices during good Behaviour, and shall, at stated Times, receive for their Services, a Compensation, which shall not be diminished during their Continuance in Office." Many federal judges involve themselves in less than "good" behavior, such as mistreating litigants they don't like and showing favoritism to certain lawyers and corporations and government agencies. This, of course, does not constitute "good" behavior, but yet they don't lose their lifetime jobs for these very common occurrences. Federal judges hold their seats until they resign, die, or are removed from office. It is almost impossible for all practical purposes to remove a federal judge as it generally takes an impeachment by the House of Representatives followed by conviction by the Senate; and since the federal judge appointments are all about politics, the politics of it makes it borderline impossible to remove corrupt federal judges. This problem could be solved if the states would be willing to put on their ballots a vote for a constitutional amendment to remove the lifetime appointments of federal judges—there should be term limits. History shows us that lifetime judicial appointments are a bad thing for the American people. Until such time that the people of this country wise up and figure out that the lifetime appointment of federal judges is a bad thing for those who seek justice from the corrupt actions of corporations and government agencies that have harmed them, the escape from that morass will be very difficult and nearly impossible as federal judges will, for the most part, continue to protect unsavory corporations and government agencies. And make no mistake about it, federal judges routinely protect unsavory corporations and government agencies—it's as though it is in their DNA.

And how about the sweet perk of retirement at the current salary? We can thank Congress for creating that lucrative deal so that when federal judges meet certain age and service requirements, they may retire and then earn their final salary for the remainder of their lives—plus cost-of-living expenses. The "Rule of 80" is shorthand for the age and service requirement for a judge to retire. Beginning at age 65, a federal judge may retire at his or her current salary after performing 15 years of active service. There is a sliding scale of increasing age and decreasing service also, for example, retiring at age 70 with only a minimum of 10 years of service would qualify. Congress put this in play via the Judiciary Act of 1869. To be clear here, this "Act" was created by Congress; it is not in the federal Constitution. Article III, Section 1, of the federal Constitution states that the compensation of federal judges "shall not be diminished **during** their Continuation in Office." The Constitution does not mandate that the amount the federal judge was receiving as a final salary should be the amount that the judge should receive for the remainder of his or her life **after** retiring. To be clear, the Constitution does not provide for a full pension set at the salary of the judge at the time of retirement. It was ludicrous for Congress to do this. Not a bad retirement package that the politicians set up for the federal judges—too bad the regular everyday working person can never get such a sweet deal. Fleecing the taxpayers by requiring us to pay for such an outlandish pension plan for federal judges is a major abuse of the taxpayers' money, and Congress should put a stop to it. This is something that Congress could change—if it wanted to. After all, Congress giveth, and Congress can taketh away. Our government does it all the time. <u>Governments Giveth and Taketh Away · Brownstone Institute</u>. State court judges do quite well also, as their salaries and benefits range from state to state. But one thing is for certain, while judges are not "royalty" by any stretch of the imagination, their salaries and benefits are "fit for a king!"

Quite frankly, the reward of a retirement pension set at the salary of the judge at the time of retirement is not appropriate. Such an outlandish perk should be eliminated. Congress has the power to eliminate it—and it should do so. It is ironic that judges making this kind of money for life have no problem in screwing over people in employment cases who sue for wrongful termination and are fighting to keep their jobs, or trying to get rightful compensation from unscrupulous employers that drummed up false reasons as a pretext to terminate them simply because the employer doesn't like them, even though they are performing their work admirably. It happens all the time, and courts are notorious for siding with employers in the vast majority of cases using warped case laws as the vehicle to do so. Judges who don't have to worry about losing their high-paying lifetime jobs have little sympathy for regular people in the workplace who want to keep making a living but are prevented from doing so by an employer who has built a pretextual case to terminate a good employee, which may not even be work related, simply by conjuring up a dubious reason to do so. Don't look for much fairness from a judge making well over $200,000 a year for life to care much about someone who is barely making enough money to make ends meet and has to fight an unscrupulous employer for wrongful termination. That person will then be inevitably forced to face a battery of corporate lawyers that the judge, in all likelihood, will likely favor. In the eyes of the judges, everything is perfectly fine as long as they are allowed to continue feeding off the public trough—the taxpayers' dime—and be damned to all of the working class people who simply want to be treated fairly when faced with the wrongful loss of their jobs. The legal community calls this "justice." I call it "injustice."

CHAPTER 16

LIFETIME APPOINTMENTS FOR FEDERAL JUDGES
A VERY BAD IDEA

"If you do not take an interest in the affairs of your government, then you are doomed to live under the rule of fools."
~ Plato

In July 2022 a group of House Democrats introduced a bill to enact term limits for Supreme Court justices in order to "restore legitimacy and independence to the nation's highest court." The proposed legislation was titled the "Supreme Court Tenure Establishment and Retirement Modernization Act" and would authorize the president to nominate Supreme Court justices every two years—in the first and third years after a presidential election. Those individuals would serve a maximum of 18 years on the bench and then retire from active service and assume senior status which would include official duties and pay. The bill was introduced by Hank Johnson (D-Georgia) along with representatives Jerry Nadler (D-New York), David Cicilline (D-Rhode Island), Sheila Jackson Lee (D-Texas), Steve Cohen (D-Tennessee), Karen Bass (D-California), and Ro Khanna (D-California) as co-sponsors. It is worth mentioning here that the United States stands alone as the only advanced democracy that does not have either a fixed term or a mandatory retirement age for judges on its highest court.

Representative Hank Johnson said the bench "is increasingly facing a legitimacy crisis" and pointed out that "Five of the six conservative justices on the bench were appointed by presidents who lost the popular vote, and they are now racing to impose their out-of-touch agenda on the American people, who do not want it." Jerry Nadler said that implementing term limits for justices is "essential" amid "all the harmful and out-of-touch rulings from the Supreme Court this last year." He also stated, "Otherwise, we will be left with backwards-looking majority for a generation or more." While I think the idea of term limits for Supreme Court justices would be a good thing for the country, I don't think the bill is going to go anywhere anytime soon and probably never will—right-wing Republicans simply won't allow it.

There is no question that the federal judiciary and Supreme Court are politicized and abusing the principles that gave rise to the concept of lifetime appointments to the federal judiciary and Supreme Court. Case in point is demonstrated in the controversy surrounding the leaking of the Alito draft opinion just prior to the Supreme Court's overruling of the *Roe v. Wade* case, a fifty-year precedent protecting women's rights to make decisions about their bodies, including having abortions, which brought the country to a tipping point. The events that flowed from the leaking of the Alito draft and the subsequent decision were very telling and cause for high alarm. The country had good reason to be in an uproar. The controversy surrounding the leaking of the Alito draft opinion taught us that the purpose of lifetime federal judicial appointments, which was to ensure an independent judiciary to prevent judges from swaying to political partisan pressures, is not working as it was envisioned at the time it was enacted. That concept went out the window when the information gleaned from the leaked Alito draft opinion revealed that Justices Samuel Alito, Amy Coney Barrett, Brett Kavanaugh, Neil Gorsuch, and Clarence Thomas each had a deep-seated desire to overturn *Roe v. Wade*. Each of them, to put it mildly, was less than truthful during their confirmation hearings when they testified under oath that it was their belief that *Roe v. Wade* was settled law and precedent that should not be overturned. Yet each of these judicial miscreants ignored precedent and overturned *Roe v. Wade* after they lied their merry way onto the Supreme Court.

It would seem that committing perjury by lying under oath during a Senate confirmation hearing would be an impeachable offense, and clearly, Alito, Barrett, Kavanaugh, Gorsuch, and Thomas did so at these hearings, yet each remained untouched. We can thank our members of the United States House of Representatives and the United States Senate for their political cowardice, as well as the political idiots who came up with the concept of lifetime federal judicial appointments, which now sticks us with the likes of such miscreant judges as Alito, Barrett, Kavanaugh, Gorsuch, and Thomas for years of judicial misery.

Previous to that leaked draft opinion, Justice Sonia Sotomayor, in an oral argument on December 1, 2021, on the issue of the 2018 Mississippi abortion law, asked, "Will this institution survive the stench that this creates in the public perception that the Constitution and its reading are just political acts? I don't see how it is possible." To answer Justice Sotomayor's publicly-raised question, the answer is a resounding NO—the Supreme Court as an institution will NOT survive the stench it has created.

Because judges in the federal judiciary and justices on the Supreme Court have generally not been operating with a high degree of trust, the public's confidence level is at an all-time nadir. It should be no surprise that a great portion of the country has a dim view of the Supreme Court and the federal judiciary. A recent Gallup Poll showed a record-low public approval rating of the Supreme Court's performance at only 25 percent—and sinking by the day—as compared to 40 percent of respondents in 2020 and 36 percent in 20121. The poll was released a day before *Roe v. Wade* was overturned. https://www.msn.com/en-us/news/politics/a-record-low-

25-percent-of-americans-have-confidence-in-the-supreme-court-poll/ar-AAYSMQF?ocid=uxbndlbing.

It is clearly time for Congress to revisit and make changes to some laws pertaining to federal judges and Supreme Court justices in terms of the concept of lifetime appointments. The good news is that there are things that Congress can do, and should do, to cure these problems; but the bad news is because of the polarization of Congress and the country, we should not expect any curing to take place anytime soon. It stands to reason that since members of Congress are very conscious of public polls and in large part react to them in the way they make their political decisions, Congress should take heed of the poll showing the public is not happy with what is going on, and that necessary changes must be made by Congress in terms of requiring judges and justices to insulate themselves from the political winds when making decisions or face the consequence of removal from the federal judiciary. And there is a way to do it as Article II of the Constitution gives the United States House of Representatives the power to impeach federal judges and assigns the power to try impeachments to the United States Senate for trial. It is a tool available to Congress to remove miscreant judges, but it is very seldom used—unfortunately.

Impeachment of judges is rare, and removal is even rarer. Since 1803, the House of Representatives has impeached only 15 federal judges—that's only 15 judges in well over 200 years. And only eight of those impeachments were followed by convictions in the Senate. Only one Supreme Court justice, Samuel Chase, has ever been impeached by the House, and he was acquitted by the Senate in 1805. No judges were impeached in the entire 20th century, and only two federal judges have been impeached in the 21st century. The first was Samuel Kent of the United States District Court for the Southern District of Texas for sexual assault, obstructing and impeding an official proceeding, and making false and misleading statements. He resigned from office on July 30, 2009 (the articles of impeachment were dismissed). The second was Thomas Porteous of the United

States District Court for the Eastern District of Louisiana for accepting bribes and making false statements under penalty of perjury who was convicted by the Senate and removed from office on December 8, 2010. Impeachment of state judges has been similarly rare. A review of studies by the American Judicature Society and the National Center for State Courts, as well as news articles, reveals just one instance of a state judge being impeached in the last 25 years. In 2000, New Hampshire impeached, but the state senate declined to remove Supreme Court Justice David Brock.

I think it is fair to say that with only 15 federal judges being impeached in well over 200 years, and only two federal judges in total being impeached in the 21st century, it is not an impressive track record. But that is what happens when the judiciary is allowed so much leeway to police itself and is also provided with so much protectionism, not only from within the judiciary but also from the politicians who are willing to look the other way and disregard the information that people are providing to them about corrupt judges. It is a significant problem. After I saw how the federal court system operates in covering up case fixing, as it did with my case, and how the politicians looked the other way, it is easy for me to understand why so few corrupt judges are impeached. It is indeed a very perverse system, to say the least.

CHAPTER 17

THE MAKEUP OF THE FEDERAL COURT SYSTEM IS A DISGRACE

"When the legislative or executive functionaries act unconstitutionally, they are responsible to the people in their elective capacity. The exemption of the judges from that is quite dangerous enough. I know no safe depository of the ultimate powers of the society, but the people themselves."
~ Thomas Jefferson

According to the Center for American Progress, there is a deep lack of female judges and judges of color, particularly the underrepresentation of women of color who have been historically excluded from the judiciary. The Center expressed that judges from different backgrounds and with different life experiences bring their unique and invaluable perspectives to bear on cases that come before them, and yet we have so few in these particular categories. The picture is a very bleak one of demographic representation across the lower federal courts. For example, across all Article III U. S. District Courts and U.S. Courts of Appeal, people of color make up only 20 percent of all sitting judges and 27 percent of active judges. In all, African-Americans comprise 10 percent of sitting judges and 13 percent of active judges, while Hispanic judges make up about 7 percent and 9 percent of sitting and active judges, respectively. Asian-Americans comprise an even smaller proportion of the lower federal courts as only 2.5 percent of active judges and 4 percent of sitting judges are Asian-American. American Indian judges and those belonging to more than one race or ethnicity each make up about 1 percent or less of the lower federal judiciary.

And in addition to the diversity issue of the federal courts, there is also a significant issue of gender disparity. A case in point is that female judges make up just 27 percent of all lower federal court sitting judges and 34 percent of active judges. Women of color comprise just 7 percent of all sitting judges and 10 percent of all active judges serving on the lower federal courts. African-American women make up only about 3 percent of all sitting judges and 5 percent of all active district and circuit judges. Hispanic women comprise between 2 percent and 4 percent of the lower federal courts, while Asian-American women make up only 1 percent to 2 percent of the lower federal bench. Native American women and women belonging to more than one race or ethnicity make up fewer than 1 percent of all district and circuit judges.

When deciding cases that affect historically underrepresented groups, judges who do not belong to such groups may have difficulty recognizing and contextualizing unique concerns or hardships experienced by those whose freedom or rights are being infringed upon, and this may, and certainly does, result in substantial miscarriages of justice. It goes without saying that questions over the courts' legitimacy arise when cases that have an impact on women and people of color, as well as other underrepresented groups or minorities, are decided by courts whose benches are demographically nondiverse. It would stand to reason that for litigants, more diversity on both the federal and state benches would offer more real substantive benefits, including fairer judicial decisions.

It's a sad day in American jurisprudence when we thump our chests and lay claim to being a country of fairness, and yet the very branch of our government, the judicial branch, that is charged with the responsibility of enforcing the people's rights to fairness itself is a body that woefully lacks the makeup of people that comprise our country. The courts should look more like the makeup of the country, but they don't, and unless and until that changes, the underrepresented and the minorities will never get the fair shake that they not only deserve in principle but that they are entitled to under the law—and consequently there will always be a continual lack of trust by the public against the judiciary as a whole.

Judge Richard A. Posner's book *Reforming the Federal Judiciary: My Former Court Needs to Overhaul Its Staff Attorney Program and Begin Televising Its Oral Arguments* demonstrates the U.S. Court of Appeals for the Seventh Circuit in Chicago as a microcosm of the entire judiciary. Judge Posner underscores in his book just how discriminatory the U.S. Court of Appeals for the Seventh Circuit is against African-Americans in terms of its hiring practices. He points out that there were virtually no African-American staff attorneys in his court and that there have been a total of only two in the last 20 years—two out of about 160 (1.25 percent). The discriminatory practices of the Seventh Circuit are a disgrace. The United States Court of Appeals for the Seventh Circuit is an iniquitous court of disgrace on many different levels, and the country would be well-served if the Seventh Circuit's doors were permanently closed shut and the key thrown away. The nefarious manner in how the Seventh Circuit operates, together with its discriminatory hiring bias against African-Americans for staff attorney positions, should easily spell finis to this immoral court, but it won't happen as this is just how the hierarchy of the federal judiciary wants it—and, unfortunately, what it wants, it gets.

I beg to differ with anybody who would maintain that a federal judiciary made up of judges that do not even come close to looking like what the makeup of the country is would somehow fit the ideals of a country that boasts about fairness and non-discrimination ideals, that such a judiciary would be considered as a treasure of judicial righteousness. How can the people expect a federal judiciary, one that discriminates within itself in terms of excluding underrepresented groups and minorities in its hiring practices, to be a legitimate judiciary when it itself discriminates against the very class of people that it is supposed to be protecting? A federal judiciary that is comprised for the most part of a politically well-connected, white male population, that hands out a token number of judgeships to minorities, is not a judiciary that can be trusted to meaningfully enforce the rights of the underrepresented class of people across the United States in their cases involving discrimination rights. Simply put, a well politically-connected white person simply cannot, by nature, recognize and contextualize the unique hardships that minorities and people of color experience when their freedom or rights have been infringed upon. We have to call it for what it is, and this is exactly what it is. There is no meaningful justice in our country when it comes to the underrepresented and minorities until we have courts across the board that are made up of a composition of judges that reflect the demographic makeup of our country. Without this type of intuition, there is no justice when it comes to the rights of minorities and people of color who seek redress in the federal courts in America.

CHAPTER 18

THE CHIEF JUSTICE OF THE UNITED STATES

THE PROTECTOR IN CHIEF OF SEXUAL PREDATOR JUDGES

"You cannot always control the powers-that-be. You just have to have faith and stand by the things you believe in."
~ Rosa Parks

When sexual harassment of employees in the federal judiciary became a hot topic in 2021, members of both parties introduced the Judiciary Accountability Act of 2021 that would provide some much-needed protection for judicial employees subjected to sexual harassment by judges and other high-level court officials, and would give judiciary workers the same rights and whistleblower protections as other federal employees. The Federal Judiciary Has a Harassment Problem—But There's a Fix (bloomberglaw.com); Text - S.2553 - 117th Congress (2021-2022): Judiciary Accountability Act of 2021 | Congress.gov | Library of Congress. However, on August 25, Roslynn Mauskopf, the director of the Administrative Office of the U.S. Courts, who was hand-picked by Roberts for this position, sent a letter to the House Judiciary Committee indicating that the Judicial Conference of the United States opposes the bill. Roberts to Congress on court reforms: We're on it - SCOTUSblog. Mauskopf wrote that the bill, "fails to recognize the robust safeguards that have been in place within the Judiciary to protect judicial employees, including law clerks, from wrongful conduct in the workplace, including protections against discrimination, harassment, retaliation, and abusive conduct." Mauskopf also wrote that "the bill interferes with the internal governance of the Third Branch...and imposes intrusive requirements on Judicial Conference procedures." https://www.uscourts.gov/news/2021/08/25/judiciary-informs-congress-its-opposition-bill.

Mauskopf's actions in opposing the bill on behalf of the Administrative Office of the United States Courts, and on behalf of Chief Justice John Roberts by proxy, in effect preserved the status quo of federal judges using the federal employees as their sex toys. https://news.bloomberglaw.com/us-law-week/the-federal-judiciary-has-a-harassment-problem-but-theres-a-fix; https://www.congress.gov/bill/117th-congress/senate-bill/2553/text,

CNN Investigation: #MeToo in the courts - CNNPolitics.] Opposing a bill that would have given safeguards to the judicial employees who were subject to being sexually preyed upon by federal judges and high-level judicial officials is hardly a unification of "administration of justice," as Mauskopf spewed in an article published by the United States Courts on September 23, 2022. The Judicial Conference: A Century of Service to the Federal Judiciary | United States Courts (uscourts.gov)

Sexual harassment in the federal judiciary was a topic in Roberts' 2018 year-end report, but it was a very sugarcoated issue. Roberts tried to downplay the significance of the sexual harassment problem in the federal judiciary by stating in his 2021 report that a panel of judges and judicial administrators had concluded in 2018 that although there had been several serious high-profile incidents, "inappropriate workplace conduct is not pervasive within the judiciary." Roberts suggested in his report that although he "appreciated that Members of Congress have expressed ongoing concerns on this important matter, he assured that 'the Judicial Conference and its committees remain fully engaged'." https://www.supremecourt.gov/publicinfo/year-end/2018year-endreport.pdf.

In an article by the *ABA Journal* on January 2, 2019, according to Chief Justice John Roberts, inappropriate workplace conduct isn't pervasive in federal courthouses. According to the article, Roberts wrote in his 2018 Year-End Report on the Federal Judiciary that when misconduct does occur in the federal judiciary, it, "is more likely to take the form of incivility or disrespect than overt sexual harassment, and it frequently goes unreported." Chief Justice Roberts: 'Incivility or disrespect' more frequent than 'overt sexual harassment' in the federal judiciary (abajournal.com).

Roberts' statements lack credibility as he well knows that there is a serious problem with sexual misconduct by federal judges. In fact, the federal judiciary is infested with perverted judges, and Roberts knows it. According to a CNN report, in 1998, U.S. District Court Judge Walter Smith called a deputy clerk into his chambers in the Waco, Texas, courthouse and closed the door behind her. The woman testified in a deposition, "He basically came over to me and put his arms around me and kissed me, and I just froze. I couldn't move." She went on to testify, "And he said, 'Let me make love to you.' And I just freaked out....And then he pulled me to him again, and he kissed me again and stuck his tongue down my throat, and he pressed himself against me...And then he started to try to touch my breasts, and I kind of pushed away and said... 'I need to go'." The next day, Smith sent her a dozen roses. The woman left her job soon after the incident. And then we have the situation in Denver where the local media began looking into alleged misconduct involving prostitutes by District Court Judge Edward Nottingham where according to the 10th Circuit's judicial council order of October 2008, the council was following up on numerous allegations, including whether Nottingham "spent more than $3,000 at a topless nightclub in one evening and that he could not remember how he had spent that money because he had a lot to drink." As an investigation was underway, another misconduct complaint came in from a woman who said she had been a prostitute and that Nottingham had been one of her clients. According to the judicial council report, the woman further alleged that "Nottingham asked her to lie to federal investigators about the nature of their relationship and not disclose that she was a prostitute whom he paid in exchange for sex." Nottingham resigned, and the 10th Circuit judicial council dismissed the complaint the next day. CNN Investigation: #MeToo in the courts - CNNPolitics.

In February 2020, Olivia Warrant testified before the House Judiciary Committee regarding sexual harassment she suffered while clerking for the late Ninth Circuit Judge Stephen Reinhardt. Warren testified how she was met with countless obstacles while attempting to report the harassment through the internal Office of Judicial Integrity. Was Judicial Misconduct Glossed Over in Roberts' Report? | The Crime Report.

In another highly-publicized sex scandal, Alex Kozinski, who was a member of the 9th Circuit U.S. Court of Appeals in San Francisco, resigned in December 2017, after six women—including former law clerks—accused him of engaging in inappropriate comments and behavior. Reportedly, one of Kozinski's former law clerks claimed he (Kozinski) asked her to view pictures of naked people. Chief Justice Roberts promises review of sexual harassment policies in federal courts | Fox News. The *Washington Post* reported that some 15 women had accused Kozinski of sexual harassment. Prominent appeals court Judge Alex Kozinski accused of sexual misconduct - The Washington Post. The *New York Times* reported that the women, many of whom had served as his law clerks, said Kozinski had touched them inappropriately, made unwanted sexual comments, and made them watch sexual materials on his computer. Chief Justice Roberts Reflects on Conflicts, Harassment and Judicial Independence - The New York Times (nytimes.com). In December 2017, Kozinski retired following the accusations. Roberts: Judiciary will review sexual misconduct policies | AP News. In the aftermath of the Kozinski scandal, in June 2018, the HuffPost reported that Jaime Santos, a former law clerk to two federal judges, organized a letter with more than 650 signatures from current and former law clerks calling for significant changes to stem harassment of federal judicial employees. They pushed for a confidential national reporting system that court staff could access. Santos said she spoke to dozens of law clerks and other court staff about workplace harassment, and the information was that it's happening often. She said, "Some shared stories about being asked sexual questions during job interviews, hearing their judge or co-clerks speak about female attorneys in derogatory and objectifying terms, and being groped or kissed in public and in private." She went on to say, "Many knew of other law clerks or employees who had been subjected to harassing or abusive behavior in chambers as well."

And then there was the slap on the wrist reprimand to Judge Carlos Murguia of the District of Kansas by the Judicial Council of the U.S. Court of Appeals for the Tenth Circuit in September 2020, for "inappropriate behavior." Murguia was found to have sexually harassed court employees, with a specific finding that he "gave preferential treatment and unwanted attention" to female employees and engaged in "sexually suggestive comments, inappropriate text messages, and excessive non-work related contacts, much of which occurred after work hours and often late at night." He was also found to have had a years-long extramarital affair with a felon on probation and was "habitually" late for court. After the reprimand, a week later, he was back on the bench. Federal Judge Sexual Harassment Case Sparks Congressional Interest - Above the LawAbove the Law - Federal Judge in Kansas Resigns After Reprimand for Sexual Harassment - The New York Times (nytimes.com).

Make no mistake about it, Roberts very well knows there's a big problem with sexual abuse in the federal judiciary, he just doesn't want the public to know about just how serious of a problem it is. Chief justice calls for judicial independence amid growing political criticism of federal courts | Fox News. The fact that Roberts doesn't want to come clean speaks volumes about the federal judiciary's concealment of sexual abuse activities by federal judges. This is what happens when we are subject to a "secret society" type court, and make no mistake about it, that is exactly what we have in this country with Roberts as Chief Judge of the United States. Judicial misconduct 'undermines confidence' in the system. That's why it's often secret. (yahoo.com).

One thing is for sure, despite Roberts' inappropriate sugar-coating of the topic, there most certainly is a major problem with sexual harassment in the federal judiciary. The country has a right to know how serious a problem it is, and Roberts has an obligation as Chief Judge of the United States to be honest with the public about it. So far, he has failed that test. We all know what happened in the Catholic Church back in the day with pedophile priests running rampant all over the country and church officials looking the other way. It appears that we have the same thing going on in the federal judiciary with the chief justice and high-level court officials similarly looking the other way, with the only difference being that the Catholic church simply transferred the pedophile priests, whereas the Chief Justice of the United States simply leaves the pervert judges in place to do their thing. Roberts has been quoted as saying that the nation's federal courts are doing a better job of policing themselves, which he called essential for the ability of the judicial branch to maintain its independence. Roberts also said that the judiciary's power to manage its own internal affairs "insulates courts from inappropriate political influence and is crucial to preserving public trust in its work as a separate and co-equal branch of government." Chief Justice John Roberts warns against 'inappropriate political influence' in federal courts (nypost.com). Roberts must be delusional if he thinks what the courts are doing with their laughable self-policing is "preserving public trust"—the people simply aren't buying what he is selling. In a recently released Gallup poll, only 25 percent of respondents had confidence in the U.S. Supreme Court. A record low 25 percent of Americans have confidence in the Supreme Court: poll (msn.com).

Roberts' resistance to the adoption of the Judicial Conference code and Mauskopf's objection to the Judiciary Accountability Act of 2021 bill are very concerning, and Roberts' thumping of his chest in making such cavalier statements about how great a job the Supreme Court is doing by policing itself, and his bold statements about how priestly the federal judges have been operating in the lower courts are very much belied by the facts.

As chief justice, Roberts is the nation's highest-ranking judicial official and speaks for the judicial branch of the federal government. He also serves as the chief administrative officer for the federal courts. In this capacity, Roberts heads the Judicial Conference of the United States—the chief administrative body of the U.S. federal courts—and he appoints the director of the Administrative Office of the United States Courts. So it should be interesting to the people who are concerned with sexual harassment in the workplace in the federal judiciary that it was Roberts' own appointment of Roslynn Mauskopf who took it upon herself to oppose the bill that was designed to protect federal employees from sexual harassment in the federal judiciary. It is very interesting that the current Supreme Court majority, led by Roberts, who were hell-bent on overturning women's rights to make decisions about their own bodies in *Roe v. Wade,* have no problem with federal judges and federal judicial officials sexually harassing female employees in the federal judiciary, to which indifference is exemplified in Roberts' appointment of Roslynn Mauskopf as director of the Administrative Office of the U.S. Courts. This is evidenced in the letter she sent to the House Judiciary Committee indicating that the Judicial Conference—headed by John Roberts— opposed the bill, and thus, leaving the employees without any protective safeguards against the federal judges and judicial officials who were sexually preying on them. For that, the vulnerable employees can thank Chief Justice John Roberts and his selection of Roslynn Mauskopf as director of the Administrative Office of the U.S. Courts for their opposition to the bill that would have protected them from the sexual pervert judges and judicial officials who prey on them.

When Roberts thumps his chest and spews that there is no sexual harassment problem to speak of in the federal judiciary, he should tell that to the employees who have been sexually victimized by federal judges and judicial officials, but who receive no protection from the proposed bill that Roberts' own appointed director of the Administrative Office of the U.S. Courts, Roslynn Mauskopf, opposed —with Roberts' blessing. And Roberts should tell that to the women of this country who no longer have the right to make sacred decisions about their own bodies thanks to Roberts and his illegitimate court that includes sexual perverts which has been shown in public confirmation hearings going back to Clarence Thomas and, more recently, Brett Kavanaugh. And we should not forget about the lying members of this illegitimate court—Samuel Alito, Neil Gorsuch, Brett Kavanaugh, and Amy Coney Barrett—who lied at their confirmation hearings in testifying that *stare decisis*—settled law—was the rule of the day when it came to *Roe v. Wade*. However, they then jumped at their first opportunity to disregard the "settled law" from *Roe v. Wade* in order to pacify their crazed right-wing political enablers. All four would be impeached for their perjured testimony at their confirmation hearings if we had a functioning Congress—which we, unfortunately, do not. Perhaps if Roberts, as chief justice, would spend more time working on protecting the people's rights in this country, such as those of employees in the federal judiciary who are being sexually abused by federal judges and judicial officials, rather than worrying about pay raises for the already-rich judges infested in the judiciary, then the public confidence numbers in the Supreme Court wouldn't be nearing rock bottom at such an alarming rate. And it isn't only the general public that is disappointed in Roberts. One of our country's most distinguished federal judges, Richard A. Posner, called Roberts a "terrible manager" of the federal court system and said he (Roberts) made "stupid" decisions. Posner's War on the Supreme Court Continues - FindLaw. It is also very stupid for Roberts to be spewing to the public that the Supreme Court is doing a great job in policing itself, and it is very stupid for Roberts to oppose an ethics bill for the Supreme Court, and it was very stupid for Roberts to have opposed the Judiciary Accountability Act of 2021 that would have provided some much-needed protection for judicial employees subjected to sexual harassment by judges and other high-level court officials, and I will add that it is very stupid for Roberts to think even for a minute that it was a wise move to allow my petition to the Judicial Conference of the United States addressing the case fixing and cover-up going on at the U.S. Court of Appeals in Chicago to be swept under the rug.

In society, there are rules and laws that govern our conduct which we are expected to respect and follow; and in all civilized societies, there are mechanisms in place for the enforcement of those rules and laws. That is part of living in a civilized society. But there is one part of American society that has no code of ethics at all: the Supreme Court of the United States. And believe it or not, the chief justice of the United States is a proponent of the Supreme Court not having a code of ethics. There have been increased calls for the Supreme Court to be subject to a code of ethics, like all other U.S. courts, but Chief Justice John Roberts has consistently opposed this, rejecting all suggestions of congressional or other oversight. In point of fact, the Supreme Court has refused for over 50 years to adopt the Judicial Conference code, or any other code, making it the only court in the United States without a formal set of ethics rules. Roberts' stated position is that the Supreme Court has "no reason to adopt the Code of Conduct as its definitive source of ethical guidance." Roberts says that "every justice seeks to follow high ethical standards" and that they may turn to "judicial opinions, treatises, scholarly articles and disciplinary decisions," and also seek advice from one another. That is laughable. Roberts should consider becoming a stand-up comedian with those lines.

We know that the federal judiciary is permeated with sexual predator judges, judges who preside over cases in which they have a conflict, judges who fix cases, and even judges, including chief judges, who protect case fixing. We know it because I have provided information about case fixing and cover-up going on in the U.S. Court of Appeals in Chicago as was disclosed to me by Judge Richard A. Posner; but the Chief Justice of the United States, John Roberts, takes the position that the federal judiciary should police itself and manage its own internal affairs in order to be able to maintain its "independence." As a society, we are subjected to such judicial corruption because the hierarchy of the federal judiciary is drunk with the power it has been given to the point that the leader of the pack, Chief Justice John Roberts, brazenly tells the public there is no need for codes of conduct and outside oversight as the judiciary will monitor its own internal affairs and "police itself." As a society, we lose when we have to put up with a "secret society" type of judiciary that is allowed to "police itself." Secrecy in the American courts is the worst-kept secret that the courts don't want the people to know about. As I previously stated, it has been written that America is like a banana republic, in that its legal system has become a "sink-well of secret proceedings" in how it is sullied with documented corruption, fake trials, and court fraud. The time has come to unlock those doors of secrecy and let the eyes of the public in, and if Chief Justice John Roberts or any other bottom feeders of the judiciary don't like it, then they should quit feeding off the public trough and go get a real job.

CHAPTER 19
THE JUDICIAL CONFIRMATION HEARINGS ARE A JOKE

"Fools multiply when wise men are silent."
~ Nelson Mandela

There is something fundamentally flawed in the way that federal judges are vetted in the appointment and confirmation process. Federal district court judges, circuit court of appeals judges, and Supreme Court justices are political appointments and are nominated by the president and confirmed by the Senate. Because these are basically lifetime appointments, senators should be much more inquisitive in the selection process. Quite frankly, the questions that senators ask at the Senate confirmation hearings of the judicial nominees are getting to be old hat and are not helpful to the concerned public in terms of the limited subject matter of questions asked.

The public has become quite accustomed to hearing the same types of questions time after time whenever there is a Senate confirmation hearing, irrespective of which political party is in power. The issues that are thrust into the confirmation hearings are always the hot-button issues involving abortion rights, gun control, and so forth, as well as a handful of other issues that may have made it to the front pages of the day. It's the same old drill every time as the senators from each party frame their questions in the manner that suits their political interests the best, and we get the standard canned responses back from the judicial nominees. And without exception, there are always several Supreme Court precedents that make their way into the questioning, such as *Roe v. Wade,* while the judicial nominees sit there looking like trained lap dogs barking out the "politically correct" canned answers—and then wait for their treat. The senators act as though there are no other issues meaningful to the public other than the regular, hot-button issues of the day. Every time there is a televised confirmation hearing, it seems like a rerun with the same old standard questions from the senators, and in return, the same old canned answers from the nominees. And this terribly choreographed rerun needs to stop being played.

I have yet to watch a Senate confirmation hearing where any senators have asked federal judicial nominees about their track record as to their dismissal of cases. I think this would be a very important question that the public would find interesting. After all, we want judges on the federal judiciary who are actually issuing fair and honest rulings in cases that people bring against corporations and government agencies. We don't want judges who are hell-bent on ruling in favor of corporations and government agencies and depriving people of their day in court by an overzealous desire to dismiss cases—and the judiciary is certainly infested with plenty of those types of judges. A judge's high-frequency rate in dismissing people's cases against corporations and government agencies is a bright red flag, and the judicial nominees should be required to answer questions about the number of cases they dismiss, but the senators don't ask questions about it. Because common lawsuits are not sensational in nature and generally don't make it onto the front page, senators don't ask questions about those types of cases, even though this issue is very important to the everyday person who may be looking for justice in the federal judiciary, but not getting it. This is incompetence of the highest degree, and any senator who doesn't want to ask a judicial nominee about his/her rate of dismissal of cases shouldn't be involved in the judicial confirmation process and shouldn't be voting on judges.

Also, far too often the public is forced to listen to legal jargon such as the words "stare decisis," which was overused in the most recent confirmation hearing of Amy Coney Barrett. https://lawreview.syr.edu/the-nomination-of-amy-coney-barrett-and-the-future-of-stare-decisis/. Most people have no idea what this ("stare decisis") means, so rather than asking questions in laymen's terms where people can understand what is going on, the lawyer-dominated proceedings are designed to impress the public with their fanciful legal jargon, while pushing through their political favorites. People would much rather listen to testimony from a prospective judge explaining his or her alarming track record of dismissing cases of the everyday person who is seeking justice rather than listening to the fanciful legal jargon which is obviously calculated to make them (the senators) look smarter than the average citizen while they are sitting in their highchairs and posing for television cameras.

Another question senators don't like to ask is if there have been any judicial misconduct complaints lodged against the particular nominee. After all, if the prospective judge is to end up on the bench for life, it would seem that the people have a right to know if there have been problems with the particular nominee's behavior that would render the nominee to be unfit. If the nominee isn't willing to discuss allegations of misconduct submitted against him or her, then that is a red flag, and the nominee should be eradicated from the process right then and there. The stakes are too high for the public to have to risk potentially ending up with dishonest, corrupt, and immoral judges, and even perverts, on the federal judiciary.

A telling example of Congress's lack of due diligence when vetting judicial nominees was the mishandled process of Richard W. Roberts who was appointed in 1998 and became the chief U.S. District Judge in Washington, D.C. NBC News reported that a lawsuit was filed by a woman, Terry Mitchell, who was a witness in a case that Roberts was prosecuting when he was a civil rights lawyer for the U.S. Justice Department. The lawsuit claimed that Roberts raped her repeatedly in 1981. She was 16 years old at the time, according to the lawsuit, and alleges that "Defendant Roberts intimidated, coerced, and manipulated Mitchell to have sexual intercourse nearly every day for several weeks." Reportedly, Roberts submitted a letter of resignation as news of the suit emerged, citing "health reasons." https://www.nbcnews.com/news/us-news/lawsuit-accuses-chief-federal-judge-d-c-raping-minor-n540556.

According to Prison Legal News, had Roberts remained on the federal bench in D.C., he may have faced a congressional inquiry as a result of Mitchell's lawsuit. https://www.prisonlegalnews.org/news/2017/jun/9/chief-federal-judge-dc-resigns-after-lawsuit-accuses-him-rape/.

The question is: why didn't Congress inquire about this behavior during the vetting process? How in the world could this guy be confirmed after engaging in such sexual misconduct with a young lady of 16 years of age? This ineptness falls on the shoulders of the senators for not doing their due diligence.

This is a loudly-rung bell, and the senators should start paying attention and start doing their due diligence when vetting the federal judicial nominees, and this means *all* federal judicial nominees at *every* level. I say *all* federal judicial nominees at *every* level because while the U.S. Supreme Court is the highest court in the land, most of the public scrutiny and press coverage comes about whenever there is an appointment to the Supreme Court, and not nearly as much public scrutiny and press coverage when it comes to appointments of the district and appellate judges. People need to realize that it is the district court judges who issue the initial rulings and conduct the trials, and it is the appellate judges who hear appeals of lower court decisions. There should be significant public scrutiny of those judges as well. And because the media doesn't provide much coverage of the confirmation hearings of the district court and appellate judges, the politicians have a much easier time pushing those judges through confirmation, and consequently we end up with terrible judges. While the U.S. Supreme Court may be the highest court in the land, it only hears approximately 2 percent of the cases it reviews each year. What this means is that the vast majority of cases that are filed in federal court are ultimately decided by judges on the district or appellate courts; for that reason, common sense dictates that there should be much more attention paid to the district court and appellate court nominees.

Senators need to spend less time on questions about the nominees' ideological beliefs and ask more questions about the nominees' records of high dismissal rates of cases and why so many people are being deprived of their day in court. Senators should also ask questions about whether there is a history of any kind regarding sexual abuse on the part of the nominee. Clearly, they missed the mark when they vetted Richard W. Roberts. Senators shouldn't just be limiting questions about a Supreme Court nominee's history of sexual abuse, they should be asking the same questions of all nominees to the federal judiciary, including nominees to the district and appellate courts where there clearly is a troubling history of it. The people are getting tired of the same old kabuki theater every time there is a judicial confirmation hearing.

Since the senators don't want to ask the right questions and prefer to proceed with the unacceptable status quo, then perhaps it might be time for the citizenry to start asking the questions of the judicial nominees. And perhaps it is time to consider doing something that has never been done before that may well be a refreshing solution to the problem. Perhaps it is time to start appointing non-lawyers to the federal judiciary. Most people don't realize that there is no express requirement that federal judges possess law degrees. There is nothing in the Constitution that requires a person to have a law degree to serve as a federal judge. And we should not forget that the Constitution is the supreme law of the land, which means that it wouldn't forbid a person with no law degree to serve as a federal judge. https://www.law.cornell.edu/constitution/articlevi.

Lord knows that we already have too many lawyers in places of power who influence decision-making—many of which are not helpful to the plain and ordinary people of our country. Perhaps it would be a good thing to take away some of that power from lawyers and start putting in federal judges who are non-lawyers, just as the Constitution permits. In discussing that there are 1.3 million lawyers in the United States and the inadequacies in the federal judiciary and Supreme Court, which is comprised solely of lawyers serving as judges, former federal court of appeals judge Richard A. Posner weighed in that "Nor should lawyers be the only candidates. A brilliant businessman, politician or teacher might make an excellent justice or judge, as long as smart law clerks handle the technicalities, which are mostly 'antiquated crap'" and that "Our current Supreme Court would be greatly improved....if, in lieu of the weaker justices, some nonlawyers took their place." 'No need for octogenarians' on the bench, including those on the Supreme Court, Posner says (abajournal.com).

The people's interests in fairness and justice would be much better served if regular people were part of the judicial process. And then perhaps the public's confidence in the federal judiciary may improve. We should give it a try. Since the senators are incapable, or unwilling, to provide us with a judiciary that actually cares about the regular people of our country rather than their own political self-interests, then perhaps it is time for the "power of the people" to step in and remedy the situation: And the remedy would be to start putting some regular people on the benches in order to cleanse the outmoded system of the judiciary's built-in prejudicial shortcomings. The lawyers need to step aside in order for the black robes to be retailored to custom fit the regular people of our country. The Constitution would allow it!

Truth be told, the whole thing is a charade, nothing more than kabuki theater. Judge Richard A. Posner warned us that the politicians don't care about the quality of judges: "They're politicians; they're interested in politics, they're not interested in having good judges." Judge Richard Posner On SCOTUS: 'The Supreme Court Is Awful' - Above the LawAbove the Law. Posner said, "Those politicians don't care about quality beyond a minimum, a very low minimum," Posner backs 19-member Supreme Court, comments on 'pompous lawyers' (abajournal.com). How much more information do we need for it to sink in that the judiciary is an outmoded, broken-down system in need of a major transformation in terms of much-needed judicial reform? Judge Posner sounded the alarm. Now, we, the people, need to take heed.

CHAPTER 20
THE SUPREME COURT IS ESSENTIALLY AN ILLEGITIMATE COURT

"No amount of evidence will ever persuade an idiot."
~ Mark Twain

Chief Justice John Roberts has been a dismal failure and disappointment in many different ways, especially so in opposing a much-needed code of ethics for the Supreme Court. Roberts has consistently defended the Supreme Court's refusal to adopt the Judicial Conference code, or any other code, making it the only court in the United States without a formal set of ethics rules. Roberts says that the Supreme Court has "no reason to adopt the Code of Conduct as its definitive source of ethical guidance" because "every Justice seeks to follow high ethical standards." Yeah, right! Supreme Court Chief Justice John Roberts gives an incomplete history lesson on judicial ethics (nbcnews.com). After all, when it comes to "ethics," let's not forget that we have Clarence Thomas, Samuel Alito, Brett Kavanaugh, Amy Coney Barrett, and Neil Gorsuch on the Supreme Court. What could go wrong? What we are stuck with now as a country is a chief justice who doesn't believe in an ethics code for the Supreme Court, and we are also stuck with several members of the court who got on the court by lying at their confirmation hearings when asked about their views on precedent, specifically whether they believe that the precedent set forth in *Roe v. Wade* should hold—they all testified that it should, but we now know they lied.

And because of the lies of these so-called "justices," the country is now at a tipping point with the Supreme Court's overturning of *Roe v. Wade* in June 2022, an action undertaken by the Supreme Court in a corrupt manner with the help of dishonest and unethical justices who lied under oath during their confirmation hearings in order to get on the Supreme Court to advance judicial corruption with the primary goal of overturning *Roe v. Wade* in order to end the constitutional right to abortion established by that decision in 1973. Make no mistake about it, that is exactly what happened here with the placement of illegitimate judges to do the dirty work for right-wing extremists. Clearly, the shenanigans that took place to get the dishonest judges placed on the Supreme Court in order to have *Roe v. Wade* overturned is, as they say in legal terms, "Exhibit A," showing that the Supreme Court of the United States is an illegitimate court. Without question, the Supreme Court has reached a real nadir.

We should not forget how we got to this point—nor should we be surprised. After all, the overturning of *Roe v. Wade* was the direct result of four justices who lied under oath at their confirmation hearings when they vowed to respect the precedent of *Roe v. Wade*, what is referred to in legal terms as "stare decisis." As discussed in previous chapters, stare decisis is a concept developed at the common law that means to "stand by things decided." Neil Gorsuch, during his 2017 confirmation hearings, testified that *Roe* was "a precedent of the U.S. Supreme Court. It was reaffirmed in *Casey* in 1992 and in several other cases. *Planned Parenthood v. Casey* was a 1992 decision that affirmed *Roe*." Gorsuch also testified under oath, "So a good judge will consider it as precedent of the U.S. Supreme Court worthy as treatment of precedent like any other." And when Senator Dianne Feinstein pressed him on whether *Roe* had achieved a status as a "super-precedent," Gorsuch said that the ruling "has been reaffirmed many times, I can say that."

And then there is Brett Kavanaugh who, during his 2018 confirmation hearings, testified that *Roe* was an "important precedent of the Supreme Court that has been reaffirmed many times." And when Senator Feinstein asked him what he meant by "settled law" and whether he believed *Roe* to be correct law, Kavanaugh said he believed it was "settled as a precedent of the Supreme Court" and should be "entitled the respect under principles of stare decisis." Kavanaugh also said *Casey* was a "precedent on precedent." He said, "It is not as if *[Roe]* is just a run-of-the-mill case that was decided and never reconsidered, but *Casey* specifically reconsidered it, applied the stare decisis factors, decided to reaffirm it."

And then there is Amy Coney Barrett who, during her confirmation hearings in 2020, weeks before the November elections, testified under oath that she was committed to obeying "all the rules of stare decisis," promising that "if a question comes up before me about whether *Casey* or any other case should be overruled, that I will follow the law of stare decisis, applying it as the court is articulating it, applying all the factors, reliance, workability, being undermined by later facts in law, just all the standard factors." She testified under oath, "I promise to do that for any issue that comes up, abortion or anything else."

And then there is Samuel Alito who wrote the majority opinion ending *Roe* who said during his 2006 confirmation hearing that *Roe* was an "important precedent of the Supreme Court." He said, "it was decided in 1973, so it has been on the books for a long time." He also said, "The more often a decision is reaffirmed, the more people tend to rely on it," and he went on to say, "I think that's entitled to considerable respect, and of course, the more times that happens, the more respect the decision is entitled to, and that's my view on that..." <u>What conservative justices said about Roe at their confirmation hearings (msn.com)</u>.

Most people knew that these judges were lying at their confirmation hearings, but there were two very stupid senators who allowed themselves to be duped: Susan Collins, a Republican from Maine, and Joe Manchin, a Democrat from West Virginia. But in the aftermath of the *Roe* decision where both Kavanaugh and Gorsuch voted to overturn *Roe v. Wade*, Collins said, "This decision is inconsistent with what Justices Gorsuch and Kavanaugh said in their testimony and their meetings with me, where they both were insistent on the importance of supporting long-standing precedents that the country has relied upon." Manchin said he's "deeply disappointed in the justices." He also said, "I trusted Justice Gorsuch and Justice Kavanaugh when they testified under oath that they also believed *Roe v. Wade* was settled legal precedent and I am alarmed they chose to reject the stability the ruling has provided for two generations of Americans." Collins, Manchin suggest they were misled by Kavanaugh and Gorsuch on Roe v. Wade (msn.com), 'Alarmed' Joe Manchin Accepts He's Been Played by Kavanaugh and Gorsuch (thedailybeast.com). And let's not forget that back in 2018, during the Kavanaugh confirmation hearings, Collins said, "I do not believe that Brett Kavanaugh will overturn *Roe v. Wade*." Susan Collins, who voted for Kavanaugh and Gorsuch, suggests Supreme Court justices misled her (msn.com).

In a floor speech defending her vote for Kavanaugh, Collins said, "As Judge Kavanaugh asserted to me, a long-established precedent is not something to be trimmed, narrowed, discarded, or overlooked. Its roots in the Constitution give the concept of stare decisis greater weight such that precedent can't be trimmed or narrowed simply because a judge might want to on a whim. In short, his views on honoring precedent would preclude attempts to do by stealth that which one has committed not to do overtly. Noting that *Roe v. Wade* was decided 45 years ago, and reaffirmed 19 years later in *Planned Parenthood v. Casey*, I asked Judge Kavanaugh whether the passage of time is relevant to following precedent. He said decisions become part of our legal framework with the passage of time and that honoring precedent is essential to maintaining public confidence." How Do You Feel Now, Susan Collins? | The New Republic.

It's a shame that we have such stupid people as Susan Collins and Joe Manchin in such high-elected positions. But that is what happens when money and political influence is in play; we end up with stupid people in power making stupid decisions that hurt people, rather than having smart people who wouldn't allow themselves to be so duped, as these two idiots were. If there was a remake of the movie *Dumb and Dumber*, Susan Collins and Joe Manchin would be perfect for the lead roles. And the really sad part is, their stupidity resulted in our country ending up with an illegitimate court with judges who got away with lying to get on the Supreme Court, gratis of Collins and Manchin, and numerous other political misfits.

And on top of having several so-called "justices" who made it to the Supreme Court under false pretenses, it is also noteworthy that two of the misfits who voted to overturn *Roe v. Wade*, Clarence Thomas and Brett Kavanaugh, were both credibly accused of being sexual predators themselves. Clarence Thomas was credibly accused of sexually harassing Anita Hill, a former aide to Thomas at the Department of Education and the Equal Employment Opportunity Commission, and Brett Kavanaugh was credibly accused of sexually harassing Christine Blasey Ford by locking her in a room and pinning her down on a bed, and also sexual abuse allegations from multiple other women when they were in high school. Also, it has been reported that Clarence Thomas groped Moira Smith when she was a young Truman Foundation scholar at an awards dinner party. 25 years after Anita Hill, Clarence Thomas has another accuser - Vox. It is unconscionable that two sexual predators would be allowed to take part in a decision that implicates a woman's right to make sacred decisions about her very own body. Clarence Thomas-Anita Hill Supreme Court Confirmation Hearing 'Empowered Women' and Panel Member Arlen Specter Still Amazed by Reactions - ABC News (go.com), Why are Republicans ramming Brett Kavanaugh on to the supreme court? | Brett Kavanaugh | The Guardian, Julie Swetnick, 3rd Kavanaugh Accuser, Speaks Out In NBC Interview | HuffPost Latest News.

And it should be noted that two of the so-called "justices," and I use that term loosely under the circumstances, were nominated to the Supreme Court by Donald J. Trump, a misfit who himself has been accused of sexual misconduct by at least 19 women. Donald Trump Accusers: Women Who Alleged Sexual Misconduct | Time. And how could we forget about Trump bragging to Billy Bush of *Access Hollywood* in the infamous recording obtained by *The Washington Post* about how he tried to have an affair with a married woman and then described how he makes moves on women as he is heard on the recording saying, "You know I'm automatically attracted to beautiful—I just start kissing them. It's like a magnet. Just kiss. I don't even wait." He also stated, "And when you're a star they let you do it. You can do anything." And he also boasted, "Grab them by the p----," "You can do anything." In speaking about a married woman who he took furniture shopping, Trump said, "I did try and f--- her. She was married." The recording reportedly occurred several months after Trump married his third wife, Melania. Trump Brags About Groping Women in Vulgar Remarks Caught on Tape, Chalks It Up to 'Locker Room Banter' - ABC News (go.com). https://abcnews.go.com/Politics/trump-caught-tape-vulgar-language-women/story?id=42655874. So the reality here is that three of the judges who overruled *Roe v. Wade* were appointed by a sexual pervert.

After the public backlash to the Supreme Court's infected action of overturning *Roe v. Wade*, in setting back women's rights to make decisions about their own bodies without governmental interference by several decades, Roberts told an audience of judges attending a conference in Colorado, "If the court doesn't retain its legitimate function of interpreting the Constitution, I'm not sure who would take up that mantle. You don't want the political branches telling you what the law is, and you don't want public opinion to be the guide about what the appropriate opinion is." Opinion | What Chief Justice Roberts misses - The Washington Post. I would say to Roberts that nor should the right-wing crazies of the Republican party or the extremists of the Federalist Society be telling the Supreme Court what the law is—which is precisely what is happening today. And as for Roberts' statement that the Supreme Court shouldn't care about public opinion, I don't think that the public at large would agree with the notion that the Supreme Court shouldn't care what public opinion is about an important societal issue. I vehemently disagree with Roberts, as I think the public's opinion should count for something, and it certainly should count more so than the opinion of right-wing crazies of the Republican party or the extremists of the Federalist Society, and should count even more than the opinions of the illegitimate members of the Supreme Court who got there by lying during their confirmation hearings, which is exactly what Samuel Alito, Brett Kavanaugh, Amy Coney Barrett, and Neil Gorsuch did—let's call a spade a spade and make that as clear as can be: they lied. So to respond in kind to Roberts' statement that "you don't want public opinion to be the guide about what the appropriate opinion is," I will wholeheartedly say that I would much rather put my faith in a conscientiously expressed opinion by the public—the actual stakeholders—rather than the opinion of illegitimate members of the Supreme Court who are nothing more than political sycophants who have no problem in lying under oath to achieve their underhanded goals to pacify certain right-wing political organizations headed by crazies and lunatics of the highest social order.

Roberts went on to whine that "Lately the criticism is phrased in terms of 'Because of these opinions, it calls into question the legitimacy of the court.' I think it's a mistake to view those criticisms that way." Roberts further griped that "Simply because people disagree with an opinion is not a basis for criticizing the legitimacy of the court." I have a news flash for Roberts, the legitimacy of the so-called "court" was called into question well before the *Roe v. Wade* decision was dumped onto the country against the wishes of the majority population. In an oral argument on December 1, 2021, on the issue of the 2018 Mississippi abortion law, Justice Sonia Sotomayor asked, "Will this institution survive the stench that this creates in the public perception that the Constitution and its reading are just political acts? I don't see how it is possible." And Justice Sotomayor wasn't the only one. In July 2022, Associate Supreme Court Justice Elena Kagan is on record telling a conference full of lawyers and judges that "The way the court retains its legitimacy and fosters public confidence is by acting like a court, is by doing the kind of things that do not seem to people political or partisan. By not behaving as though we are just people with individual political or policy or social preferences that we are making everybody live with, but instead we are acting like a court, doing something that is recognizably law-like. That is where we gain our legitimacy." In September 2022, Justice Sonia Sotomayor participated in an event celebrating the 50th anniversary of the Lawyers Club of San Diego (a bar association that promotes gender equality) and commented that the court's *Dobbs* decision which overturned *Roe v. Wade* "upended 50 years of precedent on abortion." She also stated, "When the court does upend precedent, in situations in which the public may view it as active in political arenas, there's going to be some question about the court's legitimacy." And in September 2022, while speaking to Temple Emanu-El in New York, Justice Elena Kagan raised legitimacy questions about the Supreme Court, where Kagan said, "Judges create legitimacy problems for themselves...when they instead stray into places where it looks like they're an extension of the political process or when they're imposing their own personal preferences." Reportedly, her comments seemed to respond directly to Chief Justice John Roberts' public attempts at trying to defend the Supreme Court's legitimacy after the decision in June 2022, to overturn *Roe v. Wade* and end the constitutional right to abortion established by that decision in 1973. And then Roberts had the stupidity of saying, "I think just moving forward from things that were unfortunate is the best way to respond." That's his answer, allow things to proceed in a corrupt manner, and then when things blow up, just say that moving forward from the unfortunate happenings "is the best way to respond." Here is a thought I would pose to Roberts: how about holding miscreant judges who caused the "unfortunate" things to happen accountable for their actions?

In June 2022, Representative Madeleine Dean of Pennsylvania said that the overturning of *Roe v. Wade* was done by a "corruptly seated majority" on the Supreme Court. Rep. Dean: Rights of women were overturned by 'a corruptly seated majority' on SCOTUS (msnbc.com). It stands to reason that we cannot have "corrupt" justices on the Supreme Court, and since Representative Dean has publicly enunciated that we, in fact, have "corrupt" justices on the Supreme Court, and two associate justices who are on the Supreme Court have publicly enunciated their concerns about the legitimacy of the Supreme Court, the proof is in the pudding—the Supreme Court is an illegitimate court.

In October 2016, one of the most highly-regarded federal court of appeals judges in the country, Richard A. Posner, of the U.S. Court of Appeals in Chicago, publicly stated that the Supreme Court is "mediocre and highly politicized" and that the Supreme Court is "awful" and "a quasi-political body." Judge Richard Posner On SCOTUS: 'The Supreme Court Is Awful' - Above the LawAbove the Law. In September 2017, Judge Posner, in an interview with the Chicago Daily Law Bulletin discussing the Supreme Court, is on record publicly stating, "It's not a real court. It's a political court." Richard Posner announces retirement (chicagolawbulletin.com). In discussing the Supreme Court in a March 2017, interview with ProMarket, Judge Posner described America's judicial system as "very bad." He also said, "We have a very crappy judicial system. That's the long and short of it. And that contaminates much of government." Richard Posner: "The Real Corruption Is the Ownership of Congress by the Rich" - ProMarket.

So what we have are two associate Supreme Court justices (Sonia Sotomayor and Elena Kagan) raising serious questions about the "legitimacy" of the Supreme Court; a prominent member of Congress (Madeleine Dean) who has publicly declared that we have a "corruptly seated majority" on the Supreme Court; two prominent members of Congress (Sheldon Whitehouse and Hank Johnson) who have demanded that Chief Justice John Roberts comply with their investigation into the Supreme Court's refusal to abide by ethics laws regarding shenanigans as to the religious group Faith and Action's decades-long private judicial lobbying campaign known as "Operation Higher Court"; a prominent, now-retired federal court of appeals judge (Richard A. Posner) who publicly stated that the Supreme Court is not a "real" court, but a "political" court; and of course, we have four Supreme Court justices (Samuel Alito, Neil Gorsuch, Brett Kavanaugh, and Amy Coney Barrett) who all committed perjury at their Senate confirmation hearings by lying under oath when they vowed to respect the prior precedent of *Roe v. Wade* by what is referred to in legal terms as "Stare Decisis" (a legal concept meaning to "stand by things decided"). When all of this is taken into context, indeed, the Supreme Court of the United States is an illegitimate court.

The erosion level of public confidence in the Supreme Court and disgust with Chief Justice John Roberts is so bad that James Dannenberg, a retired Hawaii state judge who sat on the District Court of the 1st Circuit of the state judiciary for 27 years and before that served as the deputy attorney general of Hawaii, and was also an adjunct professor at the University of Hawaii Richardson School of Law teaching federal jurisdiction for more than a decade, and who had appeared on briefs and petitions as part of the most prestigious association of attorneys, the Supreme Court Bar, had seen enough. On March 11, 2020, he tendered a letter of resignation from the Supreme Court Bar to Chief Justice John Roberts. He had been a member of that bar since 1972. In his letter, Dannenberg compared the current Supreme Court, with its boundless solicitude for the rights of the wealthy, the privileged, and the comfortable, to the court that ushered in the Lochner era in the early 20th

century, a period of profound judicial activism that put a heavy thumb on the scale for big business, banking, and insurance interests, and ruled consistently against child labor, fair wages, and labor regulations. In his resignation letter to Chief Justice Roberts, Dannenberg expressed that he had high regard for the work of the federal judiciary, spanning the tenures of Chief Justices Warren, Burger, and Rehnquist before Roberts' appointment and confirmation in 2005. Dannenberg went on to state that while he had not always agreed with the court's decisions, he had generally seen those decisions, until recently, as "products of mainstream legal reasoning, whether liberal or conservative." He went on to tell Chief Justice Roberts, "I can no longer say that with any confidence. You are doing far more—and far worse—than 'calling balls and strikes.' You are allowing the Court to become an 'errand boy' for an administration that has little respect for the rule of law." He continued, "The Court, under your leadership and with your votes, has wantonly flouted established precedent. Your 'conservative' majority has cynically undermined basic freedoms by hypocritically weaponizing others. The ideas of free speech and religious liberty have been transmogrified to allow officially sanctioned bigotry and discrimination, as well as to elevate the grossest forms of political bribery beyond the ability of the federal government or states to rationally regulate it. More than a score of decisions during your tenure have overturned established precedents—some more than forty years old—and you voted with the majority in most. There is nothing 'conservative' about this trend. This is radical 'legal activism' at its worst." Dannenberg went on to state, "Without trying to write a law review article, I believe that the Court majority, under your leadership, has become little more than a result-oriented extension of the right wing of the Republican Party, as vetted by the Federalist Society. Yes, politics has always been a factor in the Court's history, but not to today's extent. Even routine rules of statutory construction get subverted or ignored to achieve transparently political goals. The rationales of 'textualism' and 'originalism' are mere fig leaves masking right-wing political goals; sheer casuistry."

In lambasting Roberts even further, Dannenberg went on to say, "Your public pronouncements suggest that you seem concerned about the legitimacy of the Court in today's polarized environment. We should all be. Yet your actions, despite a few bromides about objectively, say otherwise." Dannenberg continued, "It is clear to me that your Court is willfully hurtling back to the cruel days of Lochner and even Plessy. The only constitutional freedoms ultimately recognized may soon be limited to those useful to wealthy, Republican, White, straight, Christian, and armed males—and the corporations they control. This is wrong. Period. This is not America."

And in challenging Roberts, Dannenberg went on to say, "I predict that your legacy will ultimately be as diminished as that of Chief Justice Melville Fuller, who presided over both Plessy and Lochner. It still could become that of his revered fellow Justice, John Harlan the elder, an honest conservative, but I doubt that it will. Feel free to prove me wrong." Dannenberg then told Roberts, "The Supreme Court of the United States is respected when it wields authority and not mere power. As has often been said, you are infallible because you are final, but not the other way around." And in a very powerfully worded closing, Dannenberg concluded, "I no longer have respect for you or your majority, and I have little hope for change. I can't vote you out of office because you have life tenure, but I can withdraw whatever insignificant support my Bar membership might seem to provide. Please remove my name from the rolls." The Dannenberg letter to Roberts tells us everything we need to know, and I might add, if I may, that it confirms in principle everything I have been saying for the past several years about the level of unfairness and corruption of the federal judiciary.

It is unfortunate that we have an illegitimate Supreme Court thanks to the stupidity and political perverseness of senators who helped several dishonest judges get confirmed. It stands to reason that we cannot have misfit judges on the Supreme Court, and they need to be eradicated. The question now is, what are we—the people—going to do about it? In other words, are we, as a country, going to continue to allow judges who lie under oath at their confirmation hearings to continue to be on the Supreme Court, or are we going to stand up to the politically perverse politicians and be heard? James Dannenberg did his part. He let Roberts know how he felt about the Supreme Court's misguided actions, and he asked Roberts to remove his name from the rolls. I am sure that was not easy for Dannenberg, but he felt strongly about the issue and that was his form of protest. We, the people, should now do our part, and publicly voice our feelings and opinions about the downward direction that the Supreme Court and federal judiciary as a whole are going. There actually is a remedy available to cure this problem as the Constitution provides a procedure for ousting sitting Supreme Court justices. The process is the same as impeaching the president of the United States. The House of Representatives would vote on whether to impeach the justice in question, and if the justice is impeached, there would be a Senate trial. The House needs only a simple majority to impeach a Supreme Court justice. To convict and then remove the so-called "justice," the Senate requires a two-thirds majority. So while it is not a simple process due to the politics of things, it is nevertheless an avenue that is available if the politicians of the day would put party politics aside and actually do the right thing in the best interests of the country. Unfortunately, these days the political polarization is at a monstrous level, and there are many political cronies who have contaminated Congress who would get in the way of impeaching the miscreant justices on the Supreme Court, especially since many of the political cronies currently in Congress had a hand in the placement of the miscreant judges onto the Supreme Court in the first place. That is where we, the people, can have an impact—vote the bums out!

    We are on the brink of a civil war in this country, and people had better wake up soon and smell the coffee before it is too late. The right-wing crazies have basically taken over, and we are quickly starting to lose our democracy. The crazies now have the Supreme Court in their back pockets, and as long as they own the Supreme Court, they own the country, and consequently, we no longer have a democracy. And as long as we have a federal judiciary and Supreme Court chief justice who opposes a code of ethics, the illegitimate justices of the Supreme Court will continue to erode the constitutional rights of the people to no end. This is a consequence that the people of our country will have to suffer due to having illegitimate justices on the Supreme Court and members of Congress who could remove them by impeachment but won't do so because of partisan right-wing politics and loyalty to a perverse government. When judges are allowed to lie at their Senate confirmation hearings in order to get on the Supreme Court, we are in trouble as a country. And when members of Congress allow the illegitimate judges to remain on the Supreme Court after it is clear that they committed perjury at their Senate confirmation hearings, when they could impeach those miscreant so-called "justices" but won't do so, we as a country are being let down in a big way.

Judges who lie under oath at Senate confirmation hearings and then get on the Supreme Court under false pretenses are, in essence, illegitimate so-called justices who have effectively turned the Supreme Court into an illegitimate court by their fraud. The evidence that I discussed here overwhelmingly demonstrates that for all practical purposes, the Supreme Court of the United States is an illegitimate court.

CHAPTER 21
THE BUYING AND SELLING OF THE SUPREME COURT

"The only thing necessary for evil to triumph is for enough good men to do nothing."
~ Edmund Burke

The Supreme Court's ethics (actually lack thereof) have become so concerning that on November 20, 2022, two prominent Democrats, Sheldon Whitehouse and Hank Johnson, on the House and Senate Judiciary Committees, sent a letter to Chief Justice John Roberts and demanded that Roberts comply with their investigation into the Supreme Court's refusal to abide by ethics laws regarding the religious group Faith and Action's decades-long private judicial lobbying campaign known as "Operation Higher Court." The letter raised a concern to Roberts stating, "If the Court, as your letter suggests, is not willing to undertake fact-finding inquiries into possible ethics violations that leaves Congress as the only forum. Our previous letter identified reports of conduct by justices that increasingly appear out of line with the conduct permissible for other federal judges and, in some cases, may be inconsistent with federal law." The letter came a day after the *New York Times* reported that Justice Samuel Alito leaked the outcome of a 2014 decision in the case of *Burwell v. Hobby Lobby*, a case in which the U.S. Supreme Court held 5-4 on June 30, 2014, that the Religious Freedom Restoration Act (RFRA) of 1993 permits for-profit corporations that are closely held, such as when owned by a family or family trust, to refuse, on religious grounds, to pay for legally-mandated coverage of certain contraceptive drugs and devices in their employees' health insurance plans. Alito authored the decision. He reportedly spoke about the decision ahead of its release to Supreme Court Historical Society donors who were part of an influence operation led by a former conservative evangelical leader and former longtime anti-abortion activist, Rev. Rob Schenck. Whitehouse and Johnson demanded information about a letter from Schenck to Roberts disclosing that he (Schenck) learned about the Hobby Lobby outcome days before it came down from one of his volunteers after she attended a dinner with Alito and his wife. The Whitehouse/Johnson letter to Roberts followed up on a prior inquiry Whitehouse and Johnson made on September 7, 2022, where they encouraged Roberts to adopt a formal ethics code. They also demanded answers about how many justices were provided travel, dinners, lodging, and other hospitality from donors connected to Schenck's influence operation and why the justices did not disclose these gifts on their annual financial disclosure statements.

Reportedly, meals and vacations were bestowed on conservative U.S. Supreme Court justices by a wealthy, evangelical Ohio couple in order to befriend these justices. Gayle and Don Wright of Centerville, Ohio, were part of a program called "Operation Higher Court" that recruited "wealthy donors and stealth missionaries" to befriend justices that aligned with the group's social and religious views, the program's former leader, Rev. Robert Schenk, told the House Judiciary Committee on December 8, 2022. Schenck informed the Committee that his donors hosted justices or their spouses for meals at restaurants, private clubs, or in their homes, and sometimes the justices even reciprocated. So much for the "independence" of the judiciary, as Roberts likes to spin it. Roberts has laughingly stated, "Decisional independence is essential to due process, promoting impartial decision-making, free from political or other extraneous influence." He has also said, "The judiciary's power to manage its internal affairs insulates courts from inappropriate political influence and is crucial to preserving public trust in its work as a separate and co-equal branch of government." John Roberts Affirms Judicial Independence from 'Inappropriate Political Influence' ahead of 2022 Docket (yahoo.com). Supreme Court justices who accept invitations from wealthy donors of Operation Higher Court, for which they sometimes even reciprocate, hardly fits the definition spewed by John Roberts of "decisional independence" in "promoting impartial decision-making, free from political or other extraneous influence." It is very hard to understand how such intimacy between wealthy donors from an organization called Operation Higher Court and justices of the Supreme Court in any way could be considered "impartial decision-making, free from political or other extraneous influence." And it is equally as hard to understand how such intimacy in any way preserves "public trust." John Roberts must be delusional.

Schenck told the House Judiciary Committee that at one of the gratis meals, Justice Samuel Alito gave Gayle and Don Wright of Operation Higher Court advance notice of the outcome of a 2014 decision referred to as the "Hobby Lobby" case, a case that allowed private employers to refuse to provide birth control insurance to employees if it violates the company owners' religious beliefs. Ohio couple's gifts show need for U.S. Supreme Court ethics code, congressional committee told - cleveland.com. The *New York Times* reported that Schenck used that information to prepare a public relations push and tipped off the president of Hobby Lobby, the craft store chain that the Supreme Court ruled in favor of in the case. Former Anti-Abortion Leader Alleges Another Supreme Court Breach - The New York Times (nytimes.com).

Schenck told the Committee that the "overarching" goal of Operation Higher Court was to "gain insight into the conservative justices' thinking and to shore up their resolve to render solid, unapologetic opinions." He testified to the Committee that his group (Operation Higher Court) suggested tactics like meeting with justices for meals at their homes and at private clubs to build relationships and advance their perceived common objectives. Schenck told the Committee, "I believe we pushed the boundaries of Christian ethics and compromised the high court's promise to administer equal justice." He said, "I humbly apologize to all I failed in this regard" and "Most of all, I beg the pardon of the folks I enlisted to do work that was not always transparently honest...I'm here today in the interest of truth telling." Former anti-abortion lobbyist testifies to House committee about 'stealth missionaries' at Supreme Court (yahoo.com). So what this means is that not only were the Supreme Court justices prostituting themselves for free meals from the extraneous influences of the recruited missionaries of Operation Higher Court, but they were also allowing themselves to be influenced by dishonest information according to the group's former leader. That free food must have been really tasty.

Even before Alito's penchant for free meals from wealthy extraneous influences, there was Antonin Scalia who traveled to many spots around the globe on trips paid for by private sponsors. Scalia took 258 subsidized trips from 2004 to 2014 including three to Zurich on privately-funded trips. Scalia Took Dozens of Trips Funded by Private Sponsors - The New York Times (nytimes.com). A person could easily wonder how he found any time to do any actual work. So much for John Roberts' public spewing about "impartial decision-making, free from political or other extraneous influence."

When Scalia died on February 13, 2016, he did so while staying, for free, as an invited guest at a West Texas hunting lodge owned by a businessman, John Poindexter, whose company had a matter before the Supreme Court at the time. Poindexter was the owner of J.B. Poindexter & Co., a manufacturing firm based in Houston with more than 4,000 employees. One of his companies, the Mic Group, was a defendant in an age discrimination lawsuit filed by a former employee who unsuccessfully petitioned the Supreme Court for a review.

In 2011, a liberal advocacy group, Common Cause, questioned whether Scalia and Clarence Thomas should have disqualified themselves from participating in the landmark Citizens United case on campaign finance because they had attended a political retreat in Palm Springs, California, sponsored by the conservative financier, Charles G. Koch, who funded groups that could benefit from the ruling. The disclosure report filed by Clarence Thomas made no mention of the retreat. It said only that he had taken a trip funded by the Federalist Society, a conservative legal group, to Palm Springs to give a speech. Over roughly a decade, Scalia took 21 trips sponsored by the Federalist Society to places like Park City, Utah; Napa, California; and Bozeman, Montana. The Federalist Society also paid for trips for Samuel Alito during that period, but not for any liberal justices as shown by the disclosure reports.

The Ethics in Government Act, adopted after Watergate, requires high-level federal employees, including judges, to fill out disclosure reports for reimbursements worth more than $335, but Scalia didn't have to make the formal disclosure because accommodations provided by a private individual are exempt under the rule. My, my, how accommodating! Calling it the "Ethics in Government Act" while not requiring formal disclosures that have been provided by a "private" individual hardly seems "ethical" by any stretch of the imagination. But then again, John Roberts has reassured the public that "every justice seeks to follow high ethical standards," and if anybody believes that, then they are gullible enough to believe a person when they say, "I've got a bridge to sell you."

CHAPTER 22
EVIDENCE OF THE SEVENTH CIRCUIT'S SYSTEMIC DISCRIMINATION

"What just is, isn't always Jus-tice."
~ Amanda Gorman

Let's not kid ourselves, the federal courts are essentially cesspools of injustice. Let's not get enamored by all of the showtime nonsense with the fancy engravings inside and outside of the courthouse buildings, with all of the sound-good quotes that are put there to fool us into believing that we can, and should, expect honesty, fairness, and justice in the cases that people bring against powerful and wealthy influential corporations and government agencies. The sound-good quotes that are etched into and onto the courthouse walls are a far cry from what is actually happening inside the courtrooms, especially when it comes to pro se litigants—litigants who represent themselves without a lawyer. We have a very serious problem in the country with the courts essentially blowing off almost all of the cases that are filed by pro se litigants, not because their cases lack merit, but simply because they have chosen to, or are forced to, represent themselves because they can't afford to pay hefty lawyer's fees. These are cockroach judges who cheat people out of their rights on a constant basis—and the state and federal judiciaries are filled with them.

The judiciary's disregard of the rights of pro se litigants had been a long-held secret until Judge Richard A. Posner, after retiring from the Seventh Circuit Court of Appeals in Chicago, publicly stated in a September 6, 2017, article in the *Chicago Daily Law Bulletin* that he retired from the bench earlier than he had originally planned because of the mistreatment that the judges on the 7th Circuit were giving the pro se litigants. Posner says friction on 7th Circuit bench led to his retirement (chicagolawbulletin.com). The article pointed out that Posner's move-up date of his retirement was attributed to "difficulty" with his colleagues quoting Posner as saying, "I was not getting along with the other judges because I was (and am) very concerned about how the court treats pro se litigants, who I believe deserve a better shake." Posner publicly stated in a *New York Times* article that he noticed that pro se cases tended to get very casual treatment by the staff attorneys who routinely prepare a memo recommending a disposition of the appeal. He said the recommendation goes to a panel of judges who then usually "rubber stamp" the staff attorney's memo, which is usually to dismiss the appeal. Judge Posner is on record stating in a pro se case that involved a person's death, from which he was on the panel with two other judges, that the 7th Circuit agreed with the district judge and voted to dismiss the family's appeal, and that he (Posner) dissented. Posner reportedly went on to say, "I think I was just going along with the culture of the court. None of the judges paid any attention to the pro se's, and I just never woke up to it until I saw this case." Posner went on to state, "I gradually began to realize that this wasn't right, what we were doing." He also said, "The basic thing is that most judges regard these people a kind of trash not worth the time of a federal judge." (*New York Times* "An Exit Interview with Richard Posner, Judicial Provocateur – September 11, 2017). According to an article in *Crain's Chicago Business*, a former staff attorney that he had talked to recently said that the staff attorneys, in recommending dismissals, are doing what they think the judges want. <u>Federal Judge Posner tells why he abruptly retired | Crain's Chicago Business</u>.

After Judge Posner's public revelations, then-Chief Judge Diane Wood of the Seventh Circuit Court of Appeals in Chicago publicly responded that Judge Posner's views "are not shared by the other judges on the court..." But Wood didn't go beyond her self-serving statement at all, as her statement stopped right then and there with no other information to back it up. Since Wood felt impelled to issue a public statement, then why didn't she share what the views of the other judges were on the issue? Why was she was so adamant in making a blanket public statement that Judge Posner's views "are not shared by the other judges on the court"? Since Wood failed to provide the public with any supporting information to back up her self-serving statement, it was rather obvious that those other judges were nothing more than puppets on a string for the puppeteer-in-chief, Diane Wood. If Wood's statement had any credibility, she could have easily provided some supporting information about what the views of the other judges were in substance, but she chose not to, and that speaks volumes. Judge Posner stated factual information when he made his public revelations about the Seventh Circuit's infected procedures as to the handling of pro se appeals. Chief Judge Diane Wood simply provided an unsupported self-serving public statement amounting to nothing more than utter hogwash. Once upon a time we had "Watergate," and now we have "7th Circuit-gate." At least in "Watergate," Nixon had the decency to resign his presidency, but in "7th Circuitgate," we would not be so lucky!

In Judge Posner's telling book *Reforming the Federal Judiciary: My Former Court Needs to Overhaul Its Staff Attorney Program and Begin Televising Its Oral Arguments*, he discussed in great detail the reasons that the Seventh Circuit needs to overhaul its staff attorney program so as to ensure that pro se appeals are adequately reviewed in order that a fair and just decision be rendered that could be understood with explanation. The book discusses how Judge Posner had requested from the director of the court's staff attorney program that he (Judge Posner) be provided with copies of orders that the judges had issued in cases in which a staff attorney had submitted a memo or proposed order to the judge in order that he (Judge Posner) could see how common it was for judges' orders to be issued without explanation. The director of the court's staff attorney program told Judge Posner that he would comply with his request and provide copies of those judges' orders to him; but shortly afterward, he retracted his reply saying that the chief judge (Diane Wood) had told him to "hold off" doing so.

Judge Posner discusses in the book how he had lunch with Chief Judge Wood on June 5 after previously circulating a memo on May 31 to all the judges and staff attorneys presenting his plan to improve the staff attorneys program—to which Chief Judge Wood showed no indication of opposing his proposal. But on the following day, June 6, Chief Judge Wood sent an email to Judge Posner stating, "Some of those proposals seem very good to me and I've already talked to Mike about implementing them." Then, after some rather idiotic diatribe, Wood went on to state, "I am not going to tell Mike Fridkin to institute such a system." Judge Posner's book shows a memo written by Chief Judge Wood on June 14, 2017, where Wood cavalierly states, "...I can say without hesitation that our program is the best in the country!" and "I do not believe that major changes in it are necessary." It was rather evident that Judge Posner was definitely onto something, and Wood didn't like it. In the end, rather than taking Judge Posner up on his offer to improve the process for fairness and justice for pro se's, Wood flexed her infected judicial muscle and vetoed the very concept of fairness and justice in favor of the status quo of an outmoded process of systematic unfairness and injustice. This way the infected process of continuing to collect the hefty filing fees from the pro se's could continue while at the same time not giving them the time of day when it came to giving them their right to a meaningful review of their appeals. It is essentially a system of fraud. Federal Rule of Appellate Procedure 4 explicitly states that an appeal is a matter of a "RIGHT." This governing rule doesn't give the judges of the Seventh Circuit, or any circuit for that matter, any discretion to diminish that right when it comes to a pro se appeal. Furthermore, the "Standards for Professional Conduct Within the Seventh Federal Judicial Circuit," item 6, explicitly states, "We will give the issues in controversy deliberate, impartial, and studied analysis and consideration." Item 8 states, "... that a litigant has a right to a fair and impartial hearing..." A custom of systematically dismissing pro se appeals hardly meets the threshold standard of "deliberate, impartial, and studied analysis and consideration" and "...a right to a fair and impartial hearing..."

It is a major red flag when judges aren't even willing to follow the rules of their own court. It is blatantly corrupt for the Seventh Circuit to be accepting hefty filing fees from pro se litigants and then customarily summarily dismissing their appeals simply because they are representing themselves. Systematically dismissing pro se appeals by rubber-stamping the staff attorney's memos in dismissing pro se appeals because the staff attorneys "are doing what the judges want," as Judge Posner has publicly stated, and that "None of the judges paid any attention to the pro se's," as Judge Posner has publicly stated, is a blatant form of systemic discrimination clearly demonstrating evidence of corruption by the Seventh Circuit Court of Appeals in Chicago. A custom of systematic dismissal of pro se appeals is against the law, and based on Judge Posner's public revelations, that is exactly what was taking place in the United States Court of Appeals for the Seventh Circuit—and probably still is today.

Judge Posner was on the U.S. Court of Appeals for the Seventh Circuit in Chicago for almost 36 years and was one of the most highly-respected federal judges in the country. Based on Judge Posner's public revelations, it is rather evident we have a very serious problem in the Seventh Circuit as the judges are violating the civil rights of the pro se litigants who are constitutionally entitled to their day in court. By law, 28 United States Code Section 453, every federal judge must take an oath affirming to "...administer justice without respect to person, and do equal right to the poor and to the rich and to faithfully and impartially discharge and perform all the duties incumbent upon me as judge under the Constitution and laws of the United States. So help me God." The judges on the Seventh Circuit, or any circuit for that matter, have no right to discriminate against pro se litigants simply because they have chosen to represent themselves or are forced to represent themselves pro se. This is a blatant form of systemic discrimination that violates federal law, as the Judiciary Act of 1789 explicitly states, "That in all courts of the United States, the parties may plead and manage their own causes personally." It is interesting, in light of Judge Posner's public revelations as to improprieties in the Seventh Circuit, that all federal officials, including court officials and Congress, chose to remain silent and not investigate what was going on in the Seventh Circuit despite Judge Posner's public revelations. Those violative judges should have been immediately removed from the bench, disbarred, and prosecuted. Judge Posner's public statements were very strong evidence and clearly indicative of systematic civil rights violations by the judges of the Seventh Circuit against the people, as those judges not only violated their sworn oaths, but broke the law. Unfortunately, the United States Department of Justice and all other law enforcement and judicial authorities chose to look the other way and did nothing about it. The judiciary officials, Chief Justice John Roberts, and Congress should be ashamed of themselves for not investigating and taking corrective actions against the miscreant judges at the Seventh Circuit. That is why the U.S. Court of Appeals for the Seventh Circuit in Chicago is the epicenter of injustice.

CHAPTER 23
EVIDENCE OF THE SUPREME COURT'S HYPOCRISY REGARDING SYSTEMIC DISCRIMINATION

"Get in good trouble, necessary trouble, and redeem the soul of America."
~ John Lewis

I am sorry that I have to say this, but it is time to call a spade a spade and dispel the ridiculous notion of the phrase "Equal Justice Under Law." Courts across the country, including the Supreme Court of the United States, demonstrate that there really is no such thing in the eyes of the courts. Courts know that the phrase sounds great when it is said, and it looks great when people read it, but unfortunately, they are very powerful words but have very little true meaning in the world of the actual courtrooms where the judges like to talk the talk but don't like to walk the walk when it comes to "Equal Justice Under Law"—which are basically overused buzz words that sound good but mean nothing since courts dole out very little "equal justice."

The phrase "EQUAL JUSTICE UNDER LAW" is engraved above the front entrance of the United States Supreme Court building in Washington, D.C., and yet, the Supreme Court of the United States is involved in a very disturbing and very blatant form of systemic discrimination against pro se (unrepresented) litigants—by rule, no less. It is ironic that the Supreme Court of the United States, the highest court in our land, and charged with the responsibility of ensuring that the rules and laws of the country are fair and equitable, is itself guilty of enacting a most unfair and arguably unlawful rule where the Supreme Court explicitly forbids unrepresented litigants from participating in the oral argument process. Rule 28(8) of the Supreme Court of the United States expressly dictates, "Oral arguments may be presented only by members of the Bar of this Court." This is a blatantly unfair, discriminatory, and unlawful rule pointed at unrepresented litigants who should have the same right to participate in the oral argument process as represented litigants do. The Fourteenth Amendment, Section 1, of the Constitution of the United States expressly states, "All persons born or naturalized in the United States, and subject to the jurisdiction thereof, are citizens of the United States and of the State wherein they reside. No State shall make or enforce any law which shall abridge the privileges or immunities of citizens of the United States; nor shall any State deprive any person of life, liberty, or property, without due process of law; nor deny to any person within its jurisdiction the equal protection of the laws." The Supreme Court's rule, Rule 28(8), violates the Fourteenth Amendment as this rule arbitrarily denies the pro se litigants "the equal protection of the laws."

And furthermore, need I remind the Supreme Court that the people's right to represent themselves without a lawyer is federal law of which right to represent oneself in court was given to the people by an Act of Congress! The Judiciary Act of 1789 explicitly states that "in all courts of the United States, the parties may plead and manage their own causes personally." By this congressional law, all federal judges, and yes, all Supreme Court justices, are obligated by federal law to respect the pro se litigants' rights to represent themselves, and that includes the right to conduct their own oral arguments before the Supreme Court—a right that the Supreme Court refuses to recognize. Since federal law is crystal clear that people in this country have a right to represent themselves, then the Supreme Court has no right to enact discriminatory rules preventing people from representing themselves before the Supreme Court, in any process, including the oral argument process.

The hypocrisy of the engraving "Equal Justice Under Law" on the front entrance of the Supreme Court of the United States building, while at the same time enacting a rule to the contrary in forbidding unrepresented litigants "Equal Justice Under Law" in terms of barring pro se litigants from presenting oral arguments before the court, and only allowing represented litigants to do so, is patently unfair and unacceptable as a matter of public policy, which is disallowed under the Fourteenth Amendment, Section 1. This actually constitutes "**Unequal** Justice Under Law." The Supreme Court should either remove the engraving of "Equal Justice Under Law" from the front entrance of the Supreme Court building or it should remove its discriminatory rule, Rule 28(8), and allow pro se litigants to equally present oral arguments before the court in the same manner as it allows represented litigants. It cannot have it both ways. The Supreme Court is required to follow the principles of the very laws of the land that it is obligated to enforce. In the case of Rule 28(8), it is failing to do so. Thereby it is turning a blind eye to its own discrimination against a certain class of litigants, the pro se litigants, who are entitled to constitutional protections under the Fourteenth Amendment. This is not "Equal Justice Under Law."

The Supreme Court's barring of the unrepresented litigants from this important court process is essentially an unlawful systemic form of discrimination against a class of people, i.e., unrepresented litigants. The Supreme Court happily welcomes and accepts the required $300 filing fee from the unrepresented litigants, and accordingly, it should be treating the unrepresented litigants with the same degree of respect that it affords represented litigants, but it doesn't do so. Instead, it chooses to treat the unrepresented litigants as a cash cow as a means to provide a cash flow into the court's coffers, while at the same time disallowing the unrepresented litigants from the same processes afforded to the represented litigants, all while violating the Fourteenth Amendment of the Constitution of the United States. What is so "equal" about taking people's money for filing fees and then having a rule that does not allow them to participate in the oral argument process that represented litigants are allowed to participate in? What hypocrisy!

It is not a well-kept secret that the courts are generally disrespectful of the rights of unrepresented litigants and, for the most part, do not give high regard to the merits of the cases filed by unrepresented litigants. The record speaks for itself in this regard via the overwhelming number of pro se cases that are routinely summarily dismissed, in many cases, without so much as a cursory review. Longtime distinguished judge, Richard A. Posner, of the United States Court of Appeals for the Seventh Circuit sounded the alarm when he publicly stated in a September 11, 2017, interview with the *New York Times*. "None of the judges paid any attention to the pro se's..." When I served as executive director of the Posner Center of Justice for Pro Se's, I had many an occasion to discuss this topic with Judge Posner, which was a very important issue that was dear to his heart. Hearing how serious a problem this is from Judge Posner, who witnessed it firsthand as a judge of the Seventh Circuit, and who had the integrity to publicly call the judges out on it, this certainly was a red flag as to the need for judicial reforms as to the abusive manner that the pro se's are being treated in the courts of the United States, including the Supreme Court of the United States, no less, with its cavalier rule explicitly forbidding the pro se's from participating in the oral argument process based on systemic discrimination against this particular class of people.

All litigants are entitled to fairness, irrespective of their financial or social standing, as all cases are supposed to be judged on their merits, not by the financial or social standing of the persons who bring them, nor are cases supposed to be decided on the basis of whether a litigant has a lawyer or is representing him or herself— and that certainly hasn't been happening by any stretch of the imagination. By law, every federal judge must take an oath affirming to "administer justice without respect to person, and do equal right to the poor and to the rich," and to "faithfully and impartially discharge and perform all the duties incumbent upon me as judge under the Constitution and laws of the United States." But the judges across the country and the justices on the Supreme Court of the United States willfully violate this oath every time they disrespect an unrepresented litigant in any way, especially so when they refuse to dispense fairness and justice to an unrepresented litigant simply because he or she doesn't have a lawyer and is representing him or herself. Judges who take a hypocritical oath that they don't follow are the antithesis of judicial virtue. They are in effect frauds who cheat people out of fairness in order to help unsavory corporations and government agencies that have done damage to the citizenry.

Each Supreme Court justice is in charge of a specific judicial circuit in the country. The individual justices on the Supreme Court should make each federal judge in the justice's assigned circuit understand that they are expected to treat pro se litigants with respect and without disdain in every way, and that they are required to "administer justice" to unrepresented litigants in the same manner as so-called "justice" is administered to represented litigants. But the fact that the Supreme Court shows its true discriminatory colors by putting in a rule expressly forbidding pro se litigants from the same opportunity to argue their cases as represented litigants enjoy, the Supreme Court thereby demonstrates a poor example to the federal judges around the country by its front and center discrimination by rule, no less. In other words, the lower courts undoubtedly feel as though if the Supreme Court doesn't have to conduct its business in a fair and equitable manner, then neither should they have to. Another disturbing aspect of this is that this is a bright red flag to the country that the Supreme Court, and district and appellate courts by proxy, have a preconceived notion that in the eyes of the federal judiciary, pro se litigants are essentially second-class citizens and shouldn't be treated "equal under law." So in all reality, when Judge Richard A. Posner said, "The basic thing is that most judges regard these people a kind of trash not worth the time of a federal judge," he was right on point.

Congress has a role as it has the power to remove judges who choose to violate their oaths of office, and it should do so without hesitation. Congress should underscore the importance of the Judiciary Act and make clear that complaints about violations of the rights of all litigants, whether pro se or represented, must be taken very seriously by judicial councils, and when judicial councils choose to play games with complaints that have been submitted against judges, then Congress should hold the recreant members of the judicial councils accountable as well. And that has certainly not been happening, and that needs to change.

Courts are not supposed to be a playground for lawyers and judges. They are the halls of justice for ordinary people to have their day in court, and receive justice, no matter their financial or social standing or profession. And yes, that also includes litigants who choose to manage their own cases. The law is the law.

It is very sad that the highest court in our land, the Supreme Court of the United States, the court charged with the responsibility of ensuring that the Constitution of the United States is upheld, is the very branch of government that is systematically denying our rights to the "Equal Protection Under Law" by way of an arbitrary rule that the Supreme Court itself enacted in order that there be no equal protection under the law when it comes to pro se litigants who come to the Supreme Court for the redress of their grievances but are prevented from addressing the Supreme Court at an oral argument because of their class status. That form of "Equal Protection Under Law" is reserved for the powerful and wealthy as far as the Supreme Court is concerned. The phrase "Equal Justice Under Law" is an oxymoron. The courts have consistently shown that these four words are very far from true. Supreme Court Rule 28(8) tells us so.

CHAPTER 24
THE ENTIRE JUDICIARY NEEDS A WHOLESALE CLEANSING
THE JUDICIAL GARGOYLES ARE MANY

> *"The time is always right to do what is right."*
> ~ Martin Luther King, Jr.

Without question, the judiciary is rife with corruption. History teaches us that the judiciary is infested with diabolically unfair and corrupt judges. Time and time again, we have all heard about, read in the newspapers, or seen on the news examples of inappropriate behaviors of judges. And time and time again, we learn that these miscreant judges somehow survive their stench and are allowed to keep their jobs, many times with little to no consequence for what they did. When there is a cockroach problem in a building, the exterminators are called in to fumigate the place and eliminate the cockroaches. But in the judiciary, there basically are no exterminators to eliminate the cockroaches who are wearing the black robes—and that needs to change.

And speaking of cockroach judges, there is judge, Karen Cole, of the 4th Judicial Circuit of the State of Florida, who had the gall to publicly state to a group of new young lawyers at the Jacksonville Bar Association Young Lawyers Section's annual "Afternoon at the Courthouse" CLE program that people who represent themselves in court generally fall into one of two categories: "those who aren't represented by an attorney for financial reasons and those who are "unbalanced." Cole violated the judicial conduct codes when she made such a brazen public statement against pro se litigators. The Preamble to the Code of Judicial Conduct for the State of Florida explicitly states, "Our legal system is based on the principle that an independent, fair and competent judiciary will interpret and apply the laws that govern us. Intrinsic to all sections of this Code are the precepts that judges, individually and collectively, must respect and honor the judicial office as a public trust and strive to enhance and maintain confidence in our legal system. The role of the judiciary is central to American concepts of justice and the rule of our legal system." Canon 1 of the Florida Code of Judicial Conduct states, "An independent and honorable judiciary is indispensable to justice in our society. A judge should participate in establishing, maintaining, and enforcing high standards of conduct, and shall personally observe those standards so that the integrity and independence of the judiciary may be preserved." Canon 2 states, "A judge shall respect and comply with the law and shall act at all times in a manner that promotes public confidence in the integrity and impartiality of the judiciary." Canon 3 B (5) states, "A judge shall perform judicial duties without bias or prejudice. A judge shall not, in the performance of judicial duties, by words or conduct manifest bias or prejudice, including but not limited to... socioeconomic status." Canon 4 states, "A judge shall conduct all of the judge's quasi-judicial activities so that they do not: (1) cast reasonable doubt on the judge's capacity to act impartially as a judge; (2) undermine the judge's independence, integrity, or impartiality; (3) demean the judicial office."

Needless to say, publicly calling pro se litigants "unbalanced" people clearly casts reasonable doubt on Karen Cole's capacity to act impartially as a judge and undermines this judge's independence, integrity, and impartiality in a big way. Karen Cole should have been sanctioned and directed to issue a public apology for her distasteful comments; but, yes, you guessed right, there were no disciplinary actions against this judge, which reinforces what we already know, that the judicial canons basically mean nothing and aren't worth the paper they are printed on. They are just for show.

I was so incensed at what Cole said about the pro se's that I emailed her. Here is a verbatim of the email:

Dear Mrs. Cole,

First, I must preface my message here by explaining that I cannot address you as "judge", so with all due respect, I will address you as "Mrs." as I do not believe you deserve to be addressed with the dignified title of "judge" since your recent abhorrent act of denigrating the pro se class of people. I believe you lost your right to such dignity when you publicly called the pro se class of people "unbalanced" on or about November 14, 2017 at The Jacksonville Bar Association Young Lawyers Section's annual "Afternoon at the Courthouse" CLE program when you publicly stated to a group of new attorneys that it is your experience that people who represent themselves in court generally fall into one of two categories "those who aren't represented by an attorney for financial reasons and those who are "unbalanced." This brazen and outlandish prejudicial public statement demonstrates the very real fact of your judicial bias against pro se litigants. You violated the judicial conduct codes when you made such a brazen and outlandish public statement against pro se litigators. The Preamble to the Code of Judicial Conduct For the State of Florida explicitly states "Our legal system is based on the principle that an independent, fair and competent judiciary will interpret and apply the laws that govern us. The role of the judiciary is central to American concepts of justice and the rule of law. Intrinsic to all sections of this Code are the precepts that judges, individually and collectively, must respect and honor the judicial office as a public trust and strive to maintain confidence in our legal system." Your brazen and outlandish public statement calling pro se litigators "unbalanced" certainly undermines the public trust and diminishes public confidence in our legal system. Canon 1 of the Florida Code of Judicial Conduct states "An independent and honorable judiciary is indispensable to justice in our society. A judge should participate in establishing, maintaining, and enforcing high standards of conduct, and shall personally observe those standards so that the integrity and independence of the judiciary may be preserved." Calling pro se litigators "unbalanced" certainly doesn't demonstrate "high standards of conduct." Canon 2 of the Florida Code of Judicial Conduct states, "A judge shall respect and comply with the law and shall act at all times in a manner that promotes public confidence in the integrity and impartiality of the judiciary." Your public remarks calling pro se litigators "unbalanced" certainly doesn't promote public confidence in the integrity and impartiality of the judiciary" by any stretch of the imagination. In light of this public statement you certainly cannot be considered to be impartial when you are publicly denigrating pro se litigants as "unbalanced?" Canon 3 B (5) of the Florida Code of Judicial Conduct states "A judge shall perform judicial duties without bias or prejudice. A judge shall not, in the performance of judicial duties, by words or conduct manifest bias or prejudice, including but not limited to... socioeconomic status." You clearly demonstrated your bias and prejudice against a socioeconomic status of people by publicly calling pro se litigants "unbalanced." Canon 4 of the Florida Code of Judicial Conduct states "A judge shall conduct all of the judge's quasi-judicial activities so that they do not: (1) cast reasonable doubt on the judge's capacity to act impartially as a judge; (2) undermine the judge's independence, integrity, or impartiality; (3) demean the judicial office." Publicly calling pro se litigants "unbalanced" people clearly casts reasonable doubt on your capacity to act impartially as a judge and undermines this judge's independence, integrity and impartiality in a big way. You clearly should not be presiding over any cases involving pro se litigants. I for one, as a pro se, take personal exception to your inappropriate sweeping statement against pro se's. In March 2016 I represented myself in a five day federal jury trial in Indiana against my former employer, a public school corporation, and its team lawyers. On March 11, 2016, a federal jury awarded me $203,840.39. As a pro se I beat a team of corporate lawyers in a federal jury trial. So for you as a judge to make such an outlandish public statement that pro se's are "unbalanced" people speaks volumes to your lack of personal and professional character. Furthermore, you apparently are ignorant of the fact that the Judiciary Act of 1789 is an act of Congress of which law admonishes "That in all courts of the United States, the parties may manage and plead their own cases personally." In my opinion, it is you who is "unbalanced" for making such an irresponsible and prejudicial statement which calls into question your fitness to be a judge. Your denigration of calling the pro se class of people "unbalanced" leave much to be desired and you owe the pro se class of people a public apology. If you don't feel like you can do the right thing by issuing a public apology to the pro se class of people then you should resign from your position as a judge because only a degenerate person would violate his or her obligations to the canons and insist on presiding over the very cases of the people that you so obviously disrespect and abhor. Because of your misguided feelings about pro se's and your apparent feeling for a need to publicly degenerate the pro se class of people, to a group of new young attorneys no less, it would serve a very useful purpose for you and I to publicly debate this issue in a public forum. I therefore am challenging you to a public debate as to the propriety of your public statement that you believe pro se's are an "unbalanced" class of people. An appropriate forum would be in front of the same organization that you made your degenerative comments against pro se's. Of course the general public should be allowed to attend and the media should of course also be in attendance. Do you accept? Or do you choose to run and hide?

Brian Vukadinovich

As for judicial chicanery insofar as how the judiciary brethren cover each other, the proof is in the pudding as shown in the denial of the petitions as to 83 complaints of judicial misconduct that were filed against Supreme Court Justice Brett M. Kavanaugh, formerly a judge in the U.S. Court of Appeals for the District of Columbia Circuit, which raises a serious cause for alarm in our country with respect to the need for a fair system of accountability when people submit complaints against federal judges. The Judicial Council of the Tenth Circuit In re: Complaints Under the Judicial Conduct and Disability Act before Tymkovich, Chief Circuit Judge, Kelly, Briscoe, Lucero, Circuit Court Judges, and Bremmer, Waddoups, Skavdahl, and Dowdell, District Judges issued an order denying the petitions on March 15, 2019, which underscores the impotence and protectionism of a very infected system which breeds contempt for accountability regarding investigations into corrupt activities by federal judges in our country. This so-called "Council" denied the petitions for review and reaffirmed its determination that an intervening event precluded further review of the complaints by the Judicial Council. The so-called "intervening event" was Kavanaugh's confirmation to the Supreme Court. This was ludicrous. The petitioners contended that an "intervening event" did not occur because the allegations against Kavanaugh were not moot because he was still performing judicial duties. The petitioners cited the "Breyer Report" to support that a judge remains subject to the "Act" so long as he or she is performing judicial duties. But the so-called "Council" determined that "...because the intervening event in this matter resulted in the loss of jurisdiction, this council does not have the authority to investigate or make findings upon which to base any remedial action." How convenient! However, the order contained a dissent by Judge Mary Breck Briscoe who denounced the ludicrous reasons in the decision one by one, and then added, "In my view, however, it is improper for the Council to sit in review of its own order of dismissal." Judge Briscoe makes a very valid point. And furthermore, Judge Carlos F. Lucero disqualified himself from the case "for the reasons stated by Judge Briscoe in her dissent" and further added, "I would reassign the petitions to the Chief Justice of the United States for further referral to the Judicial Council of another Circuit pursuant to Rule 26 for independent consideration of the appeals or for other dispositions as he may determine."

And then there is the Committee On Judicial Conduct and Disability of the Judicial Conference of the United States which reviewed the Tenth Circuit's decision as to the Kavanaugh matter that on August 1, 2019, basically rubber-stamped the Tenth Circuit's holding that Kavanaugh's resignation as a judge of the United States Court of Appeals and elevation to the Supreme Court of the United States qualified as "intervening events" that required conclusion of the complaints without consideration of their merits. I knew as soon as I saw that Judge Joel M. Flaum was on the panel that the decision would be a farce. Flaum came from the U.S. Court of Appeals for the Seventh Circuit in Chicago, so that in and of itself guaranteed a stain on the proceedings as far as I was concerned knowing how corrupt the judges are in the Seventh Circuit, and make no mistake about it, the Seventh Circuit is a very diseased circuit comprised of many infected judges. The decisions by the Judicial Council of the Tenth Circuit and Committee On Judicial Conduct and Disability of the Judicial Conference of the United States in coming to Kavanaugh's rescue were pathetic and reeked of malfeasance without question. Both of the infected decisions were bright red flags screaming out to the people: "Look at how corrupt we are, and you can't do anything about it!"

What I found very interesting in both of those decisions as to the Kavanaugh complaints, in terms of how they were handled, was how very similar it was to my judicial misconduct complaint against Judge Michael S. Kanne for case fixing in the Seventh Circuit, where the so-called "judicial council" of the Seventh Circuit similarly dismissed the complaint without a decision on the merits in creating a ridiculous technicality that wasn't even a rule, i.e., a dismissal based on a non-existent timeliness issue. I say "non-existent timeliness issue" because there is no statute of limitations for filing a judicial misconduct complaint against a federal judge. Yet this was the given reason that the Seventh Circuit used to dismiss the complaint. The pattern here is uncanny, and one thing is for sure, the process set up by the federal judiciary is designed to dismiss judicial misconduct complaints on ridiculous, creatively conjured-up technicalities in order to avoid decisions on the merits of the complaints—just as what took place with respect to the Kavanaugh complaints and my complaint against Kanne.

In my work as executive director of the Posner Center of Justice for Pro Se's, I ran across many instances of misconduct by federal judges where when people filed complaints against judges, they got nowhere as the complaints were routinely dismissed without so much as a cursory review, let alone a meaningful review. This needs to change if we are to have a measure of fairness in our federal judiciary, which can never be so long as we have rogue federal judges who are allowed to violate the governing standards of conduct by abusing people's rights to a fair proceeding in the federal court system, a system which not only looks the other way but acquiesces in nefariousness by its complicity. The shenanigans are many and make no mistake, it is widespread. It mostly happens in cases where individuals are suing corporations or government agencies where judges like to put the hammer down against the people while favoring the powerful. Time and time again this has shown itself to be a culture in the federal judiciary —which results in a diseased judiciary. There is no question about it, and it wouldn't take much to expose it if the House and Senate Judiciary Committees would be interested in doing so, and therein lies the problem—the members of those committees are afraid to publicly expose the corrupt judges in the country and are beholden to politics first and foremost rather than what is good for the country.

The time has come for much-needed reforms and changes for a fair and transparent system of investigation of unfair and corrupt judges in the federal judiciary. The House and Senate Judiciary Committees have been AWOL in this regard long enough. Congress needs to take notice of this very serious situation, and there should be public hearings held by the House and Senate Judiciary Committees on this very serious problem and steps put in place to ensure that all federal judges are held accountable and subject to appropriate disciplinary measures for their violations of the governing standards, and that the status quo of summarily dismissing people's complaints against the federal judges without a meaningful investigation be stopped. The time for covering up for federal judges who do not adhere to the governing standards should come to a halt, here and now. The time has come for the current outmoded system of judges covering for inept and corrupt judges to be cast by the wayside in favor of a system that is fair and non-protective of unfair and corrupt federal judges. I believe that there should be citizen input on committees in every federal judicial district where civilians, and not solely judges, are investigating and reviewing misconduct complaints against federal judges, and that the process is open and not a "secret" type process that is currently the status quo. Congress, particularly the House and Senate Judiciary Committees, should be taking action in this regard, for if no action is taken, then there is no justice. That is precisely how Brett Kavanaugh escaped any review as to the 83 complaints of judicial misconduct that were filed against him. That is precisely how Michael S. Kanne escaped any review as to the complaint I filed against him for his case-fixing activities in the Seventh Circuit. That is precisely how state and federal judges all across the country escape scrutiny for their wrongful and unlawful actions. There is no honest process in place as the current system of brethren judges overseeing the complaints and then routinely letting their brethren judges off the hook is rotten to the core. This is precisely why there should be civilian input on every committee charged with the responsibility of reviewing any judicial misconduct complaint against a state or federal court judge in this country, with a process put in place for the submission of findings of wrongdoing to be brought before a special grand jury in appropriate instances.

The instances of judicial perversion are many. In a classic case of judicial strong-arming, there is the case that took place in Michigan where a judge got upset with a Jonathan Vanderhagen during a child custody battle when Vanderhagen chose to exercise his First Amendment rights and publicly criticized the Macomb County Circuit Court Judge Rachel Rancilio on his Facebook page. In 2017, Vandergagen petitioned the court for sole custody over his two-year-old son, Killian, as Vangergagen believed Killian's mother to be an unfit guardian. The judge, Rachel Rancilio, denied the request and Killian was permitted to continue living with his mother. Sadly, Killian passed away that September while in his mother's care. Authorities came to the conclusion that a preexisting medical condition contributed to Killian's death, but Vanderhagen blamed Rancilio's custody ruling for contributing to his son's death, which he believed would not have happened had Killian been in his care—and Vanderhagen used his Facebook page to say as much. For two years Vanderhagen posted about Killian's mother, the court system, and Rancilio —at times using Rancilio's own public Facebook posts and Pinterest pins to criticize her ruling. Rancilio was made aware of Vanderhagen's posts, and an investigation was opened against him. Sergeant Jason Conklin of the Macomb County Sheriff's Office, the investigating officer, concluded in his case report, "At no point does [Vanderhagen] threaten harm or violence towards Rancilio." Nevertheless, Vanderhagen was charged with the malicious use of telecommunication services. "Malicious use" means that Vanderhagen was accused of using a telecommunications service with the intention of terrorizing, intimidating, threatening, or harassing Rancilio. Vanderhagen was ordered to refrain from engaging in direct or third-party contact with Rancilio, including sending "inadvertent messages by way of Facebook."

The prosecutors and the presiding District Judge Sebastian Lucido used the following Facebook post to accuse Vanderhagen of violating his bond conditions. The post featured Vanderhagen holding a shovel with the initials R.R., of course standing for Rachel Rancilio, the judge in the child custody case. The post's caption read, "Dada back to digging and you best believe I'm gonna dig up all the skeletons in this court's closet." According to Vanderhagen's lawyer, Nicholas Somberg, the post was created three days before Vanderhagen received his bond conditions. Somberg argued in an emergency bond hearing that Vanderhagen had a First Amendment right to criticize legal authorities; and the judge, Lucido, responded that there were "limits" to free speech. When Vanerhagen's lawyer asked Lucido to clarify which of the Facebook posts presented to the court were threatening, Lucido said that they alluded to the judge and did not explain any further. He then raised Vanderhagen's bond to $500,000. This was a ridiculously high amount for a misdemeanor alleged crime. Vanderhagen's lawyer argued that the $500,000 bond was an amount that was tantamount to one "you would expect for a murderer or rapist." What a joke of a criminal proceeding and abuse of the legal process.

Fortunately for Vanderhagen, once the case made its way to trial, a jury of Vanderhagen's peers made sure that justice would be the rule of the day and not judicial skullduggery. According to Vanderhagen's lawyer, it took a jury only 26 minutes and 8 seconds to decide that Vanderhagen was not guilty of using his Facebook account to threaten a county judge.

It was reported by *Reason* that Somberg used a portion of his closing argument to remind the jury that the case was first and foremost about Vanderhagen's First Amendment right to free speech:

> *Our Founding Fathers guaranteed us the right to a Jury Trial for situations just like this. That the founders understood absolute power corrupts*

absolutely and that we should be judged by a jury of our peers, not the government. You all should feel lucky to be sitting for such an important trial. The verdict that you come back with will send one of two very different messages to the people of Macomb County. We either have the right to free speech, or if the people of Macomb criticize our elected officials they better watch out.

This was obviously a case of inappropriate judicial strong-arming aimed at a person for exercising his right to criticize an elected official. It's a travesty and a stain against our country that we would have a system of so-called "justice" that is allowed to operate this way. But it happens far too often. This was a classic case of it.

And then there was Judge John Murphy who was presiding over a criminal calendar in Brevard County, Florida, when he grew incensed with public defender Andrew Weinstock, who had refused to waive a client's right to a speedy trial. Murphy became so angry that, in one of the most famous judicial outbursts, he challenged Weinstock to a fight. "You know, if I had a rock I would throw it," Murphy, a retired colonel in the U.S. Army Special Forces who served in Afghanistan, told Weinstock. "If you want to fight, let's go out back and I'll just beat your ass." The two men then went to the hall where a fracas ensued. Weinstock would later say he was punched by Murphy, while Murphy would insist that Weinstock was the aggressor. The scuffle only ended after a courthouse deputy separated the two men. Upon Murphy's return to the courtroom, he presided over eight criminal cases—without a defense lawyer present. More than 18 months later, the Florida Supreme Court removed Murphy from the bench. "Judge Murphy's grievous misconduct became a national spectacle and an embarrassment to Florida's judicial system," the justices wrote in an opinion issued in December 2015. The incident—which was captured on video and can still be seen on YouTube—may have been unusually public, but Murphy isn't the only jurist to engage in questionable conduct. Across the country, judges are creating embarrassing headlines when they are accused of abusive behavior toward lawyers and litigants.

In California, more than 1,200 complaints against judges closed in 2017, but no one was removed from office. Among the judges was San Diego County Superior Court Judge Gary Kreep. He referred to people by nicknames he gave them. Among them were three interns in the San Diego Public Defender's Office—whom he called "Bun Head," "Ms. Dimples," and "Shorty," who was actually 6 feet 7 inches tall. Kreep's creation and use of the nicknames "created an atmosphere in the courtroom that was too informal and lacked appropriate decorum" and didn't convey appropriate respect, the Commission on Judicial Performance wrote in an opinion filed in August 2017, but the judicial commission allowed Kreep to keep his job. While the judicial commission didn't do its job, the voters did theirs. In November 2018, Kreep lost his bid for re-election.

According to Jayne Reardon, executive director of the Illinois Supreme Court Commission on Professionalism, "Judges hold a position of authority within our legal profession." Reardon also said, "In the judicial canons, judges are called upon to be leaders when it comes to civility." State and federal codes of judicial conduct require judges to be patient, respectful, and courteous to everyone in the courtroom. Despite these admonitions, Reardon, who works to promote integrity and civility in the profession, believes the tenor and discourse among judges, lawyers, and litigants have deteriorated, as norms of acceptable behavior outside the courtroom have shifted. "What is civility in this day and age is subject to interpretation," Reardon opined. "To try and get back to a situation where we embrace civility and collegiality as a profession is a ways off." She has stated, "We call on judges not only to exemplify courteous behavior and civility but also to require that of other courthouse personnel and lawyers who come before them." Yeah, right.

But the reality is that judges don't always show those high qualities. Some of the most high-profile examples of judicial bullying have occurred in criminal cases where emotions on all sides often run high. Abbe Smith, a professor at Georgetown University Law Center has said, "Unfortunately, the system is full of bullies, even in very high places." She has also stated, "Criminal defendants are regular targets and so are their lawyers. Getting slapped down, dressed down, and put down is part of the job."

Professor Smith has written that in one of her first cases, a judge in Philadelphia criticized her for bringing up a U.S. Supreme Court case. "Are you citing a U.S. Supreme Court case in this courtroom? Do you know where you are?" he asked her. Smith, who directs the criminal law and prisoner advocacy clinic at Georgetown Law, said she was "probably struck mute for four, five seconds," before answering that the law set out by the Supreme Court applied in all courtrooms.

One criminal defense lawyer who experienced the wrath of a judge firsthand is Clark County, Nevada, public defender Zohra Bakhtary. At a hearing in May 2016, Bakhtary was arguing that her client shouldn't be sent to jail when Justice of the Peace Conrad Hafen told her to stop talking. "Zohra, be quiet," he said, according to a transcript of the proceeding. When Bakhtary attempted to continue arguing, Hafen said, "Do you want to be found in contempt?" She started to answer but was only able to get in a few words before Hafen told her again to be quiet. "Now, not another word," he said. When Bakhtary again tried to interject, Hafen ordered her handcuffed. He then proceeded to sentence Bakhtary's client to six months in jail on a misdemeanor petty larceny count—the client was later freed by a different judge. Hafen released Bakhtary a few minutes later, but four days after the incident, Hafen officially entered a finding of contempt against Bakhtary. Several months later, Clark County Judge Gloria Sturman reversed the contempt finding. Bakhtary, who currently serves as chief deputy public defender in Clark County, says her job often involves fighting an uphill battle. But she says she hadn't anticipated the struggle playing out the way it did in Hafen's courtroom that day. She said, "When I became a public defender, never in a million years did I expect I would end up in handcuffs." Hafen lost a bid for re-election in 2016. He is now off the bench but no thanks to the so-called "judicial conduct authorities" who rarely remove judges for behavior deemed inappropriate. It took the voters of Clark County, Nevada, to cure the injustice and do the job that the so-called "judicial conduct authorities" weren't willing to do.

Steve Zeidman, a professor at the City University of New York School of Law and director of the criminal defense clinic, has dealt with the ire and irritability from judges that is common in the antagonistic and often tragic field of criminal defense work. He said that judges will express their antsiness by writing out orders if lawyers talk too long or interrupt defense counsel to ask questions such as, "Is that all?" Professor Zeidman said, "There is such a focus on speed and efficiency that when defense lawyers try to slow things down to have a conversation about the facts or the law, they are inevitably seen as obstructionist." Zeidman adds that judges also can display a temper with criminal defense attorneys when their clients reject plea deals—which of course they have a right to do. When Zeidman was a young defense lawyer in Manhattan, he encountered a judge who reacted vindictively when he learned that a defendant was rejecting a plea deal. The judge scheduled the case to go to trial the day before Zeidman was slated to take a trip to Mexico. Zeidman rescheduled his trip and took the case to trial, and his client was acquitted. Zeidman says he later mentioned in a written evaluation of the judge that he was "vengeful, spiteful and tried to ram a plea down a defendant's throat." He said the judge apparently learned of the evaluation and one day he was stopped by the judge in the hallway and told, "What goes around comes around." It would seem that this would be a direct threat, a clear case of judicial bullying. Zeidman, who served on the New York Mayor's Advisory Committee on the Judiciary from 2008 to 2010 and from 1996 to 1999, says that judges are often evaluated based on their efficiency—meaning the number of cases they dispose of in a given time period. This focus on moving cases along may contribute to some judges' impatience on the bench, he said. But a lack of efficiency in his or her courtroom isn't a valid excuse when it comes to judicially bullying somebody. This is the problem when there is an impotent system in place that allows judges to cover and protect brethren judges when they disrespect the rules and abuse people.

Even where a situation goes entirely off the rails, it's not a given that judges will be removed. Lawyers who appear in court regularly and bear the brunt of judicial outbursts as part of their jobs are much less likely to lodge official complaints than litigants—in my opinion, they should man up! In California, the most populous state in the country, the Commission on Judicial Performance received 1,251 new complaints about 878 different judges in 2017. Attorneys initiated only 4 percent of those complaints, while 86 percent came from litigants or their families and friends. And in New York, the state with the most active lawyers, the state Commission on Judicial Conduct received 2,143 new complaints in 2017, with 1,832 coming from criminal defendants or civil litigants, and 53 from attorneys. Some attorneys worry that complaining will backfire against themselves or their clients. Any attorney who is afraid to stand up and speak up about judicial bullying isn't worth a grain of salt. I don't feel sorry for them.

Society frowns upon bullying—schools don't allow it, playgrounds don't allow it, workplaces don't allow it, and cyberbullying is not allowed—yet judicial bullying goes on in courtrooms all around the country on a daily basis unfettered. If the lawyers are too afraid to file complaints against the callous judges, then they are part of the problem. The above examples of "black robe disease" are only a drop in the bucket; it is a very serious and widespread problem that the judiciary very well knows exists but chooses to turn a blind eye to it, even when it is reported and evidence shown. Judges apparently believe that wearing the black robe puts them on equal standing with a king who wears a robe and that everybody in the courtroom is a peasant subject to his or her tyrannical whims. Indeed, society is in need of a cure to eradicate the "black robe disease." We need a meaningful process for the disrobing of the judges who are so drunk with power that they feel it is okay to bully people in the courtroom. And that process should include a system where judicial complaints are investigated by an independent inspector general with the power to submit egregious cases of judicial bullying to a special grand jury. Hate crimes in our country are very serious offenses that are subject to criminal prosecution and imprisonment. Judicial bullying by judges should also be considered a type of hate crime. Guilty judges should also be subject to criminal prosecution and imprisonment and, of course, removal from the bench.

According to Charles Gardner Geyh, a law professor at Indiana University Maurer School of Law, "There are judges who run the gamut from simply overly stern to downright abusive." This begs an answer to the question as to why the "downright abusive" judges aren't removed from the bench? This will always be a problem as long as there is no meaningful system of checks and balances in place. As long as the system is set up in a way to allow judges to protect brethren judges, we can expect the status quo for eternity. It makes no sense since we know for a fact that abusive judges are a problem, and that there is not a meaningful system put in place for removing these misfits. This is why we need judicial reforms and systems put in place which include members of the citizenry to sit on disciplinary investigation panels and an independent inspector general to investigate complaints of abusive judges with the power to submit charges against the abusive judges to a special grand jury. For if we continue to run scared and be silent and not demand judicial reforms, then we as a people will forever be subjected to the continuing extermination of our rights to fairness and rights to meaningful judicial redress of our grievances to the whims of the individuals suffering from "black robe disease."

Jonathan Zell, a highly-respected attorney from Columbus, Ohio, who I became acquainted with in our work in the Posner Center of Justice for Pro Se's, and for whom I have deep respect, also believes that the whole U.S. legal system is a fraud. This is because (according to Zell): "Based on personal biases, trial judges first decide how they want a case to end up and then (when necessary) concoct dishonest reasons to justify those decisions, a corrupt process that appellate courts usually cover up with their own dishonest reasoning. Lost in the process are the true facts of the case and the controlling law." I wholeheartedly agree with Attorney Zell.

And by the way, Jonathan Zell is a current member of the Committee on Ethics and Professionalism of the Judicial Division of the American Bar Association (ABA) where he continually offers common-sense proposals to rein in corrupt judges, but the pro-judge ABA keeps rejecting those proposals. Zell is one of the very few attorneys in the country who has the integrity and courage to constructively criticize the infected judiciary and actually recommend proposals to the American Bar Association (ABA) to rein in corrupt judges, and we should be very thankful to Attorney Zell for his efforts.

Jonathan Zell has no problem with confronting and exposing judicial corruption and doesn't use the standard outmoded excuse that he can't do so for fear of retaliation against his law practice. Jonathan Zell not only talks the talk, but he also walks the walk. He isn't afraid to call out corruption in the U.S. Court of Appeals for the Sixth Circuit, and he certainly has done so in publishing an "Open Letter to All Attorneys" stating, "I accuse the U.S. Court of Appeals for the Sixth Circuit of case-fixing!" On top of that, he explicitly demanded that the Ohio attorney-disciplinary officials institute disbarment proceedings against him based on his allegations of case-fixing against the trial and appellate judges. He did so in order that he could finally get a hearing on those allegations inasmuch as the judges in question denied all requests for oral argument in a certain legal-malpractice case against Frost Brown Todd knowing that their favored side would lose if these issues were aired publicly. Jonathan Zell's charges are so credible that he was not only willing to risk his law license, but he also put his money where his mouth is by offering to give the American Bar Association $10,000 to keep or donate to the charity of its choice if the ABA could find any well-respected, full-time law professor who would say with certainty that the federal trial and appellate courts did not corruptly "fix" a certain case to favor the politically-powerful "AM Law 200" law firm Frost Brown Todd. This was in addition to an offer of $100,000 to anyone who could convince three law professors of his or her own choosing that the law firm of Frost Brown Todd did not commit blatant, obvious, and wholesale perjury in that case. I have read the pleadings from that litigation, both the district court and appellate, and I can see why the judicial officials didn't want to give Jonathan Zell an opportunity for an oral argument as to his allegations of case fixing against the trial and appellate judges—the case fixing was rather evident. Needless to say, there were no takers of Jonathan Zell's generous offers—he called out the judicial miscreants and they did what they do best, they ran for cover looking for the first rat hole they could squeeze into and hide. The time has come for a major cleansing of the judiciary—from top to bottom. Martin Luther King once famously said, "The time is always right to do what is right." That time has arrived.

The chief judge of the U.S. Court of Appeals for the Seventh Circuit, Diane S. Sykes, is making a big mistake if she thinks that her complicit shenanigans in covering for her brethren case-fixing judge, Michael S. Kanne, are somehow going to be forgotten as time goes by. That won't happen. The Chief Justice of the United States, John Roberts, is making a big mistake if he thinks that his complicit shenanigans in looking the other way as to what the case-fixing judge, Michael S. Kanne, did will somehow be forgotten as time goes by. That won't happen. The director of the Administrative Office of the United States Courts, Roslynn Mauskopf, is making a big mistake if she thinks that her complicit shenanigans in trying to sweep under the rug the information I submitted to the Judicial Conference of the United States as to the case-fixing shenanigans by the case-fixing judge, Michael S. Kanne, is somehow going to be forgotten as time goes by. That won't happen. The Chair of the Senate Judiciary

Committee, Dick Durbin, and the minions on the Committee, as well as my United States Senator, Todd Young, are making a big mistake if they think that their indifference as to the case-fixing shenanigans by the case-fixing judge, Michael S. Kanne, is somehow going to be forgotten as time goes by. That won't happen. And the attorney general of the United States, Merrick Garland, is making a big mistake if thinks that his complicity in looking the other way as to the case-fixing judge, Michael S. Kanne, is somehow going to be forgotten as time goes by. That won't happen. Every one of these flying monkeys can rest well assured that I have the will and resolve to continue to seek justice and demand that the judiciary face up to the fact that Judge Michael S. Kanne had the decision of the civil rights appeal fixed, and that the chief judge of the Seventh Circuit, Diane S. Sykes, and her minions, swept the case fixing under the rug with the blessing of the aforementioned governmental hierarchies in order to conceal from the public the evidence of just how corrupt the federal judiciary is and how the governmental hierarchy protects judicial corruption.

EPILOGUE

"It is a sin to be silent when it is your duty to protest."
~ Abraham Lincoln

Every federal judge must take an oath affirming to "...administer justice without respect to person, and do equal right to the poor and to the rich" and "to faithfully and impartially discharge and perform all the duties incumbent upon me as judge under the Constitution and laws of the United States. So help me God." This is an oath required under federal law—28 United States Code Section 453. State court judges are required to take a similar oath. But as you have learned from this book, the oaths that many judges take mean nothing. The oath is sacred and should be taken very seriously by every judge, but unfortunately, the oath is very often blatantly abused without consequence. The oath is rendered with the judge placing his/her left hand on the bible and right hand held up high. It is ceremonial in nature, but it is still supposed to mean something. Deep down, however, we know that in many cases it means nothing. Many of the judges do not really believe in the concept of "faithfully and impartially" discharging their duties.

History teaches us that our judiciary is infested with incorrigible judges who are operating in a wickedly nefarious court system. I believe I have shown in this book that our judicial system is morally bankrupt.

Every time a judge, state or federal, chooses to make an infected ruling in order to help an unsavory corporation or governmental agency which in effect infringes on an individual's right to a fair decision, then that judge is an arsonist who has lit a match to burn democracy as democracies are built on the premise of a fair judiciary as part of the overall democratic form of government. When judges depart from their sworn oaths to help corrupt corporate or governmental actors to deprive the people of their fundamental rights to justice, the judges have committed an act of arson against our democracy. Corrupt rulings by judges are acts of arson against our democracy. Judicial corruption deprives society as a whole, and we, as a society, must start taking steps to insist that the implementation of much-needed judicial reforms include citizen input in the process. We cannot trust judges to monitor and discipline their brethren judges; citizens should be doing the monitoring and making the decisions as to what forms of discipline should be handed out to judges who act corruptly. Every judge has an angel and a devil on their shoulder: the angel tells them to do the right thing, and the devil tells them to do the wrong thing. Unfortunately, far too often the judge chooses to do the wrong thing, and society consequently suffers.

In the prologue of this book, I said that I would make the case for judicial reform. I believe I have made that case. I believe I showed how unfair and corrupt the federal judiciary is, and how a system has been put in place to protect judicial corruption that has permeated the judiciary at every level at every turn. I believe I showed how our branches of government breach their responsibilities to the people and go out of their way to protect the criminal activities of federal judges. I believe I showed how a federal district court judge in Indiana, James T. Moody, went out of his way to ensure that rogue police who had been tormenting me for years with numerous false arrests and brutalities would escape liability for their unconscionable and unlawful rogue actions. I believe I showed how a retired longtime federal court of appeals judge, Richard A. Posner, came clean after years of harboring guilt for throwing a decision from my appeal of the police case as a favor to another federal court of appeals judge, Michael S. Kanne, who was on a mission to make sure that I did not prevail. Kanne was determined that the trial court's infected rulings would be affirmed so that his personal animosity against me would be satisfied. I believe I showed how the chief judge, Diane S. Sykes, and her minions on the U.S. Court of Appeals for the Seventh Circuit in Chicago, conducted a sham review of the judicial misconduct complaint I filed against Judge Michael S. Kanne in dismissing the complaint without a decision on the merits notwithstanding that the judge—Michael S. Kanne—didn't provide an "on the record" denial of the case-fixing charges against him that were disclosed by Judge Richard A. Posner. I believe I showed how the attorney general of the United States and the chief justice of the United States both turned a blind eye to the fixing of the appellate decision of the civil rights case in the U.S. Court of Appeals for the Seventh Circuit in Chicago in the face of the disclosure of the judge who acceded to the wishes of a corrupt federal court of appeals judge who put the fix in motion. I believe I showed how the Administrative Office of the United States Courts went out of its way to sweep under the rug the petition I filed addressing the Seventh Circuit's corruption. I believe I showed that U.S. Senator Todd Young of Indiana played the complicity game in refusing my request that he ask the Senate Judiciary Committee to hold public hearings on the corruption that took place in the Seventh Circuit and further proceeded in an infected manner by refusing to provide me with a copy of a letter he said he wrote on my behalf, which seriously called into question his integrity as to whether he actually sent the letter as he purported, but refused to show me. I believe I have constructed a very strong mosaic of evidence of corruption in the federal judiciary.

Without question, we have many "black robes of injustice." I believe I have made the case for much-needed judicial reforms. It is now up to you, the reader, to decide if you believe we have an unfair and corrupt judiciary, and if we, as a country, need to implement serious judicial reforms. I rest my case.

ABOUT THE AUTHOR

Brian Vukadinovich is a retired educator in Indiana and has served as executive director of The Posner Center of Justice for Pro Se's based in Chicago, Illinois for retired federal court of appeals judge Richard A. Posner. He has successfully represented himself in state and federal court proceedings in Indiana and won a federal jury verdict

ABOUT THE AUTHOR

against his former public school corporation employer in Indiana in March 2016 for violating his due process rights in a five-day trial where he successfully represented himself against the corporation's team of lawyers. He has received national acclaim for his self-representation ability and is believed to be the only person who has ever won a federal civil rights jury trial by representing himself without a lawyer. Brian Vukadinovich is very passionate about social justice issues and the federal judiciary's indifference to peoples' rights to fairness and justice. Brian Vukadinovich is a sought-after speaker and was a presenter at the 2022 Martin Luther King, Jr. Celebration event hosted by Indiana University Social Justice Conference, and in September 2018, he was invited to speak to a Yale Law School class. Brian Vukadinovich has done numerous television, radio, and podcast interviews and has been a featured guest on the television program *Pro Se Nation* based in Princeton, New Jersey. He has done extensive writing on judicial corruption issues, which may be seen on his website. He lives in Wheatfield, Indiana, with his brother, Branko, who is a steelworker, and his dog, Blackie.

www.allamericanspeakers.com/speakers/451268/Brian-Vukadinovich

www.brianvukadinovich.com

facebook.com/motionforjustice

twitter.com/motion4justice

www.ingramcontent.com/pod-product-compliance
Lightning Source LLC
Chambersburg PA
CBHW030545080526
44585CB00012B/266